GROUND WORK

Ground Work

Writings on People and Places

Edited by Tim Dee

JONATHAN CAPE
LONDON

1 3 5 7 9 10 8 6 4 2

Jonathan Cape, an imprint of Vintage Publishing,
20 Vauxhall Bridge Road,
London SW1V 2SA

Jonathan Cape is part of the Penguin Random House group of companies whose addresses can be
found at global.penguinrandomhouse.com.

Introduction © Tim Dee 2018

Contributions selected and edited by Tim Dee

First published by Jonathan Cape in 2018

www.vintage-books.co.uk

A CIP catalogue record for this book is available from the British Library

ISBN 9781910702710

Typeset in India by Integra Software Services Pvt. Ltd, Pondicherry

Printed and bound in Great Britain by Clays Ltd, St Ives plc

Penguin Random House is committed to a sustainable future for our business, our readers
and our planet. This book is made from Forest Stewardship Council® certified paper.

CONTENTS

CONTENTS

INTRODUCTION

We are living – many believe – in the Anthropocene, an epoch where everything of Earth's current matter and life, as well as the shape of things to come, is being determined by the ruinous activities of just one soft-skinned, warm-blooded, short-lived, pedestrian ape.

How, then, to live on our planet in the mess that we have made? And how to do that in harmony with the rest of the world that we have permitted to remain?

Places are anthropogenic creations called into being by the meeting of humans and their environment. They are prominent among our contributions to our times and our space. We make what has been called patterned ground. Place-making is a signal of our species. We make good ones and bad ones, and plenty of neither-here-nor-there ones. Good, bad or indifferent, they operate on all their constituents.

This is a book of writing about places. The personal geographies come from as many acres as people. The writing about them shares one constant: every description and every thought arises from someone being detained – by views, buildings, sculpture, weather, chairs, churches, trees, streets, people, memories. It seems, broadly, good to be stopped by a place. And this is one way a place comes into being. Our attention to them makes places significant. They are inhabited. Seen this way, these places are all cultural landscapes of one sort or another. Seen this way, they are vital for life. What follows, therefore, are various relief maps: they show what places might look like to themselves, but also how places work on us.

There is succour here. And this is important because most of the time most of us are *unplaced*. Even when we live somewhere that we

1

can call home, we spend much of our time away. We traffic along roads, through airports, in offices, hospitals, supermarkets – all non-places where the most we can hope for is a relatively frictionless passage. The success of these zones is measured by their throughput, their flow, their footfall. The sinuous path many airports have imposed around their entrances and exits via their duty-free shopping areas might define this world. I want nothing to do with it, yet here I am joining the conga.

An oblong of flat glassy space is now our most common go-to place. Young children, scrolling their fingers, attempt to enlarge images in books as they can on a screen. I've seen that. Digits working the digits. Some might try the same outdoors. Why not? Unfold the clouds. Bring me my bow. Mediation is not new. Magnification has long assisted birdwatchers. Ted Hughes's killer thrushes in his poem were, I am sure, seen through binocular lenses. But optics can distort as well as enlarge. The very tools that take us in close are also keeping us, ultimately, from any happily muddying contact with the hard matter of the world. Objects, as it says on North American car mirrors, are closer than they appear. We fail to notice this when mediation is all.

One of the most depressing places I have been in recent years is Bellaghy in County Londonderry. Seamus Heaney is buried there near his childhood home: the great poet of the personal omphalos, the navel stone that might mark the centre of the world, hence the most important place of all. His grave was young when I was there, still bare and earthy. The town was something else. A flesher's survived, J. Overend & Sons, and I shivered at the name and the family's tasks, but many of the other shopfronts were boarded up, or rather blinded with window-sized stickers of garish leafy scenes, manipulated images of healthiness and happiness, screens of greenery elsewhere.

To talk about trees in dark times, Bertolt Brecht wrote, is almost a crime. As more and more people in the world seem to have no place of their own, it has got harder, rightly, for the fortunate to linger in any sort of sacred grove. The Jungle at Calais was certainly a place. And in the knowledge of such places, to extol Birnam Wood or

Burnham Beeches or any other sylvan spot would seem like an escapist romance, an umbrageous avoidance of the issue, that few can afford. Masking economic and social collapse and failure with digitised verdancy seems comparably culpable. Natural beauty once guaranteed the status of a place. Not now.

The threat to our understanding and valuing of place is not, then, the heaped-up world of the built environment. That is our habitat and has been for thousands of years, perhaps, as Mark Cocker has suggested, ever since we shared caves with swallows where their 'procreant cradles' gave us an idea for mud bricks. As long as we've been settlers we have been place-makers. We've made *pied-à-terre*, we've lived *in situ*. What saps the possibilities of rooted or detained or placed life is the untextured places we increasingly live among: the unmuddy world of the depthless screen and the sealed space. How many accumulated years have I lived in a car? Even before virtual life threatened lived life, the *place-ness* of place was under threat in this way: specificities have been dulled, local habitations and names globalised, the instress or haecceity of every street or field driven from common memory. It was house martins, the swallows' cousins, that King Duncan saw breeding on the battlements of the Macbeths' castle. It seemed propitious to him that the birds shared a home with his hosts. But it wasn't good news for Duncan, and now the martins too are struggling on British houses where the eaves are so made these days that there is little purchase. The birds' mud nests cannot stick.

*

Two thoughts – on the forecast end of places and on their observed persistence:

> This ... is less a warning than a prophecy of doom: the prophecy that if what is called development is allowed to multiply at the present rate, that by the end of the century Great Britain will consist of isolated areas of preserved monuments in a desert of wire, concrete roads, cosy plots and bungalows. There will be no

real distinction between town and country. Both will consist of a limbo of shacks, bogus rusticities, wire and aerodromes, set in some fir-poled fields.

Ian Nairn, from 'Outrage', *Architectural Review*, 1955

I live in a community whose members are scattered piecemeal around London (some of them live outside the city altogether); the telephone is our primary connection, backed up by the Tube line, the bus route, the private car and a number of restaurants, pubs and clubs. My 'quarter' is a network of communication lines with intermittent assembly points; and it cannot be located on a map.

Yet place is important: it bears down on us, we mythicise it – often it is our greatest comfort, the one reassuringly solid element in an otherwise soft city. As we move across the square to the block of shops on the street, with pigeons and sweet papers underfoot and the weak sun lighting the tarmac, the city is eclipsed by the here-and-now; the sight and smell and sound of place go to make up the fixed foot of life in the metropolis. Place, like a mild habitual pain, reminds one that one is; its familiar details and faces – even the parked cars which you recognise as having been there in that spot for months – assure us of a life of repetitions, of things that will endure and survive us, when the city at large seems all change and flux. Loyalty to and hunger for place are among the keenest of city feelings.

Jonathan Raban, from *Soft City*, 1974

*

Places, 'An anthology of Britain', edited by Ronald Blythe (and made for Oxfam), was published in 1981. It is rich in fine writing about beautiful places. There are poems and essays from, among others, Ruth Pitter, John Betjeman, Susan Hill, Alan Sillitoe, R. S. Thomas, Jan Morris, Dirk Bogarde and John Stewart Collis. Its prevailing mood is wistful and elegiac. Almost everywhere described is either no longer fully there or is remembered from childhood. It seems twentieth-century life has sent place-writing adrift. In one memorable formulation the historian Richard Cobb, writing about his Essex childhood, describes how he has always preferred facing backwards when travelling because the world appears more honest as it is disappearing. It's a rationale for a historian's methodology (the ghost of Walter Benjamin's Angel of History is perhaps hovering nearby), but it also describes the myopia about the present that is common to many of the contributions in the book. Throughout its soft-spoken pages the writing intimates its underlying subject: the long and continuing impact of industrialisation, the severance from the perceived sustenance and verities of the rural past, and the alienation of urban life. There is some writing about London, but it seems that in general today's places – cities and towns and all the living zones – are not places to be written. It is as if something isn't working, as if Britain, estranged from itself, couldn't make places any more.

The injuries continued, and another book looked to staunch some wounds and advance an argument. In 1984 Jonathan Cape published *Second Nature*, a 240-page collection of essays and illustrations edited by Richard Mabey (with Sue Clifford and Angela King). The book was made for the charity Common Ground, and its jacket declared the organisation's then purpose as being to stem the tide of destruction of much that was wild and natural in Britain, by providing a fusion between the arts and nature conservation.

The editors assembled an impressive collection of words and images, and divided the contributions into three sections headed Personal Landscapes, Nature and Culture, and Beyond the Golden Age. Among the writing commissioned were pieces from John Fowles, Ronald Blythe, Fay Weldon, Peter Levi, Norman Nicholson and Kim Taplin. Intersecting the essays were illustrations of artworks by, among others, Henry Moore, Elisabeth Frink, Richard Long, David Nash, Norman Ackroyd, Andy Goldsworthy and Fay Godwin.

Common Ground was looking forward, but most of the writing in *Second Nature* still looked back. The historical analysis in essays by John Barrell, John Berger and Raymond Williams reframed the past. But the book stood, as it declared, at the end of things, beyond a golden age. The ancient continuities were still just about graspable, but the incoming tide of destruction was running high. The old natural world was dying and, although imminent, the new man-made world, which had killed it off, had yet satisfactorily to be born, at least in prose. It is more than a collection of elegies, but most of the book's literary efforts were put into accounts of what had been lost. Common Ground was only a year old and much of the writing in the book (the visual arts are less constrained) makes for sunset songs, or requiems for the end of the long, lived-in (and perceived as mostly benign) entanglement of a people and their (mostly rural) places.

The poem isn't in the book, but much of what is there has the same odd tense of the pressingly posthumous of Philip Larkin's 'Going, Going':

> And that will be England gone,
> The shadows, the meadows, the lanes,
> The guildhalls, the carved choirs.
> There'll be books; it will linger on
> In galleries; but all that remains
> For us will be concrete and tyres.

How the value of place-writing has shifted, and what, more generally, has happened to ideas about place since the 1980s is, I hope, evident in this book. Concrete and tyres, the man said. We now understand that the paved world can be as articulate as the vegetated. Philip Larkin's poems themselves announced that. What has changed is that we are now prepared to consider as meaningful habitat places previously ignored or written off. Modernity has shattered our world like never before, we are more deracinated than ever, but because we feel most places to be *nowhere* we have also learned that *anywhere* can be a *somewhere*. All of our habitat is relevant: not just the pretty bits. It turns out, counter to prime-ministerial sound-bites, that we are all at once citizens of nowhere and citizens of the world. In one extraordinary essay in Ronald Blythe's collection, Russell Hoban questioned what a place might be: 'Place itself may not be possible at all ... all the place ... is may well be no more than the moving point of consciousness in us.' Whether we call this place doesn't matter (Heidegger and Merleau-Ponty's ideas are stalking somewhere about Hoban), but, whatever it is, it 'provides a cross-over between the seen and the unseen, between the potential and the kinetic energies of that space we move in which is not simply space: perhaps it is the soul of the universe; and perhaps we are the organ of perception required by that soul'.

A place, then, as ever, might be a hollow tree or the dark end of a street, a childhood bedroom, a roundabout, a refugee camp or a sewage farm. In the last thirty years all sorts of *anywheres* were promoted in the collective consciousness and could be written as places. Despite this, none of them were secure. All places are challenged by modern times, yet none will go quietly, even those hedged with simulacra or trampled under real feet. Places, meetings of people and world, remain stubbornly *there*, itchy, palpable, determining. Good or bad, they are felt on our skin and get under it too. Time, the deer, is in Hallaig wood, said Sorley MacLean (as translated by Seamus Heaney). Birmingham is what I think with, said Roy Fisher.

Among the pieces collected here, the art of Richard Long and Greg Poole does some place-holding for me. All three of us are Bristol people. Greg and I have birdwatched together for more than thirty years. We don't do so much now, and the place we most often meet is just behind his garden where his micro-meadow is up and coming. He tries again and again to get my non-bird naming – flowers, butter-flies, moths, dragonflies, bats – up to scratch. I stake a claim to Richard Long's work. The polished stone behind his text here is the product of generations of Bristol bottoms sliding down a smoothing slope of rock between the old observatory and camera obscura on the top of the Downs and the approach-way to the Clifton Suspension Bridge (subject of Patrick McGuinness's piece here). For an hour of most Sundays for years of my youth my sister and I would add our shine.

A green city, Bristol has been called these past years, a green capital even. Green capital is what it has. One of the reasons I like the place is because from almost anywhere locked within its streets and buildings, you can see beyond to a green rim, where the city ends. It talks to its opposite in this way. My grandfather was a clerk in the old Fry's chocolate factory in Keynsham. From his desk he could see a summit ring of trees on a round hill south towards Bath. They kept him going, he would say. And the green belt fed Romanticism too. The poems of the *Lyrical Ballads*, first set in type in Bristol, were for Coleridge and Wordsworth made *out of* that West Country green.

At its simplest or starkest the effect of a cultural landscape is expressed in a poem fashioned from another west. Seamus Heaney, in his last book, *Human Chain*, translated 'A Herbal' by Guillevic, the great twentieth-century poet from Brittany, who was also a civil servant in the French Ministry of Finance. Towards the conclusion of the poem, which lists the grasses and flowers of a western headland, is this simple, somewhat stony, couplet:

> I had my existence. I was there.
> Me in place and the place in me.

It is striking how few of the places described here might be thought special other than to their describers. There are no grand houses, no Georgian cities, no national parks, no demarcated nature sanctuaries. Beauty spots – remember those? Preserved territory or reservations like these perhaps lose the quintessence of place, the co-evolved mutuality of people and surroundings, which many of the writers notice here. Places are better unplanned, when thay are feral spaces where things and lives can get on, more on less, like the entangled bank where life thrives, that Darwin described in the last paragraph of his *Origin*. Calculated attempts to make places often show only the dead hand of management. New public spaces often suffer in this regard; public art, too.

Striking, too, is how ugly and broken many telling places are. We paint with distemper when, as now, the time is felt as out of joint. In much of Britain everyone navigates what Ian Nairn called *subtopia*. The *drosscape*, Alan Berger's American term for the *splurge*, is perfectly at home in the UK, and extends for many miles in most directions.

8

Topographical phenomenologists and cultural geographers have found things to say in the non-places – those zones where we, unwittingly, spend much of our lives, where indeed we mostly live, but where no one feels at home. There are books on shopping malls, the M25; there is Jean Baudrillard's *America*. But it is scant fare. Recently the leftovers, the ends of places, have been more arresting and have offered better nourishment. W. G. Sebald was an unlikely tour guide, but showed many readers some ways back into the richness of rot, the humus of memory meeting an evanescent world.

But long before Eeyore walked East Anglia, Richard Mabey (the presiding genius of this book, its own spirit of place, and the only writer common to this and the other two place books I've mentioned here) had directed our attention to *The Unofficial Countryside*. Following him, Patrick Wright botanised on asphalt in *A Journey Through Ruins* and Paul Farley co-wrote *Edgelands* and re-launched a habitat. Ken Worpole studied suburban cemeteries and paved-over front gardens. The whole of Essex seemed brought to book. J. A. Baker's *The Peregrine*, like a radioactive pellet, the product of a sick man tracking a sick species in a sick place, became a holy text. Werner Herzog teaches it. Things fall apart and many of us like it that way. Analogue scratches on vinyl speak of a relationship between sound and listener as no digital dead air can. Ghost walks, hauntings, landfill, the draw-down of silting tides – all have made for copious place-based literary deposits. Edward Thomas has steered Matthew Hollis; the Thames estuary flooded Rachel Lichtenstein; Hayden Lorimer is excavating a pet cemetery on the North Sea shore. A kind of grit, the granulated ordinary past, has become a common currency. Copper pennies on the tongue are obols for many a traveller. Julia Blackburn, just out of Essex, knows the old money. David Matless mapped made-up landscapes and our inherited fantasy localisms in his *Landscape and Englishness*. Tim Ingold read into the lines on the land. We learned to call the scuffed marks that we've footed into a place desire paths. These have been Richard Long's *arteries*, ever since he created *A Line Made by Walking* fifty years ago in Wiltshire.

Places call up the places they were; that is part of what makes a place. Aside from Milton Keynes (which feels olde worlde these days, as old futuristic sci-fi films do, or the words *Betamax* or *escalator* or even *sci-fi*), is there any city in Britain that is more twentieth century than nineteenth? I can't think of any. But we have new ideas for these old places. Ruin lust is one of them. Entropy tourism. I recently joined the pilgrims to the modern ruin of a 1960s seminary at Kilmahew on the Clyde: as striking a place now as it falls down as it was when built up. Jonathan Meades made a tremendously *ferocious* TV film about rust. A recent book by Caitlin Desilvey is called *Curated Decay*. 'Nothing in his life / Became him like the leaving it' – so Malcolm describes the death of the Thane of Cawdor in *Macbeth*. We might say the same of most of our places today. The ones that matter to us are still often going or gone. Ozymandias truncated says more than the whole man would. We don't want to know how the garish Greeks painted their palaces. Filters on our phone cameras will age an image before our eyes. But modern life has always done this. These fragments, quoted T. S. Eliot, I have shored against my ruins. W. H. Auden was drawn to old human junk in rocky places. Rimbaud liked trash and kitsch. We laughed at a president for fixing a new marble penis on a dismembered Mars. The broken place speaks louder than the perfect place. Even the National Trust finds visitors more interested in the kitchens of the great house than their ballrooms. Downstairs tells more truth than up.

There are many places noted here, many other conversations with natural places as well as nurtured places, with other people, and with other animals: Michael Viney has been writing dispatches from a shifting Irish shore for decades; Fiona Sampson moves house; Tessa Hadley looks outdoors from inside on a new view; Helen Macdonald accesses her *girlitude* in western Surrey; Andrew Motion goes fishing; Richard Holmes gets drenched; Peter Davidson raises the ghost of one of the first in Britain to consciously notice and capture an ordinary place; Marina Warner remembers being ushered into a landscape by Peter Levi; Andrew McNeillie digs over his allotment and thinks of his plot; Sean Borodale goes underground; Alexandra Harris sets out to learn about a place and asks where it leads her; Hugh Brody maps his British childhood onto his adult life in Arctic Canada; John Burnside stops at some wayside shrines; Sean O'Brien plays out; Adam Thorpe lets a muddy puddle take a cast of his mind; Nick Davies wonders what birds make of their places; Barbara Bender logs how communal memories can be preserved; Adam Nicolson digs up his own; Philip Marsden passes down river; Phillip Hoare goes out to sea; Dexter Petley asks what the salt water gives back.

*

In the summer of 1801, Coleridge often went walking in the Lake District. On 18 June he found a rest stop:

> A Hollow place in the rock like a Coffin – a Sycamore Bush at the head, enough to give a shadow for my Face, & just at the Foot one tall Foxglove – exactly my own Length – there I lay & slept – It was quite soft.

Before the tide ebbs a grazing limpet heads home ... to its home scar: the shape of its shell can grow to precisely match the contours of the rock it fixes to. The limpet has marked the rock; the rock has marked the limpet. Jen Hadfield has written poems about the home scar of a limpet. It's a nice term for a nice idea. Richard Pearce has been counting the same in north Cornwall ever since the oiling disaster that followed the sinking of the *Torrey Canyon* in 1967. He showed me Porthmear beach where there are, he has counted, one million home scars.

*

This collection of new writing about places draws on the ideas and ideals of Common Ground. Common Ground gave Britain the concept of *local distinctiveness*, and this book is made for the organisation that has worked since the 1980s to revive, preserve and celebrate the diverse, local and intimate connections that people and communities have had, and might yet have, with the landscape that surrounds them.

11

Thirty years ago, Sue Clifford and Angela King set up Common Ground to help us understand where we are vis-à-vis nature in Britain: both to acknowledge our footprint, the tyre tracks, a paved country, its concrete overcoat, and to encourage some repairs, interventions, preservations and some newfangledness, and to do this in the belief that a relationship with our local outdoors environment – even as we have clobbered it to within an inch of its natural life – remains fundamental to human health and happiness.

The genius of Common Ground is precisely its understanding that *genius loci* is all important: that, in our ever-more internationalised, corporatised, mediated and de-individualised world, the spirit of a place, the sum of the meeting of people and land, remains of vital importance. Crucially, as Common Ground saw and sees it, place pertains and operates most and best at a local level, and on a scale we still might call human. Consequently, their efforts were not about restoring the wolf, or rewilding by managing facilities for nature: they were about looking at and growing a feeling for those less dramatic times in our lives when we cross the path of our own community; moments when old ways seem still operative; times when dormant traditions wait to be woken; times when our lives mesh with those of others who share the same weather; moments of intense and personal response to familiar corners.

The strong *presence* of both Common Ground's directed projects and the spontaneous manifestations of the same ethos elsewhere, their tang and their *multum in parvo* feel – a great deal in a small space, much in little – is even more important today in our vastly accelerated and denatured times. When Common Ground began no one anywhere in the world knew of the internet. But throughout its life the organisation's engine has been and remains the creation and inspiration of site-specific work for what it recognises as site-specific lives. Most, though not all, Common Ground projects have happened away from metropolitan centres. While it is fully understood that rural Britain is as man-made as urban, the parish scale has proved to be the most fruitful ground for the organisation's ideas. Where this scale can still can be felt in the big towns and cities, projects that promote local distinctiveness can be as life-enhancing there as anywhere.

Common Ground's work (art commissions, community projects, practical assistance) is made with an understanding that people and place are entangled at all levels – functionally (e.g. the built infrastructure of the country and farming and food); emotionally (novels, painting and music, flower arranging); intellectually (planning and philosophy); physically (walking, knitting, hang-gliding and working the land); and genetically (the home phenotype). Giving *a local habitation and a name*, Common Ground repeatedly declares, is neither yesterday's thing nor just a job for poets ...

Common Ground is still at work. In the last few years Sue Clifford and Angela King have handed over to Adrian Cooper. The rich archive of the charity's accomplishments to date is being prepared for study and exhibition, but its energies are still current, with its intentions little changed.

It has mostly failed, of course. As all our best-laid plans will. The world is still, substantially, to win. But its successes are many and have also been writ large into the wider world. One of the reasons why nature writing is resurgent today is because of Common Ground's steadfast belief in the value of exploring what the natural world – even the broken-down, rubbish-dump world – means to us. One of the reasons why almost every poet in Britain has written a blackbird poem is because Common Ground has reminded the country that local looking is as valuable as any panoptical survey – that the imaginative work that will address climate change, say, will come not from windy pieces blowing vatically around the planet, but from attending to what is close at hand.

There is still much to worry at. That tide is even higher, with the sea level rising, and lapwings, skylarks, even starlings and house sparrows, depleted beyond the imaginings of 1984. Larkin's concrete and tyres are even more in the ascendant. But to answer this has come passionate and articulate energy born of new ways of seeing that are less wistful and more animated, that demonstrate that fallen man can, by understanding his fall, be more vital than any heavenly body; that, for example, the edgelands might come to the centre of our lives and mean as much to us as any wilderness ever might have done.

We are on the far side of the river now, and no amount of looking back is going to help the guildhalls. A kind of singing in the dark times has begun. It says that the state we are in is worth as much attention as the world we have lost; that there is masses to do, and many struggles and obstacles ahead, but also that a renewed diligence and attention to what remains, and what it means to us, can help us live more fully, happily, healthily, wisely, more humanly, and better placed to know why we should step back from finishing off our planet in our own cracked image.

My thanks go to all those who have written here. The idea of writing something for Common Ground made many say yes very willingly. Some wouldn't, and I also failed to find anything other than white contributors. There are lots of gaps, and there are countless other places. But I hope something of how we live now is ahead.

Tim Dee
2018

Notes from a Devon Village

Barbara Bender

Until recently I lived in Branscombe, a small seaside village in East Devon. I lived there for nearly thirty years, which is the longest I've ever lived anywhere. As the child of German refugees who arrived in London in 1939, I never felt much at home, or that I really belonged. My mother did her best, but I always seemed to wear the wrong clothes, never seemed to know the right way to use a soup-spoon or fork, and, longing to conform, was mortified by my school friends' remarks about my mother's accent. My suburban childhood was, in retrospect, very lonely. Things got better, of course, as I got older. But Branscombe is the nearest I'll ever get to 'belonging' or being in place. I'll never be an 'insider': for that you'd have to be born in the parish, or have married in, but that's all right.

What's it like, this place? A tucked-away 'picturesque' landscape. Small streams from three steep valleys flow together a mile or so from the sea, meander through a narrow flood plain, skirt a high shingle bank that almost blocks the valley mouth, and peter out amongst the pebbles on the beach. The bay is a wide-open scoop with tricky currents that makes fishing difficult. To the east of Branscombe Mouth, chalk and sandstone cliffs rise steeply above an almost sub-tropical undercliff created in 1792 when a large stretch of land slipped down. You can take a narrow path through the undercliff lined in May with gentian-blue gromwell flowers, and if you're lucky watch peregrine falcons and ravens disputing the crags overhead. In contrast, to the west, the cliffs

15

are dark red marl with a thin topping of chalk and sandstone. During the great gales of 2014, slides of red mud came down and glistening bands of pink gypsum suddenly appeared.

Inland, the valley slopes are parcelled into small odd-shaped fields. It's pasture land, and the slopes are so steep that there's never been a reason to uproot hedgerows or enlarge fields. On the higher slopes, and along much of the cliff top, the grass gives way to unkempt woodland. Only the segments of plateau between the valleys have larger fields – now, more often than not, slobby pig-lands.

Once upon a time five hamlets dotted the main valley, but over the centuries they were stitched together by small rows of terraced houses. Even so, there's still a strong distinction – if you live 'up' Street your pub is the Fountain Head; if you live 'down' Square, it's the Masons Arms.

These words don't begin to describe what season or weather does to this place – a dusting of snow with footprints of birds or foxes, moon paths across the sea, long winter shadows sharpening tump and hollow, low sun haloing sheep. It is heart-wrenchingly beautiful. And yet, a couple of years ago, we moved over the hill to the next village. Why? Partly because, as we got older, the hills got steeper and the garden larger. More acutely, there was a sense of malaise. Branscombe had been 'discovered'; in estate agents' parlance it had become 'iconic'. The kiss of death. More and more houses have become second or third homes or holiday lets. Thirty-five per cent of the houses are unoccupied for most of the year. Come the winter, most of the cottage windows at Street are dark, the lanes eerily quiet. It feels as if the village is hollowing out.

Finally, two years ago, the Post Office was sold. The old owner had wanted to find a buyer who would take it on; the new owners said they would. But they'd just wanted a cheaper house, and after six months they closed it. It was the end of a long, drawn-out process. Talk to the old villagers and they'll tell you stories about half a dozen small shops:

Wynne Clarke & Rita Saunders: Mrs Hopkins, she used to wear a shawl around her shoulders and a little sort of hat. She didn't use to walk like we do; she was more of a shuffler. She'd go out for the paraffin, then come in – didn't wash her hands – for the cheese. She'd cut the bacon with the knife, she'd dig the sweets out of the bottle with the same knife ...[1]

Shops and front-room tea rooms, a bakery, blacksmiths and cobblers, carpenters and coffin makers, fishmonger and market gardeners. By the time we arrived, in the late 1980s, they'd mostly gone, but the Post Office-cum-shop, hub of the long, straggling village, where you met and caught up with the news, where, alongside pensions and stamps, tickets were sold for village entertainments, was still there. Now a visiting post office sets up in the Village Hall for a couple of hours once a week.

One of the reasons the place is 'iconic' is because it appears 'timeless', and that's because much of it is 'owned' by the National Trust. They've preserved it, and pickled it. They say that they want to work with, and for, the community, which may once have been true, but isn't now. They used to let their cottages to villagers, but the rents have soared far beyond the range of local people. They used to house their warden in the village and pay local people to do conservation work. Proposals that they might offer – at a reasonable rent – a small building to serve as Post Office or farm shop or exhibition space are brushed aside. Time, energy and money is spent stamping their corporate image on their properties and, by extension, the village, but contact and consultation are minimal (and, more often than not, bad-tempered). Not good for them, nor us.

So we decamped to the neighbouring village of Beer – less tidy, more mixed, much busier, with shops, a doctor's surgery and a Post Office.

Beer is a good place to live, but Branscombe is still *my* place. Partly, of course, it's about knowing people. Partly because my heart still lifts when, taking the steep road down into the village, I catch a first glimpse of the hillside and hedgerows rearing up on the far side of the valley, or, swinging seaward, wait for the moment when the sea – and our old house – comes into view. But more, it's because I *know* so much about this place. My Branscombe landscape is a *depthy* place ingrained with stories that go back thousands of years.

Twenty-five years ago, a group of us set up the Branscombe Project. We were aware that the old villagers were getting older and that their children had often moved away. When we started there were at least forty people who had lived in the village all their lives; now, perhaps, there are ten. Alongside the affluent incomers, they have often seemed marginalised.

We began to record their voices and memories. Lillie Gush, the first person I ever recorded, was born in 'an hundred and one' (1901). With no teeth and a strong Devon accent, she wasn't easy to understand, but it was clear she was very angry. She'd lived in the village all her life, she'd looked after her family. Now there was no one left and no place for her, and she'd been sent to a care home some distance away. Not really anyone's fault, but still she felt it was unjust. She knew all about inequality and village class divisions. She remembered when the first water pipes were laid and how, though they passed through her parents' garden, 'they didn't even give we a tap. But', she added, 'they'll get their deserts where they've gone now!'

We wanted to do more than just siphon people's memories into cassettes. So we began to unwind their stories into annual exhibitions, wrote and published booklets, and ended up with a capacious website.[2] We also host well-attended winter talks.

Some of the best moments come as we pore over old photographs or postcards, or manipulate a digitised map[3] so that people can mark their favourite places or landscapes and wonder at each other's choices:

John Marchant: Pits, School Lane – the view to the sea and the sea of wild garlic flowers in the spring.
David Strange: South end of Stockhams Hill – a fantastic spot for star-gazing.
Betty Rowson: Goosemoor, where I lived as a child. I was happy there.
Mike Fielden: Up at Weston – as a kid going there. My father used to launch his glider up there – with an elastic band and a Jag.

18

Other good times are spent walking the landscape, stopping and poking around, old villagers and incomers talking with one another, remembering things they'd quite forgotten, often contradicting each other. Moments of communal gathering-in; theoretical or techy know-how twining with people's intimate local knowledge.

After we'd transcribed the old gravestones in the churchyard we put on a performance. Masked ghosts (old villagers and new) emerged from behind the gravestones to recount the life-stories of the deceased. At one point, Ralph Cox suddenly stopped, swept out his arms to embrace the graves – 'Thirty-five of them, thirty-five, all my relatives!'

We went on from oral history to working in the archives, and to field-walking. We pieced together stories that went back 700, even 5,000 years. Where the chalk-lands of southern England come to an end, on the east side of Branscombe Mouth, you can see the bands of flint nodules in the cliff face. It's a beautiful black flint highly prized by prehistoric people; they would have scavenged the beach and scaled the cliffs for it. Inland, you find spreads of waste flakes, cores, scrapers and points. Once, when I was walking with a fellow archaeologist on Bodmin Moor, he pulled out a flint point from the side of the path – Branscombe flint! Even 5,000 years ago, people and things moved long distances.

Working with maps is another way of exploring time and space. Recently we ran workshops[4] with about thirty people in which we compared the 1840 tithe map, an early Ordnance Survey map and a current map, and plotted changes in the social and economic landscape. For example, on the 1840 and 1880 maps every farmstead was surrounded by orchards. In spring the parish would be flushed with sweet-smelling apple blossom. But, until the beginning of the twentieth century, the farmers turned the apples into fairly gut-rotting rough cider which then formed part of the farm workers' wages. Not great news for the household economy. By the 1960s farmers were being subsidised to grub up old orchards.

We also used maps to trace the changing fortunes of footpaths and tracks. They leave the best traces of past generations of men and women going about their daily business. Paths taken by the farm workers as they walked to and from the farms and fields, climbed the hills to the quarries and lime kilns, or made their way down the zig-zag paths to the cliff-plats or beach. The five shutes[5] that mark the spring-line along the lane through the village were where the women came to fetch water and gossip. Other paths took them to work in service in the big houses, or to Barnells where John Tucker, the mean-spirited entrepreneur who enforced a monopoly on their Honiton lace-making, lived. He paid them a pittance, and made them buy their goods at his overpriced truck shop.

Although many of these paths have gone and those that remain are often deserted, it's still true that the best way to get a feel for the topography of a place, what was in view and out of view, the activities that went into the making of landscape, is by walking the footpaths. If you take the coast path from the beach, up the steep west hill to the cliff top, you're following the donkeys that carried the coal landed from Welsh colliers up to the Berry lime kilns. Further along the cliff top the path broadens out into Kiln Lane and you'll find huge flint spills, debris from the old lime quarries, or occasional pieces of coal or brick from one of the long-dismantled kilns. Eventually Kiln Lane meets the lane by which farmers 'from away' came by horse and cart to fetch the lime.

Most of the old zig-zag paths down the cliff to east and west of the Mouth have fallen away or become overgrown, but a few remain. At Littlecombe Shoot you're walking smugglers' paths that date back to the eighteenth century. 'Littlecombe Shoot', wrote a Customs officer in 1807, 'is a good landing place, and a road [Kiln Lane] leading up to the head of Branscombe Village. The fences in general very indifferent, so that the smugglers may cross them in any direction that best suits their purpose to avoid the Officers.'

An old smuggler recounted this story late in the nineteenth century:

My brother was landing tobacco at Littlecombe, when the coast-guard boat rowed out gently from the shadow of the cliff ... The three men hearing the noise turned round & rowed smack out to sea. That was Friday night, & by Sunday afternoon they had rowed to Jersey and sent the goods back to the consigners. I call that acting honest.[6]

Some of the smugglers, and many others as well, put these same paths to more legitimate use. On the cliff faces where the land had slipped, there were patches of soil which, aided by sea breezes and the sun on the cliff face, and manured with seaweed from the shore, produced very early crops. Farm workers renting the plots could grow early potatoes, vegetables and flowers. They called themselves cliff farmers and used their donkeys to carry the produce up the cliff and off to market. It gave them a modest, but much prized, independence. But it was hard work, and by the mid twentieth century the plats were abandoned.

But not quite. Some of the stone linhays the cliff farmers had built for their donkeys were turned into holiday huts. When these new cliff-dwellers were asked to mark their favourite places on our map, it was nearly always 'their hut':

Flo Pearson: It's our hut – it's been part of my life always and is my favourite place in the world. My dad's ashes are there, plus years of plants we've tried to protect from the brambles.
Adrian Symons: Recently my mother and my sister counted about thirty or forty different types of wild flowers.

And that's not the end of it. In 2007 a startling bit of Branscombe history was made when a huge container ship, the *Napoli*, breaking up in the channel, was beached at Branscombe below Littlecombe. Overnight the wind came up and nearly 200 containers slipped into the sea, many washing up on the shore. They contained an eclectic assortment of BMW engines, motorbikes, cosmetics, personal belongings, oak barrels, nappies, dog food and Xhosa Bibles. A microcosm of world trade.

The popular press castigated the white-van people 'from away' who arrived a couple of days later, for the wild scenes on the beach. Before

21

that, however, the local lads had already appropriated most things of value. They easily avoided police cordons and guards by using the same old cliff paths. One night, Jamie Lambert and his mate were scouting the containers at Littlecombe when they suddenly saw the guards:

'Run!! Let's get the hell out of here!' The search lights were going and the people were chasing us. Pulled ourselves up the rope, started going up the cliff. We didn't use torches and we managed to run zig-zag all the way up the path. But, obviously, those security guards ain't local, they would struggle to believe that anyone could negotiate those cliff paths without a torch, so they spent the next twenty minutes ripping apart the chalets, going through the hedgerows. We were long gone!

Same footpaths; different histories.

Final story: not long ago we took an inland walk with a group of villagers. We were walking in the footsteps of Harry Layzell, village blacksmith-cum-chimney-sweep-cum-postman. Sometimes he'd deliver the post by bike, but mainly he walked, and sometimes it was a good eight miles. Jenny Newton, now in her seventies, used to ride on his shoulders, and as they went along he'd be singing Methodist hymns at the top of his voice. So, with Jenny, we walked part of his round. Down the steep hill to Hole Bottom where the owner of the former mill came out to tell us about the ghost of a lady in a red cloak, another man showed us the millstone that marks his threshold, and Angela Lambert brought out a polished chert axe found in the stream-bed behind her house. Then up the steep hill to the disappeared farmhouse at Hooknell. Ross Wilmington, the farmer's son from up the road, remembered that his grandma had lived here and that, each day, she'd walk up to the farm to fetch her bread. We stopped at another disappeared cottage – faint traces of wall foundations, different sorts of vegetation where the postman's path was barely visible – then trudged up to Hill Arrish for tea and buns.

Hill Arrish is a grand new house built on the footprint of a 1930s Indian-style bungalow. Pulling down the bungalow revealed a cache of newspapers. Copies of the *Black Shirt* and *Action* dating from 1935 to early 1940. Sitting out in the sun, reading these obscene anti-Semitic rags, the hairs rose on the back of my neck. The then owners of Hill Arrish, Rafe Temple-Cotton and his mother, Lucy, had been ardent fascists, and Rafe was chief south-west organiser for Mosley.[7] He ran a large market garden and was considered a good employer, but his innocuous white delivery van also served as a grandstand for him to spout his fascist views – in Sidmouth and Hyde Park. Villagers still remember him and some at least were not unsympathetic. In Sidmouth the locals threw him in the river.

It's a truism that history's always in the making and that we're part of the making. Sometimes, being on the spot, you can offer small interventions.

In 2014 came gales so fierce you couldn't stand up, a sea so wild that spume from the waves topped the Sea Shanty café. The waves took out the foundations of the beach chalets to the east and tore away the trackway to the west. Natural England and the National Trust showed little sympathy. For them, the wooden chalets were a blot on the landscape. Far better, and all part of the national Shoreline Management Plan, to allow cliff and beach to revert to their 'natural' state. The owners of the chalets and café offered to pay the costs of reinstatement. To no avail: the pebbles were not to be moved because they might disturb the elusive scaly cricket (which, it seems, had not been much disturbed by the beaching of the *Napoli* or the heavy clean-up operation that followed). No 'foreign' stone could be imported to shore up the trackway. They envisaged that as sea levels rose and breached the pebble bank, a fine estuarine habitat would be created. In the longer term they may well be right, but in the meantime the chalets are part of the landscape, much loved, and they and the café are important to the local economy.

Moreover, just as we recognise that the gale and its aftermath are not 'natural' but are caused by climate change due to human activity, so the notion that the cliffs should be returned to a pre-chalet 'natural' state is nonsense. So we have helped make the case for a *cultural* landscape. Had they not noticed, for example, the stands of white buddleia that mark the old cliff plats? Or the remains of a donkey linhay and lime kiln. Permission has reluctantly been given for 'temporary' repairs.[8]

That's it. For me love of place comes with the detail, and in trying to understand the stories and histories that go to make a living landscape; comes, too, with a sense of belonging.

Bringing this piece to a close, I realise that I've hardly cited any significant landscape literature. And thinking about it, I find myself wanting to bypass more recent writings, to return to the people who first fired my imagination and helped form my understanding of place and scape. To W. G. Hoskins[9] for his pleasure and skill in explaining why a road takes a particular bend, or what a faint field trace might mean. For insisting that 'Any small tract of England [makes] a marvellous study under the microscope of the local historian'. And to Raymond Williams[10] for teasing out the way cultural perceptions and social and economic relations play off one another, and for shifting easily between micro and macro: 'history active and continuous: the relations are not only of ideas and experiences, but of rent and interest, of situation and power; a wider system'.

And John Berger for not only insisting on how subjective our understanding of the world is, and how caught up in unequal social relations, but for his ability to 'hold things dear', to feel gratitude, and to engage with other people.[11]

Perhaps, before we uprooted from Branscombe, we should have reminded ourselves that history *is* always in the making. Our sombre assessment of parish and community is already open to question. For example, it's noticeable that, being able to work from home, and with the council making efforts to rent out council houses to local people, there are now more young people in the village. The primary school begins to look less like a basket case. The young ones have successfully fudged traditional events – Apple Pie Fayre, Harvest Festival – with new ones to create a Harvest Fair that's re-enthused the community. New stewardship schemes have begun to address environmental and social issues. A local environmental group is in the making, wanting to talk within the community about climate change, bio-diversity and sustainable energy. 'Bad times' spur new energies.

24

Notes

1. Barbara Farquharson and Joan Doern (eds), *Branscombe Shops, Trades & Getting By* (Branscombe Project, 2000). In the context of village and Project I use my married name, Farquharson. It seems more comfortable than Bender, my professional maiden name.
2. www.branscombeproject.org.uk
3. The digitised 'Favourite Places, Favourite Landscape' map, and a discussion of what it was that people chose, and why, is posted on the Project website.
4. This project, undertaken in conjunction with the East Devon AONB and English Heritage, was known as the HEAPS project – Historic Environment Action Plan.
5. The shutes are pipes let into the roadside banks to tap the spring-line water.
6. Ephraim Perryman, talking to J. A. Morshead in 1893.
7. Todd Gray, *Blackshirts in Devon* (Mint Press, 2006).
8. These issues are taken up in the last chapter of *Cliff and Beach at Branscombe* by Barbara Farquharson and Sue Dymond (Branscombe Project, 2014).
9. W. G. Hoskins, *The Making of the English Landscape* (Pelican, 1955).
10. Raymond Williams, *The Country and the City* (Chatto & Windus, 1973).
11. John Berger, *Ways of Seeing* (BBC & Penguin, 1972); with Jean Mohr, *A Fortunate Man* (Canongate, new edition 2016); with Jean Mohr, *A Seventh Man* (Penguin, 1975).

A Box of Old Shells

Julia Blackburn

I was walking along the beach. Sunshine and a cold wind. Nobody, and then a couple sitting very still side-by-side on the upturned concrete bunker close to the water's edge. Two dogs milling softly around them, and I was sure I had seen exactly this scene before long ago, but I couldn't remember when.

I had a slight sense of hurry because the tide was coming in and it was possible to get cut off, with the steep cliffs at my back and the waves biting at my toes. Stepping quickly over sand and pebble and the shiny expanses of exposed clay, I sometimes looked out towards the mirage of distance, but mostly I looked down, hoovering the solidity of surface with my eyes.

I noticed a man walking towards me from out of the distance. He was also looking down, and stopping every so often to pick something up. He was carrying two bright-green plastic shopping bags that appeared to be rather heavy. As we passed each other I said, 'Treasure?'

'No,' he replied, as if this was not an odd question: 'lead' – and he opened one of the bags to reveal a tangle of lead piping. 'I get fifty quid a week, some weeks,' he said.

'Ever find fossils, bones?' I asked.

"Undreds of 'em. Got me garage full. Three years back, under the forest bit of the cliff, it was all bones, scattered on the sand. I got a vertebra as big as a table top' – and he put down both his bags to define the size of the vertebra. 'Sold it on eBay for two hundred quid. Gave a lot of stuff away a few weeks back – a young girl who's interested in fossils, and now she's studying 'em at college, and I reckon she'll become a palaeowhatsit.'

I told him I was writing a book about Doggerland and all the lands that came before it, and he turned his head vaguely towards the soupy grey of the North Sea as if he was looking at the country I had just referred to.

I felt bold and said I'd love to see his collection, and he said, 'Come any time! You can 'ave what you want from it. It's no use to me.' I wrote his phone number into my mobile. His name was Ray. He lives in Pakefield, not far from the Pontin's Holiday Park.

I phoned him a couple of days later and his wife answered. 'Ray! It's that lady you met!' And so I arranged a visit.

They live in a little bungalow in a loop of little bungalows, shoulder-to-shoulder like biscuits in a tin. The people in the house next door had a life-sized black panther in their garden, sitting upright. I think it must have been made of fibreglass: it was too smooth and shiny to be the painted cement of garden gnomes.

There was no bell on the front door, so I followed a concrete path round the side. The two of them were in the kitchen, close to the window, and they looked up and waved as if we were old friends. Ray opened the back door with the front-door bell in his hand. 'It's broke,' he said.

'Making a noise all night,' she said.

He is not very tall and has a nice quiet manner to him, like an old-fashioned idea of a bank clerk. She – Gail – is round and jolly, like an old-fashioned idea of a schoolteacher. I had brought them a book and a packet of biscuits. 'That looks nice – I like reading,' she said. 'Ray will eat the biscuits. He'll eat anything sweet. Me, I eat crisps. Crisps are my downfall.'

We went into the sun room and Gail brought us mugs of coffee. I sat in a big upholstered armchair with flower patterns on it. A smattering of polite conversation, and then Ray pottered off to his garage in the garden and returned with a little pile of plastic ice-cream boxes. He pulled the lids off and lifted out small objects he thought might interest me, each one in its own sealed pocket.

'All this lot's from Covehithe – the beach, the cliff and the private land behind the lake. I've permission to go there from the lady of the house.' We started with medieval seals and then moved on to Anglo-Saxon buckles. I paused to admire a broken bit of worked metal: some kind of belt clasp, on which the crude outline of a running dragon had been scratched, or maybe etched is a better word. Unmistakably a dragon, and done with a sort of familiarity as if from life. I said how lovely it was.

'Have it,' said Ray. I was rather taken aback, but I thanked him and put the dragon on the side table next to my mug of coffee.

Now lots of Roman coins. The faces of emperors, one after the other. Hadrian, with the word *Aegyptus* on the reverse side, and a naked female form which I thought might have been Cleopatra. And then a really tiny coin that would balance comfortably on the tip of my little finger, and very shiny as though it had just been polished, holding the perfect image of a round-faced and rather insecure-looking emperor, but I couldn't find his name.

Ray gave me a broken clay pipe. 'There you are,' he said, and I put it next to the dragon.

He kept going out and coming back with more stuff and saying how much he had given away or sold. 'There's a good market for the seals. I gave stuff to the Norwich Museum, but when I went to have a look, they said they'd lost it. Lent them stuff to be identified and now they can't find that either.'

His collecting began when he was given a metal detector forty years ago. The first thing he found with it was a gold coin. He brought out the coin from its plastic bag. He keeps it in a box lined with red imitation-velvet. It looked as fresh and beautiful as a wild flower still growing in a field, thin and delicate, and it seemed impossible it could have survived undamaged for so long. On one side there was a rather snaky-looking boat riding some rather snaky waves, and a king was standing in the middle of it, almost as tall as the central mast. He had a pronged crown upon his head and a kingly, or perhaps a saintly, expression on his face I could distinguish the Latin letters that circled the king and his boat, but I couldn't read them because my Latin wasn't up to it.

'1362,' said Gail. 'Edward III.' She paused and then said, 'You hold it in your hand and you think, it's not people like us who ever owned something like this. We took it to the coroner, but he gave it back. He didn't want it, so we kept it.'

I wanted to ask about the nature of finding – the compulsion of it, perhaps, or the quiet that comes from looking without knowing what you are looking for, but Ray wasn't interested, and all he would say was, 'If conditions aren't right you still got to go, because you don't know, do you … When I find something that's been in the ground all that time, it's a marvellous feeling. But the thrill for me is the finding of it. I don't need to keep the stuff.'

Ray's father was one of seventeen children. They all grew up in Covehithe, but Ray moved to Kessingland later, which I think was something to do with his mother dying. It was in Kessingland that he met Gail and became a slaughterman.

He spoke of Covehithe as if he could see its past history from having found so many traces of what had been, and perhaps also because his family had lived there for generations and it was still the place where they all belonged, dead or alive.

He explained that in medieval times Covehithe had been very wealthy: lots of rich people, traders; there was a port there, and he was shown an aerial photo in which you could make out a sort of square shape in the sand. 'You can see where it was if you know what you're looking for. You follow the little path past the pigs; through the narrow bit, and then there's that notice board and a bent tree, and you look across towards the reeds and there's a sort of dip, almost an outline. Boats came right in at high tide, and they'd unload when the tide went out.'

Ray kept going to the garage and returning with more boxes, more talk, more little gifts for me to add to my heap. He did have a Papal seal from 1100: Pius I, he thought it was, but he sold that, and some years ago, after a storm, he found a medieval well. 'A circle as big as that' – and he held his arms out as if he was embracing the air – 'lying there on the sand, just the base of it, and it was made of wood, and there were black things all the way round the sides, and at first I thought it was a bear trap.'

That had been the day before Christmas, and he'd contacted his friend Paul Durbridge and together they'd dug the well out. 'A bell-well it were. Double layer of wood nailed together and made from parts of barrels. The mouth of it was at the top of the cliff, but of course the edge was much further back in those days. The people who made it had dug all the way down, fifty feet or so, until they reached the water level, and the well ended in a point at the bottom. There were pots in there, some of 'em near-perfect, and the wood was as good as new, and you must be talking six or seven hundred years. It was a work of art.' Ray wondered why they'd dig a well there in the first place, because surely it must have been filled with salty water. There was no answer to that.

While he went to get more boxes, Gail told me she wasn't really interested in his treasure hunts, but they kept him happy, and anyway she and an old school friend went out quite regular to a place called Potters for a girlie weekend. They laughed a lot. So she has her fun too.

Ray returned with some worked flints. He said the lake at Covehithe, which is known as Benacre Broad, was once a stream, and an archaeologist told him the stream was a tributary of the Thames. 'Archaeologists are a bit like zoo keepers,' he said then, remembering the conversation: 'they think that because they're paid by the taxpayer and have got stuff, it all belongs to them. They take over. They don't like it if a member of the public gets in the way and knows more than they do.'

We were moving back in time. The flints were followed by a card-board box filled with clam shells, all of them stained in gentle shades of cream and ochre and a sharp yellow like clear honey. Some were filled with a coarse-grained sand, packed in tight. 'After a really big storm the sand can go right down, and there's scouring at the base of the cliff and you get about four foot of these shells. You only see them for a while and then they're gone.' He said these ones were 2 million years old, and they were soft when he first got them, but he dried them out and now they were hard.

'There was a chap came with sacks and a sack barrow, and he'd collect the shells and dry 'em out and go through 'em with a magnifying glass, and he found some teeth of a mouse that was unknown and he named it after his wife. He was big in fossils, he was – he had a bone that came out from the sea and he thought it were a pelvis, but it were the top vertebra from a giant deer. D'you want 'em?' – and the box came to sit beside my chair.

Then he told me that once he was walking at Covehithe and on that day the layer of grey pink marl that is part of the old riverbed was smooth and flat, lovely it was, and he noticed these white markings in the clay, and that was an animal, about six foot long and four foot wide, and it was complete, but he couldn't tell what sort it was. The white markings were the lines of its skeleton, like a beautiful drawing, and as he watched it was erased by the incoming tide.

He went out one last time and came back with a cardboard box filled with mammoth bones. 'These any use to you?' he said, and I said they were. 'There you are then' – and he set the box down beside the box filled with shells.

There was a final rush of giving, and I received a bit of mammoth tusk, dark brown and shiny, and he explained how you could tell what it was by the texture of it; two belemnites; a lovely piece of pale fossilised wood, and a sea urchin that had been partly crushed, maybe trodden on by some heavy beast, before it was transformed into a lump of golden-coloured flint. He'd had it for years.

'You don't mind if I give her this, do you, dear?'

'No, dear, it's been on the side of the sink long enough.'

They called each other dear, very sweetly, with a tenderness floating in the word.

I said my goodbyes and they accompanied me outside, the dragon and the broken clay pipe in my pocket and all of us carrying everything else in cardboard boxes. There was something odd about my car, and we saw that the back wheel was flat. I'd only had the thing for a couple of months and didn't even know where the spare tyre was hidden.

'Don't worry – Ray will do it, won't you, dear?' said Gail. And so she read the instruction manual to him, while he crouched on the pavement and did the practicalities of removing the wheel and fitting its replacement. I looked on and felt foolish. 'Me and Ray are a good team,' said Gail.

'She reads books,' he said, struggling to undo a nut. 'All I ever read is the *Metal Detector* magazine.'

Before I drove off, Ray promised he'd let me know when he next hears from his friend Fred, who has lots of worked flints, beautiful ones. He's sure Fred would like to show them to me: we can meet him together.

When I got home I laid out the shells on a long pale table in my husband's studio and they looked like music, or a story without the need of words.

I Am Still Yesterday

Sean Borodale

The moment when a feeling enters the body is political.
This touch is political.

Adrienne Rich

House

Rain like a fog. River pounding. Scent of blossom smashed up. I surprise
a deer; it bounds away under the fence into the boggy corner of the
field where the flag iris grow. Stack wood in the woodshed for it to dry.
Bring dry logs into the house. The slightly fermented smell of cherry
as the dampness dries off. In this wet, tangible land whose sour earths
are the decay of meadowsweet, scabious, knapweed, the windfall of
apples, the sloe leaves when they turn yellow, how does a beehive occupy
site? I look at the bleached boards of the box on its stand to the north
of the house. A point of dissonance: its assemblage of stackable supers
reminds me of Le Corbusier's vision for a new Paris.[1] A modernist tower
block, endlessly repeatable, honed to the right angle, aligned to the
vertical. BS1300: 1960 is the 'Modified National' endorsed by the
Ministry of Agriculture in the 1920s. The 1920s: when Rudolph Steiner
warned that modern apiculture might be devastating to the honeybee.

The terrain here is rough, unkempt; but I can see invisible fields and
points of attention that echo Le Corbusier's 'relational lines' – the hidden
geometry that connects distinct elements in the architectural scheme.
'Relational lines' inhabit the footprints of ancient settlements.

Architecture has lifted them into the vertical as regulators in the organ-isation of facades. These relational lines of architecture haunt stage-craft, too, as they are worn into my theatre of writing across site. Repetition, tangible forces, worked and reworked like glances between actors on stage; honed through revisiting sites (the walk from the house to the beehive, or the entry into the confines of a particular cave), becoming paths of assertion as force-fields, gravities, 'spots of time'.[2] The place is actor: we perform together. I try language to X-ray the earth and the air. Writing live is like working with wood; a mobile joinery of motion respective to grain of moment attempted. Writing almost quiet; a mime bound to earth's substance through exertion, the labouring body in the field of its work is collaborative: unit of footstep, angle of turn, reach of arm, capacity of ear.

Cave

I have gone into the dark; entered the mouth of the cave uphill taking Sophocles' *Oedipus at Colonus* with me as torchlight and guide; as equip-ment for seeing darkness.[3] The process of recovery has been in the field of language. The poetic voice. All that is dark, coveted, hidden by the earth, in state of burial or decay, is brought to exposure in the flickering wings and poetic speech of the dimension of light. Insects metamor-phosing in darkness unfold wings and take flight. Flowers sing or scream. The air into which speech is given broadcast is where bees fly. Speedier than the slow-urn of burial-time. Working boots of children rise from scoured river-silts and are lit: enigmatic as the keeping of bees.[4] What lies in the dark is darkness itself; rare as a mineral; bones, teeth, bodies, toxins. The river is metaphor for the direction of transport. Time is transport, but convoluted here: an alliance with the anticline on which this valley rests.

Cell

The bees hatch from cells built by bees. In *Krapp's Last Tape*,[5] the cell is the closed apartment in which Krapp hears the memory of himself. His only actual location: 'a late evening in the future'.[6]

I imagine a locked apartment in a tenement or tower. The load-bearing of the singular voice in isolation is an audio honey; memories of a springtime. The voice which meets its own ghost-echo, isolation. This is the voice that steps out, as it moves towards the beehive and finds its singularity tested in what is modular. The beehive stands as the pragmatic symbol and principle of the cell's multiplicity. Memories and formative sensations locked in combinations that – by simply walking through a site – parts of the lock align and open into emotion. How does honey encrypt time? How does language transform itself? How does the terminology of beekeeping diminish a symbiosis? Why am I forced to say: 'national hive', 'queen bee', 'colony', 'worker'?

Asylum

The honey in the stacked supers and brood frames can be taken as a microfiche for the data of a locality, environment, weather, flora, pollen, meteorological condition. The river silt here is not nearly as nutritious as it looks: leaves grow with difficulty; roots remain shrunken and woody; beans aspire to grow but are most often severed at the root by earthen mice and wilt suddenly. What am I made of eating this landscape? A place of repetitions that equivocate the bearings of continuity. Tonight, I took peelings out to the compost, then up to the beehive to cut the long grasses away from the entrance. Grasses gone mad, everything on bowing stilts. Apples in this valley taste of coal tar: sour and vinegary, blotchy red, a black lichen growing over them like coal dust.

Everything has happened in this ground; the place is a physical archive of caves, quarries, swallets, mines, Neolithic burials, Mesolithic cave cemeteries, Bronze Age barrows, Cold War bunkers. What am I in? A thirty-mile ridge in north Somerset, twenty miles south of Bristol, running in an east–west direction with a northern trend towards the west where it falls into the Bristol Channel at Brean Down. In the east the karst landscape of the Mendip high plateau breaks up into the hills of the coalfields between Frome and Radstock. 'Mendip' is cognate with the Welsh *mynydd* (hill), echoing *mine deep* and *men dip*'.[7] I hear in the word *asylum* the refuge of archive; collecting voice-prints from sites of darkness into accession for a future unknown, for a use not yet recognised. Recording the instant of lyric unconscious: the edge of the unheard, recording incidentals of noise, action; decay, generation.

Riverbed

The bees hum in their box as I lower down fully into the river water, neck-deep, cold gripping me, a whole skin-suit of prickles like nettles stinging. Immersed at the lowest point of the valley, I watch the black river flow below the level of everything. Bits of moon: what else was there underneath flowing past, crouching in the unseen where otter have been and in water which flows from a pike pond four miles upstream? Too alert to fingers and toes numbing in the depths of crayfish and all other imaginings, I step back onto the soft land.

Deciphered scrawl I made in the near-full moonlight, but darkened by trees, rough writing I can barely read. I remember smelling mint, water mint – I must have crushed it underfoot. Contingent essence. How can I write the smell of water mint?

Presence

I kept busy to evade the calm which shows up absence: I took a wall apart, baked a cake with coconut and sultanas, made popcorn for a 'makeshift' cinema with the children. I made a lunch of bread, cheese and a grated celeriac-and-apple salad, I made a chicken stock, I cooked a supper, mowed lawns, read. At midnight a white moth was upside-down in the bath tub. I took it out and put it on the side of the bath. Watching it being still, a barn owl in miniature, brown flecks and freckles along its wings; a furry head, large feathered antennae. Pure white. The dips of its eyes glinting, tiny inverted rubies shone back at me when I rotated it in my hands and looked in. I thought it was dead. I took it with me on a piece of paper. When I woke there was only the page, no moth; the absence of it a greater statement.

Time-Exposure

Late summer. I hope to take some honey out of the hive. Blue scabious in the two fields nearby – a haze of blue not unlike the blue of eyes – somewhere between the knee and the ankle, in the afternoon sunlight; wading perfect seawater but airy and field-borne. Look up the steep hill into the air full of aslant sun, thousands of insects, crane flies; like being underwater, thick with life, deep and gelatinous air of living flight. A steep scarp rises from the bee field: once a cave holding a Neolithic teenage couple hunched before a hearth: burnt hazelnut shells, elder twigs, pointy-jawed faces whose bone fragments are boxed, numbered, archived in Wells Museum today. How does time run in such a world? Like Beckett's 'hold about five seconds' as I find myself looped into this evening, trying to cross its mire ...

And the sun risen, white and flaring and brilliant, at that waiting spot, the only level, where the cows steam, like a damp chorus on a hillside threshing floor in ancient Greece. So they waited for the sun: all night they stood vigil and sculptural and waited, perhaps believing in its arrival, trusting the minute it would sear up and create the pasture again, and now it hangs in cobwebs and grasses laden with dew barely able to stand up, and the pools of white fog absorbing all organisms.

Mask

Incident carries a rhyming meaning; a constellation of harmonics across language in modulation. Transcript: a tower block of text. The lyrigraph on its printed pages scattered over the floor of the attic; Borges' map of the world. Its ratio 1:1 text to lyric-kinetic time and place. How does the field of text differ to the field of spoken voice? When I put on the beekeeper's 'costume' and mask, I earth myself into being something here. When I put on the role and voice of Hestia at the stove, I ground myself in function.[8] I exist as a shadow otherwise. The lyrigraph is born of a shadowy set of instruments – in my records of this place are the experience of a shadow.[9]

The road twists downhill, its A-road banking and hard verge rubbish-strewn. It will always be the road on which I caught the swarm of bees; it will always be the road from which I picked up the dead black cat stiffened with rigor mortis. The road snakes around the line of the Fosse Way, the Roman road which cuts through the coalfields of the valley. Deaths of forests under the stone and grass and worms of the present country. It is the landscape where I have tried most to formulate a physical poetics not of poetry but of the experience of writing poetry – the *lyrigraph*. How writing on location is set up, how it happens live through the presence of body: the task which is also the play, the game which is the art, the act of uttering which is writing ...

Faucet

A tap in the corner of the kitchen is bound up like a wounded hand. A small well which I pass each day overflows quietly and runs under the track, under the garden, a hole keeps opening. There was once a leaning apple tree, its apples were huge black with light, frothy flesh. I never found the name of it. It fell one spring after a heavy rain, most was burnt in the fireplace. They burnt slowly, its limbs often a whole day's fire, putting an aromatic smoke into the air above the place which gathered the light and grew them first. I have a damp notebook which I left out where I was clearing the tree, now retrieved and to be deciphered. I left it where I'd crouched down to watch a leatherjacket laying her eggs in the grass. A clock ticks. A Black Forest clock from the 1930s with a pendulum which swings and runs fast. Here, time is always out. Darkening along the rill which ran from the ground close to its roots and calciferous water, anything which dropped in it or grew near (nettle roots, leaves, twigs, coins, toys, left for months) encrusted with a grubby white stone. Roots thick with the bone-white scale, twigs inside it rotting away to hollow negative spaces like pieces of old clay pipe if snapped. The road crackles with cars, like a great long twisted aerial laid down over the valley floor. Rolling marbles down a metal sheet, tyre noise and wake of sound falling in pitch ...

Duende

Digging out the bank to rebuild the wall, black granular soil down to the ochre clay which lies in bands of colour, black roots of horsetail; a copper slow worm, a bracelet bent open. A badger came out at dusk and spoke its strange language to me: rough and like a radio from France drifting badly over the Channel. Going back to my own excavation: five centimes from 1997 and a dark yellow rib, the corner of a plate with a piece of flight on it, perhaps a bird, its wings up, like an angel's; blue wings. A plate. What else do I have from the ground here? A gold locket with two locks of hair, a jet ring-stone, a small porcelain dove, a lead songbird, small blue bottle, a bone paper knife. Memory and digging. I go down. The spade cutting neat slices, until I have the bank re-defined, a foot back from where it's to be. Notebooks are like batteries; full of charge. Lorca: 'Whatever has black sounds, has *duende* ... a power, not a work ... a struggle, not a thought.'[10]

Blitz

Quarry workings within earshot. 13.01. The air-raid siren; Gurney Slade or Stoke St Michael quarry. It is permanent sound, pitch winding and braiding, but also as it moves the wind rises, hushes, whines. I feel it. A thing across my face and neck. The wind brings the sound closer and further. A variant on the unchanging. The noise of wartime. People rushing down into dark underground spaces, shelters, terrors, some irritated, some frightened, some mourning, some feeling the random community of possible survivors they might become, all feeling uncertainty. Or perhaps it has become normal. Seventy or more years ago. It is 13.06. Five minutes have passed. Trespass through sound into the shudder of time. Underground of time. A song of the air-raid siren. I remember what I cannot remember. Fragments of readings, takings, gleanings into a composite imagining. It phases, the sound, made of two twisting notes of exactly the same pitch but not quite synchronised. The siren falls, drops, empties of itself. 13.08. I do not feel the blast.

Honey

Honey dripping off my hands as I walked back to the house away from the hives. Bees circling around me; and I so calm the bees could barely 'see' me. Sentences moving around. The wind moaning through wire fencing, a refracted wind.

On the old midsummer: noise at the river, otters, a two-week-old fawn running, trying to swim out. Thoughts of Albion, Avebury, Blake, turfs brought to Bronze Age barrows from elsewhere. Such places at this time of year. All those lives and our lives. Here now. The grass grows ... bright sward from the jaundiced, fragile grass-coat on winter's muds. The house a machine for living in, yes; the theatre of place a machine for writing in. I woke to quarry noise at Gurney Slade; they used to burn stone to send down to Torbay sewage works. A use for limestone. They make tarmacadam for B-roads now. Roadstone. Aggregate for concrete. The water runs into the low stream of the little steep valley, milky water, barely any direct sun, frost all winter, ill-looking grass. Small, hunched houses on a steep track. A single brown pony. The sound: aching joints.

Opened the hive. The bees looked very fine; feisty and so many. I had to improvise a smoker. Packed with honey, packed like a battery; some from the winter too, still in the comb: a red, dark, sticky clump of cells in the middle of the clear, bright, new summer's honey. A light-emitting-diode display of honey; matrix of rooms brightened variously. A metropolis of power. Five frames out, and a big operation in the kitchen with the children helping but mostly licking fingers and spoons, closed doors, scraping the honey off, straining and bottling. About nine jars. Most left for the bees in the hive. Thankful for flowers, nectar; had Turner's *god is sun* in my head, we melt the bee's-wax down into a pristine buttery-yellow block.

A closed-down pub by the main road; a man always with his back to the sky in a nearby field, bent over the scratchings of his chickens; no lefts or rights but meanderings between changeable obstacles and allures and creatures at various stages of their cycles and lives. Trying to hear stars, seeing a fish leap in the dark flow of the river swirling its lace shapes, its tension and contortions; a gauze woven of swirling flies. I go in from the damp field. I am a piece of the grass and the failing last colours of a dusk reflected in the north. Saw a coppery iridescent moth: midnight creatures all disappeared into grass from the heatwave of day.

Nkisi

A hornet flew into the room and onto the table. I tried to catch it under the table lamp with a glass and a card. It died, struggling slowly and heavily, almost as big as my hand. The dream precipitated by a queen wasp crawling out of logs in the wood stove that had been lit, and then falling headfirst into flame as I rushed to find a glass to catch it, and of course perishing; we listened to it hiss. Then a huge ashen hornet fell out onto the ash pan, long dead. I took it up to the attic on a piece of paper to observe later – I think its kinship absorbed the energy of the dying wasp, and ran into my hands and pursued my dreams like one of those African sculptures. What are they called? With iron nails in their heads, glass mirrors in their stomachs.

Changed into thick thorn-proof clothes and went out with a wool hat on my head and gloves on: into the green chemistry of the over-grown. Struggling with nettles I revealed an earth world of tiny bright insects and caterpillars with copper heads and one dying comma butterfly so slowly interposed between the morning and afternoon that I couldn't tell what state it was in. A spider crawled across its underwing. I find myself trying to use – not write – an autobiography to cast pieces of my study of them – the insects – against a roughly human scale of need; to set it at an odd, vague old, imagined or dream-held state. Made notes in the damp air on notebook pages. More earth than words.

Insulation

Typing slowly today. Centipede words, centipede sentences that struggle: pale, soft, not fully alert. Not fully born. Insects that are dead or are dying. Most of them that I encountered, however: wayside stragglers, seeking refuge, or failing mid-step, or shaking near the place where they will drain of consciousness.

A dandelion growing from the pedal of a child's bike. I started to transcribe a moth. I move about aching in time, aching in time like the body aches in certain positions: is it positions of time I ache in? Mary Wordsworth: 'Left William in bed hurting with a sonnet.' I was thinking of insects, wondering how I will make the transition of them as remains of bodies and expressions of being into images that are theatrical, held, uncovered, inside out, performed. The small radio in the head will attempt to tune into the thoughts of insects. Quiet under the stars, under the pantiles of the roof. Tiles made in Bridgwater a hundred years ago. Every tile I put back up on the roof of this house: hung on batons I nailed down on roof felt I unrolled and chalk with a taut chalked string snapped against it to mark a line straight. Inherent warmth. Sheep's wool insulates the roof, big grey sections of it, like Joseph Beuys' felt.[11]

There is nothing rehearsed here, nothing that comes with a script; only the damp stones, mud, dead grass, river silt, deer, badgers, the stag running heavily up and down in the dark close to me breathing shortly, withholding my presence. Scrolls of ice oozed from split hemp agrimony stems. I stand on the creaking of ice and hear the faint signal of bees pulsing like a star; near *and* distant. The hive is a tower. The bees are ions, electrons, magnetism. Flux in a society of units of repetition. Their wild organisation has entered the machine of the house. Hive walls symbolic of improvement, advancement: 'the plan is the generator'.[12] I think of Beuys' *Honigpumpe am Arbeitsplatz*, its tubes of pumped honey: machine as symbol of creative intellect in society.[13] Here it is: the beepump sucking nectar from the flowers and concentrating it here for use more slowly. It makes a sound and the boards of the hive smell of its sound. At night in this valley it is heard more easily, like the incandescent lights of rooms seen through windows. It enters my body.

Notes

1. Le Corbusier, *Towards A New Architecture* (John Rodker, 1931).
2. William Wordsworth, *The Prelude*.
3. Sophocles' play, *Oedipus at Colonus*; the cave is Cockle's Wood Fissure.
4. 'Perhaps you noticed something about the entire nature of beekeeping, something, I would say, of the nature of an enigma.' See Rudolph Steiner, *Bees: lectures; with an afterword on the artistic alchemy of Joseph Beuys* (Anthroposophic Press, 1998).
5. Samuel Beckett, *Krapp's Last Tape and Embers* (Faber, 1960).
6. Stage direction preceding *Krapp's Last Tape*.
7. Robin Atthill (ed.), *Mendip: a new study* (David & Charles, 1976).
8. Hestia is a persona lying at the back of the voice in Sean Borodale, *Human Work* (Jonathan Cape, 2015).
9. 'Lyrigraph', a word I coined from the Greek *lyric*, concerning the lyre, and *graphos*, writing. The lyrigraph is a counter-poetics to the closure of a finished poem, in which the moment of writing is an intentional performance. The writing itself *is* the live performance. The text is its record; a transcript of live experience *of* the performance of writing. The performance of writing the lyrigraph is not the same as the latent performance in a playscript. I made (and printed) texts which scripted the attempt to write about place, in situ or on location. I felt a need, in creating this term *lyrigraph*, to move away from the deadweight of making the poem appear *fait accompli* and into the moments when I felt most alive as a writer. See also Introduction to Sean Borodale, *Bee Journal* (Vintage, 2016).
10. '*Duende* climbs up inside you, from the soles of the feet ... it is ... a question ... of spontaneous creation ... It brings to old planes unknown feelings of freshness, with the quality of something newly created ... All arts are capable of *duende*, but where it finds greatest range, naturally, is in music, dance, and spoken poetry, for these arts require a living body to interpret them, being forms that are born, die, and open their contours against an exact present.' Federico

García Lorca, *Teoría y juego del duende* (Theory and Play of the *Duende*), (Maurer, 1998) pp. 48–62.

11. Joseph Beuys, artist, for whom felt was an important element in his art and theory of social sculpture.

12. Le Corbusier, *Towards a New Architecture.*

13. 'Honeypump in the Workplace', *Documenta* 6 (Kassell, 1977). I discuss this work in more detail in 'Unity in Diversity', *Tate Etc.* issue 38, Autumn 2016.

A Story of Arctic Maps

Hugh Brody

There's no place like home. No other territory that can remind you of childhood feelings – of belonging, and of constriction and loss; nowhere else defines the forces that shape you, and that you need to get away from; the landscape that is both wonderfully familiar and rich in primitive heartbreak. The place that can make you long for elsewhere.

*

Peoples who live by hunting and gathering do not leave much evidence of their occupation and use of their lands. The Inuit of the Canadian Arctic lived in houses built with stone and whale-bone insulated with chunks of sod, or in the famous igloo, shaped in a spiral of blocks of wind-packed snow; and, in summer, in tents made from animal skins. They did not build monuments or mark the boundaries of their territories with any kind of wall or fence. Apart from the delicate evocations of a figure in the landscape, the *Inuksuk*, that was put up as a marker of a trail or used to divert migrating caribou towards waiting hunters, they left almost nothing on the land to show they had been there. And they did not want to change the land itself. Hunting peoples need their world to stay the same – knowledge of it is their most valuable tool. They did not have a way of writing down this encyclopedia of knowledge – their histories and experience – but passed these on in what they said, through the stories they told. Theirs was the life of the mind and the voice.

Minds and voices leave indelible marks on the next generation, but not on the land itself. There are hints of occupation – a ring of stones shows where a tent had been pitched, the broken circle of rocks and sod where a winter house was made, a curve of boulders across the shallows of a river where a weir had been for trapping migrating fish, and the *Inukshuit*, small piles of stone that, in the words of one Arctic traveller, redeemed the empty wastes of their loneliness. Empty and lonely; Arctic wastes. These are terms, a way of evoking the north, that suggest that people have made no difference to it and, indeed, are absent or irrelevant.

The Inuit claim to these empty wastes had to deal first of all with that stereotype, and then with the overarching problem of evidence. They could say this was their land, but could they prove it? Could they show that they were more than perched at the edges of the vast expanses of tundra, wild fjords, and winter ice? No one would deny that the Inuit were the people of the north, but how much of it? Where in truth had their way of life given them a basis for making a claim? Which bits of the Arctic could be said to be their homeland? What areas of this forbidding landscape could be shown to be a territory that had supported life 'since time immemorial'? This was the legal requirement: the Inuit must show that they had a way of life, an economic system, that linked them to specific lands, and that all this had been in existence for many generations, and at least since well before any southerners arrived. What was their way of owning their world?

The attempt to answer these questions, to find the evidence, to make the invisible visible, began in the Arctic in 1974. The Canadian government funded a project that would set out the nature and extent of Inuit use and occupation of their lands. Milton Freeman, a British-born biologist turned anthropologist who had lived in Canada all his adult life, and had done extensive research in the far north, was given the job of coordinating this work. It was to be an independent study, aiming to give definitive answers to the questions raised by the Inuit claim to the Arctic. Lawyers were asked to give their advice: what did they need to know in order to develop the legal basis for a claim? Their answer was simple enough: everything – they needed every possible fact about Inuit ways of using their lands. Freeman decided that the way forward was to make maps of every Inuit hunter's life history – a biography that would show on a map, or a set of maps, all the places he or she had been and all the hunting and gathering he or she had done there. Freeman set out the objectives of the study: as close to 100 per cent coverage of the population, with a map biography for every person who had used the land.

Through all its history as a nation, Canada had been calling for the assimilation of its 'Native Peoples' into society as a whole, or into some idea of a single Canadian society. There had been repeated declarations, as at so many colonial frontiers, that 'Native' people at the margins, 'primitive' peoples, must somehow be absorbed into the body politic, or at least protected against their inherent ignorance and 'lack of development'. Maps would refute these notions – they would make the wealth and sophistication of Inuit life visible and undeniable. They would show that the Inuit, like all the indigenous peoples of Canada, lived at the centre of their worlds. To see the extent and nature of their ways of life would show strength, not weaknesses; riches, not poverty.

The Arctic was divided into regions. A list was made of every creature and plant that could have been hunted, caught or gathered. This list would be used as the basis for the mapping: each hunter and gatherer would be asked to mark on a map where every resource had been found. Older hunters would be asked to make separate maps for earlier times – the era before there was a trading post, the time when there was a trading post but not a school, and then the time since the school came. These are the phases of modern Inuit history. Three different ways of relating to the place where they continued to live. The maps would show how the way and extent of using the land had been affected by these historic changes brought from far to the south.

The project also aimed to make maps of cultural sites – the graves of ancestors, an area that figured in important stories, trails and travel routes, ancient villages, the bays and headlands where the distant ancestors of the Inuit had lived, reaching back several thousand years. This

47

understanding of ancient history was also part of Inuit knowledge, of their links to their lands. This would be done on another set of maps. As if this were not enough, maps would also be made to show how the people understood the biological and environmental relationships that their system depended upon. Routes and patterns of caribou migration; areas where polar bears would make their dens to give birth; ways in which the structures and movements of ice explained patterns of seal hunting; connections between movements of walrus, narwhal and killer whales. This level of information – the ethno-scientific – would emerge in ways and with details that could not be foreseen; but as it did emerge, further maps should be made to show as much of this as possible.

I was given responsibility for the mapping in the North Baffin region. The first task was to put together the topographical map sheets that would include the widest possible extent of the land use of the Inuit of the communities of Pond Inlet and Arctic Bay. I had an idea of this from my time in North Baffin, both listening to accounts of hunting and travel across the region, and being taken out on trips at each time of year with some of the most active hunters. I knew it was a large area: when I came to put the map sheets together, I discovered that we would have to map onto a base that extended over 450 miles from east to west, and 400 miles from north to south. This area was made all the more extensive, with all kinds of possible travel, by its fractured topography: multitudes of bays, inlets, islands and mountains meant that those who used this land would be travelling routes that twisted and turned, headed out across spans of open water and far inland along both dramatic fjords and long river valleys. I knew that many families often had travelled to hunt with or visit relatives and neighbouring settlements that were 150 miles away; and one family I knew had made an extended journey of over a thousand miles, moving from one Inuit community to another, all the way to the edge of the tree line, far to the south-west. Putting together this extent of land use meant making a set of base maps that was five feet across.

In house after house people squatted and crouched around this great area of virtual territory. We went through the list: can you mark all the places you have hunted for ring seal, bearded seal, harp seal, walrus, narwhal? And the places you hunted for caribou, hare, polar bears? And trapped foxes? And fished for arctic char, trout, cod, sculpin? And gathered clams and sea urchins? And hunted eider ducks, snow geese, tundra swans; or collected the eggs of Arctic terns, murres, gulls, black guillemots? And found blueberries, cranberries? Show us all this for when you were living out on the land before the school was set up. Now all the places since the school. And where were the graves of your ancestors, the camp sites you used, the places you put your tents? Then the ecological knowledge: the bears' dens, the way cracks formed in the ice and meant that seals and narwhal could be hunted in open water. Which way did the caribou move in spring and autumn; where did they have their calves; where was their favourite summer grazing? Someone mentioned spiders – were there many in this particular place? Or butterflies? Someone had picked mushrooms – where were they usually found? And a journey – to trade one year, to visit a sick relative another, to travel for the fun of travelling. Along this shoreline, across that mountain pass, then down the coastline there. These were the places we stopped. Here there was a bad storm, and across that headland the ice was always piled high in early spring so it was slow and difficult to use that route. And here is where you can find the bones of my grandparents, or the grave of a southerner who came to trade, or the wreck of an old whaling ship …

One map biography could take two days, and then be added to with extra visits, more stories, another set of memories. We worked and worked, all of every day, for weeks on end. The maps became filled with circles, lines, notes; and the maps piled up. To our surprise, everyone was able to find themselves on these maps – they could see their world in these representations from above, as if the bird's-eye view, which they could have had only in flights of the imagination, was as easy for them as any other way of seeing their lands; and the setting-out of all this experience and knowledge was to discover what it had meant to be a hunter and gatherer in these territories. For all their clutter or information, crossings-out and corrections, lines going in all directions in many different colours, the maps were astonishing, compelling and beautiful creations. They showed just how intense, extensive and rich the Inuit relationship to their world had been, and still was.

The people of North Baffin revealed this to me, the outsider who had brought this inquiry into their homes. They also showed it to one another. No one did their mapping in solitude: members of the family sat and watched, neighbours who were visiting joined in. This was work that celebrated experience and skill. Everyone was delighted to show, tell, share. Everyone took pride in what was being revealed. Each group had its set of hunting, fishing, trapping and living sites. Inuit life had been built around a seasonal round, with winter seal-hunting areas out on the sea ice where a number of households would gather; then a scatter to spring hunting places; a further scatter to summer caribou hunting inland or coastal hunting where kayaks and skin boats could be used; then a move to autumn fishing places at a river the char would be migrating up; and back to the winter seal hunting. Each group had a set of such places. In winter some groups might overlap; for much of the year each group would move between its particular set, along its distinctive seasonal round. As we made the maps, everyone could see that between them they had created a large and widespread system of interconnected patterns of hunting, fishing, gathering and trapping. And of culture. Each family would only speak for its particular part of the large pattern; but to see the pattern as a whole was to understand the brilliance and completeness of Inuit use of their lands and their stories about their lives. When all the maps were put together, every possible harvesting area and living site had been used; everywhere and everything seemed to be known and understood. Stories became maps; maps turned into a new kind of story.

*

During the years I worked and lived in the Arctic I went home, or parts of home, for long visits. I did my writing there. I was in my thirties. My parents were in the north of England; my girlfriend lived in London, where we shared a small flat in Bayswater, at the edge of Hyde

Park. I had new friends in Ottawa, and old friends in England. All the sources of life, all the things that make up the contexts and circumstances of home, were far away and scattered. But when living in the Canadian north I felt alive, or felt that I was able to be who I wanted to be or to experience myself as I really was. I would have the use of a bunk bed in the house of Inuk and Inuya, the family where I always stayed, in a row of low-cost government housing in Pond Inlet, looking out at the mountains and glaciers of Bylot Island, across the wide inlet where I would be taken hunting, moving in winter and spring across the sea ice on a sledge pulled by skidoo or dogs, and in small, open boats in summer and autumn. I was taken to rivers and lakes to fish, and up onto the tundra to look for caribou or geese. By the time the mapping project got under way I was able to live and work in Inuktitut, speaking the language of everyday without too much difficulty, able to learn about most aspects of hunting without needing an interpreter, dreaming in the language; and able to wear the clothes, eat the food, share the routines of my adoptive family without making too much of a fool of myself. I was sometimes miserable with cold or with fear when out on the land. But when I was there, immersed in being there, I did not want to be anywhere else.

The mapping was the most pleasing and, at times, exciting work I had ever done. There was clarity and a fundamental simplicity to the task. We helped people to show on paper what they had done and what they knew. It was obvious what to ask, and it made perfect sense to those who answered. Every map produced surprises: no one had ever known the extent of each family's use of the land; there was a spread of long journeys that people had made that had never been recorded; and I had never seen the systems and patterns of life across an immense area of the eastern Arctic. The work led to real, material results: map after map covered with facts, names, bits of stories, history, culture. The invisible made visible. It was possible to make journeys across it all without going beyond a room where I laid out a set of map sheets.

So I did not give much thought to elsewhere, to the people or places that were 'home'. I never imagined that I would live all the time in the Arctic. It was as if I had no home; or could find enough of a home in a form of homelessness – in being immersed in the Inuit idea of home, and by taking intense issue with the ways in which I could disregard the extent to which I might be homeless. I did not have a phone; there was no such thing as email; the post came in once every two weeks, weather permitting. I could have found ways to be in touch: the radio-phone at the government office could be used, and there was a postal service. I did write occasional letters, with descriptions of what I had been doing or, at times, with expressions of loneliness and missing – these being the times, the states of mind, when I would want to write a letter. But they were few and scant. I gave little thought to the difficulty this might cause to those who had wanted to make homes for me.

I am not sure if anyone worried about me: they never said they did. And there was nothing to worry about. I did not look for danger; every day was an adventure, but I was given the safety and comforts that came from this being a home to the people who took me out onto their lands. Part of their sense of place, and my discovery of the north, came from it being shaped by knowledge, by stories, and not by any remodelling of the physical world. In this sense it was a wild place; though, for the Inuit, and for anyone who followed them into their territories, everything was shaped by their voices and knowledge and a way of living that gave everyone the same kind of connections to the world. A place that took sharing and equality for granted; and where no one staked an individual claim, but all individuals shared in the system as a whole.

When I returned to England, and went again to the Derbyshire hills where I had grown up, or to the London where I continued to be based, I looked out at a world that was shaped and built and understood through private ownership, permanent sites of all kinds, and exclusion. Even the open spaces of the north of England were caught in this net of transformation and class. The walls and hedges marked where land had been worked into fields, and where boundaries had been set up. Bare slopes, moorland and bracken, were the result of deforestation and grazing of the farmers' sheep. The intricate mazes of property.

These were landscapes of social and economic exclusions, the basis and expression of great inequity.

I would look out at this, my childhood home, and understand a bit more about why I had needed to leave it; and what I had experienced in that other way of being human, in the Canadian Arctic. At times as I walked in England, aware of its particular kinds of beauty, I would have a sense of a screen between my eyes and all that I saw; and I would imagine onto this another kind of place. Having been immersed in the lands and the lives of hunters, I needed to see, at least in my mind's eye, a land unmarked by boundaries, open to all, rich with names in a very different kind of language.

In Arizona

John Burnside

Wayside Shrines

On the hard shoulder of Highway 86, halfway between Tucson and the Tohono O'Odham Indian reservation, you might come across a simple wooden cross decorated with trinkets, dusty Valentine hearts, scraps of faded tinsel and a single, magically untarnished Dr Pepper can. It will not be dissimilar to the wayside shrines you have seen in other parts of the world, home-made memorials to the casual dead in Mexico or rural Italy, strangely poignant in spite, or perhaps because, of their crude construction, and as transient as the lives they commemorate. Yet what distinguishes the shrines of southern Arizona is the way in which they differ, not only in number (and they are painfully common sights on this stretch of 86), but also in their remarkable inventiveness, their elaborate decoration and – most of all – in their oddly haunting beauty.

The shrines are not a new phenomenon in this landscape, but their construction has evolved, over years, into a local art form. More often than not, what began as a simple marker has developed into a thing of beauty: ringed around with blue, or red, or yellow painted stones, or draped with Christmas-tree lights and ornaments, a stark white cross gradually becomes a local description of home – a home both real and imagined, drawn, as all American homes are, from television, popular magazines and the myth of a better time, where the deceased may be sensed as continuing in the usual way, his can of Dr Pepper or an old-fashioned Coke bottle in pride of place amongst the knick-knacks, as if he might come back at any time to finish it off. Some of the crosses bear heartbreaking messages – 'Killed by a Drunk Driver', or 'We Love You Daddy' – but most are silent, anonymous, a private treaty between the one who has passed and those who are left behind. Yet even as those unnamed dead continue, they are also magically transformed, like the dead of prehistoric times. The roadside shrines are not official, they have no orthodox function, yet they are the true focus of the region's most authentic funeral rites: better than Church, better than anything the state can provide. Here, mourning, and the process of regeneration, are home-made, just, and true to the dead they honour.

It must be admitted that many, if not most, of these shrines have fairly banal histories. In this part of Arizona drunk-driving is commonplace, especially on the reservations, where poverty, humiliation and boredom are the banal facts of life. The standard vehicle is the old and painfully dilapidated pick-up: a vehicle which should seat three at most in the cab, but which is often used to transport whole gangs of reckless partygoers, men, women and children perched in the back of the truck as it cannons along an empty road in the dark, the driver out of his head on cheap liquor, or exhausted after days of celebration. It's part of the culture, anyhow, to be fearless: life is too poor, too dull and too little prized by the outside world to be overly careful about, consciously at least. A short drive through reservation land confirms it: even the police here are careless road-users, and they sometimes tolerate the drunk-driver who meanders blindly along the empty highway at dawn, weaving from lane to lane or sliding off into the chaparral to sleep it off, if he is lucky, in the shadow of a tall saguaro. If he is lucky.

The unlucky ones kill themselves, or others, or both and, equals in death, are marked by wayside shrines tended by their wives and children, or their parents, or their workmates, through feast days and holidays. The shrines are painted red and decked with hearts on St Valentine's Day, draped with the Stars and Stripes for foreign wars and days of remembrance, twined about with tinsel and hung with tiny coloured bells at Christmas. On birthdays and special occasions, the families drive out with cakes and sweets and canned drinks, yet nobody ever sees them, just as nobody ever sees the careful relatives and friends as they tend the shrines, making them, with each short visit, ever more beautiful and elaborate.

The stores and service stations that line Highway 86 have caught onto this grave culture. Here, the gas stations have a wide selection of plastic flowers and decorations, everything from tinsel to coloured ribbon to Christmas-tree baubles, alongside the car accessories and snacks. Yet – and this really is spooky – nobody is ever looking at these displays when my friends and I stop in for road supplies, and the locals we encounter, the thin old grandfathers in cowboy shirts and hats, the obese children in sweatshirts and cutaway pants, are both shy and suspicious when we loiter at the plastic flower stall to stare, with surprising reverence, at the unacknowledged grave goods. Oddly enough, notwithstanding the very exposed nature of the wayside shrines, death, and the honouring of the dead, is not a public matter here.

In a strange way, the shrines are just as private. This is a country where nobody stops on the road unless death or chance intervenes. As my friends and I pull over to look at one particularly beautiful shrine, I feel awkward, somehow blasphemous, as if I am about to rip open one of those sacred Dr Pepper cans and steal precious liquid from the memorialised father, or son, whose death marks this particular spot. It is hard not to feel that I am being watched, as I hunker down to read the message – a simple 'We Miss You' – on a red, white and blue painted crucifix. When I look up, however, nothing is there, not even a passing car. Only the desert, stretching away as far as the eye can see. This stretch of Arizona is a land of ghosts, a land of those who have died violently, but for as long as I watch it stays silent, empty, utterly peaceful. For a moment I allow myself to hope – perhaps even to pray – that this silence, this peace, gives the unseen mourners who built this shrine some kind of solace. Then I stand up and hurry back to the car, relieved, and disappointed, to be on my way.

Place, or, something there is that doesn't love a wall

Where, or what, is Arizona? For that matter, what is *place*, anyway? How do we know where one place ends and another begins? Where is America? Mexico? Do we find place, or do we make it? Perhaps both: we find a place, we give it a name – our name – and we begin to change its intrinsic nature, more often than not transforming it into property. We plant a flag. We draw up deeds. A man says, 'This is mine,' and does not even consider the absurdity of such a position. One of the main reasons for changing a place is to facilitate this process of acquisition. Our first relationship to place, then, is a betrayal. After that, the only question is: where do we build the wall?

Though non-native (whatever that means here), my Arizona friends do not belong to that species known as 'snow-birds' – town people from the north, usually elderly, who drive south in the winter to save money on heating and other bills. No – they live in the desert all the year round, working from home and accommodating themselves to their various neighbours, with a strong sense that they are newcomers there, and ought to practise respect for those older inhabitants. I still recall the first night with them when, exhausted after my long journey, I headed off to their spare room, only to be offered some advice about the morning schedule that involved a little more than where to find my favourite cereal. Knowing my penchant for rising early and getting out of doors as soon as I can (especially in perennially overheated America), my friends advised me that, if I did go out early, I should remember to put my boots on first. 'That way, the rattler won't catch you barefoot,' they said, with a grin.

It was true: they had a rattlesnake as their closest neighbour, a sizeable fellow who often climbed onto their porch to catch the morning sun. Other locals included coyotes and roadrunners, straight out of those old Chuck Jones Wile E. Coyote cartoons that satirised not only our insane love affair with technology, but also the absurd pace at which we choose to live. Meanwhile, there were bigger and scarier critters to be avoided further afield (diamondbacks, bobcats, mountain lions). The real beauties of the desert, however, are its birds, from tiny hummingbirds to red-tailed hawks to the strange, and oddly cartoonish, burrowing owl, a creature that seems to live in a constant state of wide-eyed surprise, and the only owl species known to live underground. My friends tended a large garden, and I saw a huge variety of birds just by sitting on their porch and waiting for what passed through each day, but they told me that, if I really wanted to see birds, the place to go was Arivaca.

Arivaca. The town itself is nothing much, but the nearby *cienaga* (a marshy area at the edge of grassland where, in this case, several waters meet) was like a dream of heaven. Yellow-billed cuckoo, Swainson's hawk, Lucy's warbler and black-bellied whistling duck breed here, along with thick-billed kingbirds, rufous-winged sparrow and the rare buff-collared nightjar. When we think of desert, we tend to picture mono-tones – sand, rock, dry arroyo, scree – but wherever water is present the daily round turns miraculous. At the same time, when birds find water, they tend to linger, and they are easier to watch for longer periods of time. So many bird encounters are teasing and elusive – walking a rocky trail, I have heard the song of the canyon wren (to my mind, one of nature's most beautiful sounds), but that doesn't always mean I have seen it, while far too many warblers have passed by like restless spirits, filling my head with song, but flitting away into the reeds or the shadows before I quite caught sight of them. Though I have to admit that part of the reason for this is that I am not one of those patient souls who spend whole days in well-camouflaged hides with binoculars and photographic equipment that makes space travel look amateurish. I'm not a real birder; I prefer to saunter.

I should be more disciplined. For stillness offers rare treats now and then: like the day I sat, alone, utterly still, at the edge of a dry arroyo and watched as a passing roadrunner gave me a curious, but far from fearful look, before moving on along the muddy track. It was a good moment, a rare instance of proximity, even a kind of intimacy, and I was about to store it away and carry on my walk, but something held me there and, a few minutes later, a not very wily-looking coyote appeared, obviously trailing the bird, albeit in rather nonchalant fashion. It wasn't like the cartoons at all: speed was not a factor, or wouldn't be, at least, until much later in the game, and it reminded me, once again, of the patience of animals – and of how impatient we are. Then, without further ado, I stood up, and walked back to the point where my world began, a realm that all at once seemed endlessly frenetic, for reasons I was no longer so sure I understood.

Songbirds of Pima County

I am glad you love the blossoms so well. I hope you love
birds, too. It is economical. It saves going to Heaven.

Emily Dickinson

With so many ways for them to fall,
there are days when I cannot bear
to hear them singing.
Yet I look up and, always, the light
is larger than my gaze,
making of each cottonwood a house
of many mansions, where they come and go
from this world to the next.

If, once, I could not raise my hand to stop
the older boys from emptying a nest
and pinning each cowlicked chick
to the bars of a gate,
I still couldn't run for safety, crying
murder, there was too much happening
and, whether by choice or not,
I was involved.

Later the bunting's song would lead me
out into the dark viridian
above a stream, where willows huddled in
so close, it seemed a room in which the mind
could lose itself, the way the heart was lost
in love, when love
was still that kind
of story.

Now love is mostly song
and song

is mostly reminiscence: not
a true account, but something writ
in cypher, like the local
dialects of vireo, or towhee, or a secret
history of mourning dove
and shrike, it speaks to us

in ways we do not care
to understand.
Yet I would understand them, if I could,
the red-tailed hawk sucked
clean into the wheels
and dragged for fifty yards along this desert
road, its last cry
drowned out by the screaming of the tyres,

or later, when we pull in by the creek,
a full moon in the giant
cottonwood, where who knows what
is roosting
and the voice out in the dark
is one part whippoorwill and three parts
grief for something
none of us could name –

though grief is natural, where there is time,
and time is in the music, when we hear
the canyon wren
at daybreak, or the raven
quartering the land, the cottonwood
expanding into light, a red-winged blackbird
calling from the reeds in the *cienaga*:
insistent and lusty, persisting and passing away

as we drive across town to the sun-tiled
diner, where a local is telling the usual

story of how, in the old days (and this is true),
the fishing was good, and the birds
more numerous; while, somewhere, out in back,
a radio is playing to the sunlit
kitchen, and the waitress sings along
so lightly, you could almost love again.

Florida

'Is there a brick wall getting in your way? Fine. That happens. But you have a choice. You can walk away from the wall. You can go over the wall. You can go under the wall. You can go around the wall. You can also obliterate the wall. In other words, don't let anything get in your way. Get a balance, and then let the positive outdistance the negative.'

Yes. That *is* Donald Trump, in his 2010 book, *Think Like a Champion: An Informal Education in Business and Life*. I don't imagine the boys my friend met in the Sonora Desert had read that book, but they had surely absorbed something of its aspirational thinking, or why would they be standing there, in the middle of nowhere, with little or no supplies to speak of, when my friend arrived (her work involves travelling around the remoter corners of this wide country)? Asked where they had come from, they did not reply. Asked what they were doing there, they said they were 'waiting for a friend'. Offered water and a little food, they accepted warily. Then, opening up somewhat, they expressed the concern that their friend might not be coming – they had been waiting for two days. Finally, as my friend made to leave, she asked if she could help them in any way, maybe drive them somewhere, or make inquiries about their lost companion. They shook their heads in unison, and then one boy, the shorter of the two, asked her to point out which direction they should take for Florida.

A few days after I heard this story, I spent a day in the Gila Desert, wandering amongst vast stands of organ pipe cactus. Then, when nightfall came, my companions and I made our way to a small motel on the edge of Ajo, not far from the Mexican border. Given my aforementioned aversion to overheating, I do not linger in hotel rooms easily; more often than not, I am up and about by daybreak – and that overnight stay was no different. After a long dinner at the local Chinese restaurant, I had gone to bed fairly late, but I was out of my cabin by six the next morning, sitting on the tiny porch area and staring off across the yard, towards the desert beyond. A few feet away, an unhappy-looking dog turned and looked at me wearily, but he didn't bark, or come to see if I had anything to offer him, he just lifted his head for a moment, checked what manner of beast I was and then, clearly disappointed, settled back into the dust. It was more or less day already. The yard was partly separated from the desert beyond by a row of parched, twiggy shrubs, and though I knew that makeshift hedge for what it was – one of the *thin places* known to the Celts as borderlines between this world and the other – I let it be and stayed on my porch, feeling the morning cool on my skin and enjoying the fact that, for once, my mind was empty of noise. Twenty paces would have taken me through that invisible borderland into the mystery beyond, but I stayed put and studied to be quiet, and it was a long moment before I realised that I had grown apprehensive of something, though even then I didn't know what. And, of course, it was nothing major: for a local, I later discovered, it was even a commonplace, but to me it was both magical and tragic. At first, I had no idea what was going on, but as I stood gazing into space, I became aware of movement, and then, of a line of people, maybe fifteen or more, coming through one of the many gaps in the hedge and hurrying across the yard: men, women and children, clutching bundles to their chests, following a tall, very thin man who looked no better-off or sure of himself than they were, but who must have been a coyote, nevertheless, one of those professional guides who lead bands of migrants across the border and up to *El Norte*, where the money lives. When they saw me, some of the people in that line looked startled, not because they were afraid I might be a border guard or a busybody, but because I would have looked like an apparition to them (apparitions being common in the thin places). Nevertheless, most of them kept their eyes fixed on the man who was leading the way, hoping they could trust him, possibly wondering where they were and how far it was to safety – and I understood, suddenly, that while apparitions might be a source of fascination for me, for them, hurrying from nowhere to nowhere, and hoping for work and such dignity as life affords, such things were a needless luxury. Some of them would make it (or so I hoped), but most would be forcibly returned, sent back across a border no more real than that straggling line of dusty shrubs at the edge of the motel yard, to begin the journey again. Those who did stay would be confined to other forms of borderland, where someone like me would not linger and, when they stood at the edge of their world, gazing out, their eyes would be turned, not towards the desert, but to the streets and houses that, able as I am to take them for granted, I am always a little too eager to leave behind.

SPRING GENTIANS

Mark Cocker

I'd long heard about Upper Teesdale in County Durham. For botanists, for almost 400 years, it has been a holy grail. The pre-eminent story of the place is the chance it offers to see the ancient plant life of this country at a point when its great carapace of ice had finally begun to slip off. It is the early Holocene at its most tender and pristine. In truth, I was moved to visit when I chanced on pictures of its totem flower. The spring gentians looked like strange, furled tongues of ocean blue bulbed out of the Earth from who knows what depths.

On a whim I set off, but not all wildlife excursions are successful. Yet none is ever wasted. On the drive to the car park at Cow Green I stopped briefly in Langdon Beck. The weather seemed too brutal and the river too swollen with run-off even to get out. Instead I sat and watched a scrap of black plastic – the defining foliage of the oil age – that had somehow escaped the farmer's control. It had snagged across eight tines of a barbed-wire fence.

While its iron-claw grip anchored that sheet down, the gusts wanted to take it and I was mesmerised by the physics of their contest. Minute corrugations in the fabric relentlessly rippled across the surface so that it resembled molten lava freshly setting, or perhaps the black motile liquid from which it was originally made. With each lull the sheet's ragged edge slumped under gravity. Then battle resumed and the plastic bellied out and heaved, and I noticed how its upwelling dark shapes momentarily resembled the wider contours of Cronkley Fell immediately beyond. It was strange to reflect how that rippling crag was made from the same kind of elemental arguments, but over a period of 295 million years.

From the Cow Green car park there were just two small receding eyes of snow somewhere on the high slopes of Great Dun Fell. At 2,782 feet it is the second highest hill in the entire Pennines, and the average May temperature is the same as London's in January. Then the cloud mass rolled steadily down from those northern English vertebrae and the snow eyes were obliterated and the light fell.

I braced myself for the walk while the wind snuffled at the car's underside. I could feel the whole vehicle rock with quiet violence on its axles, but I had not thought through the angle at which I had parked, so when I finally opened the door it was snatched from me and there was a hideous crunch as it whanged against the hinges. Then I got out and my hat flew off 50 feet before coming to Earth. I raced after, having almost to fight for each in-breath against the pull of the wind.

I retrieved the cap and set off along the track by the spot where the gentians are seen. I found it hard to conjure anything so rare or so colourful in this landscape. In fact it was hard to imagine any plant, of any description, in flower today in this vile weather, when there were just the leached sand tones of dead grass and the leached russet of dead rush and the long dark cloud brood passing east.

Cow Green Reservoir was on my right as I headed towards the dam head. The westerlies scoured the down slopes and jack-knifed off the water, sending clean white mare's tails across the surface. The rain never stopped until I got back to the car two hours later, and with each gust it clattered at the surface of my waterproof. I dragged the hood down, but the wind found a way to squeeze in and prise it off my head so that rain could sleet full in my face and coat my spectacles in blobs of water. When I arrived at the vehicle all down one side, sleeve and trousers, was slathered cold and wet onto bare skin.

In between the blur I picked out this handful of details: the way the elements had hollowed out the wooden fence posts until only the hardest lignin cores remained. Yet each post top had its own headful of grey lichen, and between the skeletal uprights were strands of barbed wire, buckled and snapped with rust. In my notebook I wrote:

> There were few flowers but probably dried remnants of last year's bog asphodel and sundew without their fly-trap stems. Withered and desiccated lichen and drab heather, but no fresh green anywhere: only winter recoil. Spring was not here. The single sign of recent human was an apple core crushed to the path. Cow Green was entirely free of vertebrate life, aside from two curlews blown slantwise and silent across the cloud race. And me.

You realise that while this has been a site of constant human traffic – the old adits of the lead mines and the reservoir's 1,700-foot concrete dam were proof of that – the elements test everything to destruction. Cow Green admits of nothing that is not weighted to the place. And you are always aware of wind: either its imposing, even brutal, presence or, occasionally, its momentary lack. It affects the grand – the clouds over the Pennines – and the trivial – stray wool strands wittering at snags in the wood posts. Like a tongue in a tooth cavity it is incessant and erosive. All is shaped and made fit to meet it, gravity and mass holding everything to the landscape – stone, water, tree, plant – until it is entirely true. Temporarily.

A few weeks later

As I head for Cow Green at dawn, with the sun at my back, the whole landscape is cleanly engraved by low-angled soft light. Below and immediately above Middleton-in-Teesdale is that stock northern blend of cattle and sheep pasture segmented by drystone wall or stout wind-slanted thorn hedge. The River Tees flows by the town and at intervals bends close to the road as I climb west, all shallow blue shimmer and white-flecked stone. Then it is lost to view in the valley; the cattle fall away; so too the ash and the sycamores towering over the fields, while the lime-washed white cottages grow more distant from their neighbours. I pass the High Force Inn, where botanists have stayed since the 1840s, and just after the turning for Force Garth Quarry I ride out on to the upper reaches of the dale and the grandeur of it all seizes me.

Even as I absorb the panorama, a lapwing in full display blusters like a wind-slewed cloth just in front of the car, and even through the glass and engine drone I can pick out the ecstatic sweet ache of its song. A pair of pied wagtails flushes up from the road edge, and the cold dawn glow fringes all their feathers so that the two birds look as if they had just been freshly minted from bright light.

But nothing equals the impact of the marsh marigolds. In the roadside fields, which weeks ago had been the pastel shades of snow-burnt grass, they are spread in such profusion that they embody the ideal of the colour yellow. I'm heading for Widdybank and Cow Green, but the flowers immediately unravel my programme. I fling the car door wide open. Within a minute the knees of my jeans are swollen with ground water (despite a plastic sheet I roll out to lie on), but there is also the joy of photography: forcing you to get on eye-level terms with flowers.

Our friend Polly Monroe (partner of Richard Mabey) calls the same species by their old Norfolk name – 'molly blobs' – which evokes the way that the stems and leaves of her local plants rise up with robust, water-filled, lily-like fleshiness. Here in Upper Teesdale, marsh marigolds are wind-sculpted creepers. I find a patch that has grown just high enough to meet my wide-angle lens, and behind their crisp detail is the blurred lustre of the yellow pool; beyond, a whitewashed gable end to a farm and, blurrier still, the Whin Sill plateaux of Cronkley and Widdybank Fells. The smothering of flowers reminds me of what has been lost with the destruction of 4 million acres of herb-rich meadow, of which this is such a singular, breathtaking example.

I have never seen its like before, and I am pitched into an elevated state of mind so that when I arrive, a few moments later, at a flower-lined trickle just by Langdon Beck it feels nothing to stop again. Weeks ago this very spot was a foam-flecked torrent, and the sound of angry water had been obliterated by the insane skitter of black plastic snagged in barbed wire.

Now I am straight across the brook and flat on my front before bird's-eye primroses. I saw the basal leaves last time – star-like rosettes of pale waxy green, prostrate to the ground – but here the plants are a spring song of exquisite colour. The petals are gently notched in their outer fringes so that a central yellow eye, formed by the cluster of pollen-bearing stamens, is encircled with five hearts of deepest pink. Almost without end they quiver in the breeze, and it is more than an hour before I align everything to my satisfaction: the blood pulse of my own hands, the detail of the flowers, a lull in the wind and then May sunshine coming and going between white cloud. As I lie to attend to this scarce resident of Upper Teesdale, I can listen to the sky songs of its most abundant bird neighbours – the lapwings and snipe, whose displays are fletched higher and higher by the morning's warmth and sunlight.

That hour with the primroses reflects how the whole day goes – a seven-mile distracted meander right around Widdybank Fell, which occupies me until seven in the evening, entirely alone, through scenes of overwhelming beauty punctuated with moments of absolute joy: the five-bar gates mottled white and grey and crusted along their upper beams by intricate gardens of fruticose lichens; the weathered slabs of Whin Sill, so empathetically curved to the human rear you would swear they were hand-cut stone benches (yet the upper planes of the dolerite are entirely smothered in a lichen cartography. My favourite, which I photograph over and over and later select as screen saver for my computer, is a Rothko-like blend of desert sand with islands of black-flecked ginger or grey).

I have my lunch sitting on such a stone with the white rush of Cauldron Snout boiling down beside me and my senses immersed in its force-drenched music; and despite its power, a dipper, nesting in the crag above where I sit, manages to pierce the heart of all the water noise with song.

Around teatime a short-eared owl, wafting like some kind of finned sea creature from the depths, performs a slow-savoured display that makes it seem larger than it truly is. I notice as it passes over the outcrops of sugar limestone, which are the colour of an Aegean shore, how the whole of the owl's underwing acquires its own calcareous glow. Then it swims away with the breeze and across the predominant rust-infused straw of Widdybank's wider vegetation, and in direct sunshine the bird is oat-white like setting steel.

This is all preparatory to the gentians. In a sense it has taken more than 300 million years to create the conditions for this flower. The decisive element is the Whin Sill itself, which began as lava from deep within our planet's core around 295 million years ago. On its journey through the crust it met strata of Carboniferous limestone, sand- and mudstones, which had been laid down around 33 million years earlier when this part of England lay near the equator.

The magma extruded through faults in the older sedimentary rocks and, as it rose, so it cooked the adjacent limestone layers to a coarse crystalline marble. When the latter weathers it acquires the consistency of fine sand or, according to geologists, of white sugar granules; hence the name: 'sugar limestone'. The surface outcrops of it are found only on Cronkley and Widdybanks Fells, and it is these that in large measure give rise to the botanical significance of Upper Teesdale.

The special nature of the flora was noted by the late seventeenth century, when the pioneer botanist John Ray published records of shrubby cinquefoil, which grows in Upper Teesdale and in only one other English location, the Lake District. By the early nineteenth century botanists had found most of the famous Teesdale plants, including alpine bartsia, alpine bistort, alpine cinquefoil, alpine meadow-rue, alpine penny-cress, bearberry, bird's-eye primrose, bog orchid, hair sedge, hoary rock-rose, hoary whitlow grass, holly fern, another fern called kobresia, mountain avens, Scottish asphodel, sea plantain and three-flowered rush.

On paper the most special of all is a tiny tufted, glabrous perennial called Teesdale sandwort *Minuartia stricta*. Yet the five-millimetre flower is entirely insignificant. Were it not for the fact that the species grows on just two isolated patches here at Widdybank, and nowhere else closer to these islands than Norway, it would be hard to be aroused.

Not so the gentians. And I find them eventually in good numbers. And I know, instantly, exactly what they are. Here's one. Quite soon, they surround me. I am routinely amused by the way in which a naturalist sets off with a long-brewed sense of longing for some rare organism – a bird or a flower – which one dreams to see; and then the ever-so-casual manner in which that anticipation confronts reality. There is no drum roll. No climax. Not even fumbling excitement. You simply pass quickly, efficiently almost, from one existential state to another.

With the gentians there may be no dramatic transformatory moment, but there is indubitably the life-lasting star-like beauty of them. It is not hard to see why they are the ultimate botanical symbol for Upper Teesdale. It is the colour. Of her own Californian gentians, the writer and pioneer feminist Mary Austin, a woman seldom lost for the exact word, could only pile up the one hue for added impact: 'blue–blue–eye-blue, perhaps'. One is not surprised to learn, she added, 'that they have tonic properties'.

It is a blue so much more striking than the sky, or the sea – as blue perhaps as the Earth when seen from outer space. The gentians are eyes of intense happiness in a brown and wind-troubled place. I drop to my knees to meet them.

Bodleian Library, Oxford; Aubrey Manuscript 17, Folio 12r

Peter Davidson

I am writing about a place which I have never seen and which I know by heart: gently sloping parkland falling to a stream, with the fields on the other side of the valley bright with new grass. It is one of the coloured drawings (technically limited, even amateur, but eloquent in their love and sorrow) which John Aubrey (1626–97) made of his family house, grounds and farmland at Easton Piers, near Kington St Michael in Wiltshire. He may have begun by testing a perspective device for landscape drawing, at some point before-and-after fantasies of an Italianate recasting of house and garden entered the series, but the sequence of drawings seemed to change purpose and atmosphere about halfway through. The change almost certainly came at the point when Aubrey realised that his inheritance was going to be dispersed because of the lawsuits which had ruined him at the age of forty-four. Once he knew that everything was going to be sold, his purpose altered to the making of a series of tender records of the estate as is was in reality, a series of captured moments and places from the April of the year 1670.

This loss called forth from him an intensity of identification with place. Depth of feeling is embedded in these coloured drawings, a sense of devotion to the sheep-cropped slopes and small, stream-scoured upland valleys. Memory inhabits their coppices, stone shelters and field gates, as well as their grand, cloudy Wiltshire distances, recessions of

71

wooded ridges seen at evening from the high ground behind the house. There is an intensity here which transcends aesthetic limitations: a fragile, personal set of notations set down in the pocket drawing book – a portable memory book for a landless, migratory future. This can be felt in Aubrey's notes in the margins: 'my grandfather Lyte's chamber wherin I drew my first breath', 'a thin blew landscape'. What is recorded by his careful, unsophisticated work is a kind of memoir of youth and young manhood, a history of walking the fields, dog at heel, year after year, combined with an exceptional degree of natural observation.

It is this passion and closeness of observation which are extraordinary, seeming to belong less to the era when the drawings were made, than to the intense relation to English place which marks the years after the 1780s. Some of the drawings even speak to times and moods nearer to our own, wholly unlike the formalities of the estate and prospect poems which were the seventeenth-century ways of writing about landscape. The last drawing is sepia monochrome, a haunting prospect eastwards across fertile, well-wooded land towards the spire of Kington St Michael, the church school where Aubrey had his first education. A spring rain shower is passing over from the south, the trees and hedges are in leaf. The little figure of Aubrey is walking away from his lost inheritance, a stick over his shoulder. His dog Fortune, running ahead of him, turns back to look up at his master. *Mine now, his tomorrow, after that nobody knows whose*, is the English version of the motto which Aubrey wrote on the title page of this little book of drawings.

On this overcast late-winter afternoon, the sheets of paper which Aubrey carried around the Wiltshire field paths in the blue spring days of 1670 lie on the table in front of me in the Weston Library, part of the Bodleian Libraries in Oxford, the university which Aubrey attended until the civil wars put an end to his studies. He remained associated with Oxford all his life, and is buried somewhere in the church of St Mary Magdalene, at the other end of Broad Street from the Library, four minutes away. Little of his work was printed in his lifetime, so the manuscripts now in Oxford are his real legacy. In their varying degrees, all of these manuscripts of Aubrey's are beguilingly unfinished – a disordered, mysterious and poetic world of jottings about people and places and inventions and anecdotes and rumours and hauntings and antiquities. Inevitably every reader is sooner or later seduced by the feeling that if only these fragments could be deciphered (the hand is difficult, the papers dishevelled) and set in order, then the past would somehow be all but tangible and the voices of the dead would speak at the frontiers of our hearing, their shadows linger at the other door as we come into the room. You don't know Aubrey as a writer: you are drawn into knowing him as a collaborator in his great unfinished, unfinishable work. In a curious sense, he remains our contemporary, as though he is in some way still alive, out there in the green south-western quadrant of England, kept in being by the seductive incompleteness of his work. Thus, reading him makes you somehow his contemporary, or him yours. It is a strange, satisfying, sleep-troubling, dream-invading, unique relationship. (Part of the success of the recent, peerless edition of Aubrey's *Brief Lives* is its subtle assent to this process.)

The manuscript is on the table in front of me, the grey and white stripes of my shirt cuff are beside it where Aubrey's own hand must often have rested. I work with such things regularly, and have grown almost insensitive to the way that manuscript brings you into physical contact with the past and its inhabitants, the way that the individuality of a script long outlives the hand which shaped it. But Aubrey's works, and especially this manuscript, where he has dared to commit such defenceless love to the page, is an exceptional object which compels you to think of its paper as a contact with Aubrey, paper which has rested on his knee at the end of a field path. We are still aware of his hand under-drawing the scenes in the brownish ink of the seventeenth century, then setting the colours of coppice and sky, his brush hand hovering carefully just where my hand is now above the page as I turn to the twelfth leaf of the little bound book.

I gaze long and carefully at the saddest and most powerful of the drawings: we are looking down a sparsely wooded slope to a small stone building with a mono-pitch roof – some sort of cattle shelter or 'sheep house'. A hedge runs along the bottom of the valley, hinting at the presence of a stream. Another hedge divides the coppice from a field of grass to the right, entered by a wooden field gate. At the bottom of this field here are shadings and monochrome brushstrokes which outline small rocks breaking the surface of the grass.

Green slopes rise gently on the other side of the water. The more you look the more you see: a strong line of vertical light lies on the right-hand side of the tree trunks as if the sun is now low in the sky, shooting light along the valley. I think that it is growing cold as evening draws on. The tree shadows are strongly patterned on the ground. The under-drawing is in sepia ink, which shows through now-fading watercolour almost like the prefiguration of the autumn which will follow the partings to come. The brownish colouration dominates the page, for all that the sky is very blue. A green pigment must have faded from the sloping field on the other side of the valley, which once must have been bright with new grass. As the colour has gone, the hedgerows have dimmed and umbered. It is spring on the page, but the day is ending, and the shadows cast by the trees grow very long. You half catch Aubrey's murmur: *Nunc mea, mox huius, sed postea nescio cuius.* He must have gathered up his brushes and colours as the sun dipped below the horizon and, calling his dog to him – *Fortune, Fortune* – set off up the hill.

I take a last look at the sloping field in the westering sun, and turn the pages gently for one more glance at the sepia drawing of Aubrey and Fortune walking away into the green April evening. I close the manuscript, put on my jacket, hand the little oblong book in at the issue desk, then go downstairs and out through the peaceful, enormous hall. It is dark now and the evening air strikes with a chill like water on the skin. Bicycles whisper swiftly through the dusk. Opposite is the golden stone ensemble of theatre, museum and the endearing provincial baroque of the stone piers crowned by giant heads of the Roman emperors (I wish I could have seen this 'ragged regiment' in their 'wonderful state of decomposition' in the mid twentieth century[1]). These contrast with the stark grandeur of Hawksmoor's Clarendon building, which is tough and melancholy and belligerent all at once. Blackened lead statues of the Muses patrol the roofline – pitiless executives of success and genius and fame. *Fortune, Fortune.*

I start to walk home along Broad Street, past the closed gates and the concert posters. I glance across to Trinity, Aubrey's college, sitting far behind its screen of railings, beyond lawns and trees, like a country house. I turn south into Turl Street – in the panelled front room of the Turl Street Kitchen the first customers are eating an early supper by candlelight. Streetlamps and college windows shimmer dimly on damp flagstones. Now the smart shops pass: jeweller, bootmaker, dandy's tailor, whisky shop with its window full of names from the uplands around the house where I once lived in Aberdeenshire. Light strikes upwards to the brass chandeliers and high stucco ceiling of the church turned library on the corner. *Fortune, Fortune.*

I cross the High Street at the lights. Then down bricky Albert Street, round the corner by the Bear, where the lamplight is playing on the polished wood in the bar. Out into St Aldate's and threading through the crowds at the bus stops – the buses for Wantage and Abingdon, setting off into the damp night and through the lighted villages. I walk down past the front of Christ Church, Wren's Gothic tower high above me, through the breath of wood smoke from the pizza van at the college gate, and across the wide road. Brewer Street is dim, sheltered by the bulwark of the old city wall, by Pembroke's high buildings. The main road falls behind with every step, more removed still as I push open the outer door of Campion Hall and slide the tab against my name to IN.

I think that only in this college are there three choices: IN or OUT or AWAY. (Given the early history of the Jesuits in Britain it is hard not to associate AWAY with phrases like *gone beyond the seas*, or *fled to his kinsfolk in the North*.) *Fortune, Fortune.* A smell of polish and flowers and good, careful cooking. Past the great polychrome and gold carving of Ignatius and his companions, through the dim dining room (with habitual glances at the weekly menu, and at Augustus John's nervous, brilliant portrait of Fr Martin D'Arcy). Through the lobby with its paintings from Flanders and Peru, and into the library. Panelling above the broad stone fireplace, books from floor to ceiling, pools of light under the standard lamps. The room is profoundly still, and this quiet house grows quieter at evening. It is almost as though it grew more

75

remote, when the lamps are lit in the library and the fire in the common room. It becomes like a manor house, silent at evening, remote and westerly and enfolded by wooded hills. The buds of the birch tree rustle in the dark like the gentlest rain. And I am thinking of John Aubrey, still walking away northwards through the green land, the shower over, the drops glistening on new hawthorn leaves, dog Fortune dancing at his heels down the green lane.

Note

1. The state of the Emperors before renovation is described by Nikolaus Pevsner in Jennifer Sherwood and Nikolaus Pevsner, *The Buildings of England: Oxfordshire* (Penguin, 1974) p. 256. He borrowed the phrase 'ragged regiment' from William Morris who borrowed it in turn from the traditional description of the royal waxworks in Westminster Abbey.

From the Old Tower Hide on Wicken Fen

Nick Davies

From the top of this old tower hide, I have a cuckoo's-eye view of Wicken Fen. My horizon is encircled by waving reeds. Nine miles to the south-west lies my home city of Cambridge where, as a young student nearly 200 years ago, Charles Darwin eagerly awaited the barges that brought the reed and sedge harvest from the Fens, for among the debris he found many rare species of beetles. When I was a Cambridge student in the early 1970s I too sought fenland treasures, but my passion was birds, and not collecting but watching. As often as I dared, I escaped lectures and laboratories and cycled out to Wicken, and here, in the reeds fringing the waterway right below this hide, I saw my first cuckoo chick. It was in the nest of a reed warbler, the cuckoo's favourite host in the fens, and the foster-parents seemed to risk being devoured themselves as they bowed deep into the enormous orange gape to feed a chick that was five times their own weight. Why, I wondered, were these little warblers being so stupid?

That memory remained fresh, so when I returned to Cambridge six years later to teach and do research I was drawn back to Wicken to try to solve the puzzle of how cuckoos trick their hosts. I have always felt at home out in the Fens, perhaps because I imprinted on a flat landscape during my childhood days on the Lancashire coast, where wide skies and skeins of pink-footed geese calling over the marshes seemed to me then, as they do now, the most wonderful sight and sound there could ever be. Young cuckoos also imprint on the habitat

77

where they were born and on the host species that raises them. It pleases me to think that we are both drawn here by the same impulse to become watchers on the fen.

This wooden tower has been a focus for my watching and wondering ever since my student days. The narrow windows invite me to look out on the world rather than in on myself, and I now often come here to plan my experiments. Many biologists begin by wondering, having been inspired by new theory; then they find a suitable study animal to watch in order to test their ideas. For me, it is always the watching that comes first; whenever I see a bird doing something interesting, I then wonder why. As I survey the fen, I think of the female cuckoo sitting in the treetops beside me, also hiding and watching to plan her summer of trickery. Perhaps this is a good place for me to plan precisely because of my cuckoo's-eye view. From this height I am better able to see the fen through her eyes and to imagine the problems she faces as she looks down on the reed warbler nests below: how to monitor their progress, so she can time her egg-laying, and how then to slip unnoticed past host defences. As my mind plays the part of the cuckoo, I imagine the costs and benefits of her alternative options, and I wonder what might be the best way for her to trick her hosts. These thought experiments simulate just what natural selection does over the generations, favouring the most effective behavioural strategies. Perhaps this is why imagining oneself as your study animal often provides insights into evolution.

The first adult cuckoos arrive on the fen towards the end of April, just as reed warblers are arriving and setting up territories for the summer, and their departure in early July coincides with the time when most reed warblers cease to start new nests. So the cuckoos' visit matches exactly the period when there are opportunities for parasitism. During their first few weeks here in May, I watch the fen become transformed from winter's canvas of yellows and browns to one of bright green, as the stems and leaves of new reeds come to dominate and provide cover for reed warbler nests. In the bright reflected light from this green and watery landscape, splashes of colour come as a surprise: on the banks there are patches of pink marsh orchids, yellow iris and creamy meadow rue, and then sudden flashes of red and blue as dragonflies dart across the water. The reeds provide a uniform soundscape too; against their gentle whispering in the wind other sounds are magnified and catch you unaware: a burst of chattering song from a reed warbler hidden in the reeds, or a loud and haunting chuckle cry from a female cuckoo in the bushes nearby. All senses are on alert out here in the fens.

For a female cuckoo, every bush provides a hidden perch for observing reed warblers from above, but it is harder for a human to remain concealed here, and in any case my power of observation can never match that of a cuckoo, so I look for nests by walking along the banks and parting the reeds with a stick. Along the best stretches, there is a nest every twenty metres or so. Those nearest bushes are most likely to be parasitised, and my view from the tower shows why, because they are the ones that the female cuckoo can most easily find and watch from her secret look-out perches.

She has wonderful natural camouflage: her contrasting dark upper-parts and pale, barred underparts enable her to blend in with the vegetation and to avoid detection. I have often sat in this hide and watched her sitting motionless on a high branch as visitors walk by, unaware that Nature's most notorious cheat is just a few metres away. The cuckoo might sit for an hour or more as her egg passes down her oviduct in readiness for laying, and then she awaits a perfect moment to parasitise the nest. It is an agonising wait for me, too, and I dare not look away for fear of missing the action because it takes her just ten seconds to glide down to the nest, remove a host egg, lay her own in its place and fly off. Her egg is greenish in colour and spotted, just like the reed warbler's eggs. So when the warblers return to their nest, nothing seems amiss; there are the same numbers of eggs as before and all are similar in appearance. But they are now sitting on a bomb set to explode in eleven days' time, one that will destroy their chances of reproduction. For the cuckoo chick will hatch first; then, just a few hours old, and still naked and blind, it balances each of the other eggs on its back, one by one, clambers up the inside of the nest to the rim and, with a flick of its tiny wing stumps, heaves them overboard.

It is only a short flight of fancy from imagining you are a cuckoo to becoming one yourself. My colleagues and I soon realised that the best way to test how the cuckoo fools her hosts was to play the part of the female cuckoo by placing model eggs in host nests. Our experiments revealed that the cuckoo's egg mimicry is vital for fooling the reed warblers, because they are on the look-out for any egg unlike their own. When we 'parasitised' a nest with a model egg that we had painted to be different in colour and pattern from the reed warblers' own eggs, most were quickly ejected. Only model eggs painted like their own were likely to be accepted. However, the female cuckoo's speed and secrecy is important too: when we alerted the warblers by placing a stuffed cuckoo on their nest, they were more likely to reject even a good-matching model egg. So to succeed, the female cuckoo not only needs to hide her egg, she needs to hide herself too.

Adult cuckoos return to the same territory each year. Perhaps getting to know a particular area well enables them to exploit it better; they learn where the hosts' nests are, the best food sources and the local dangers. This is surely why I, too, return here each year: as I learn the best places for my observations and experiments, I work the fen better and so become more attached to this place. Repeated visits also create my personal songline of treasured memories, woven into the landscape as firmly as any reed warbler's nest. Whenever I pass a particular bush or patch of reeds, I thrill once more to the replay of special moments: a male Montagu's harrier, Britain's rarest bird of prey, sailing close by on a surprise visit one day in May; a flock of black terns hawking insects over the mere and then rising high into billowing white clouds to continue east on migration; and one spring dawn a nightingale singing with a cuckoo calling close by, when, for a magical few minutes, they were accompanied from the heavens by the melancholic bugling cries of a pair of cranes soaring overhead.

Attachment to a particular place also alerts you to change. Since I first visited Wicken Fen in 1971, some new birds have arrived: as a student, I hitchhiked to southern Europe to see my first little egrets, but these have now spread north throughout Britain and are common residents here. Other species have increased in numbers: populations of resident Cetti's warblers and long-tailed tits now flourish because of better survival in our milder winters. But there have been many losses too, especially among our summer migrants. In the 1980s I brought my two young daughters, Hannah and Alice, to this tower hide to show them their first cuckoo. I cupped my hands to make a sound chamber, blew a loud 'cuck-oo', and to their delight a male cuckoo immediately flew in and circled close by, uttering a 'kwow-wow-wow' in annoyance at the unseen intruder. He then landed in a treetop right next to us, his tail cocked and wings drooping, the characteristic posture of a territorial male, and he called continuously for several minutes as if in triumph.

Today, my calls are often met with silence, for in the last thirty years we have lost two-thirds of our English cuckoos. In the early years of our studies, in the mid 1980s, about 20 per cent of the reed warbler nests on Wicken Fen were parasitised; since 2005 this has plummeted to 5 per cent or less. There are just as many reed warblers now as in the old days. It is cuckoos that are disappearing.

Satellite tagging by the British Trust for Ornithology has revealed that this decline is linked to increased mortality in southern Europe during their migration to winter quarters in the Congo rainforests. Our studies have shown the challenges cuckoos face during the breeding season, as they try to overcome host defences in a continuing evolutionary arms race. But cuckoos face equally tough challenges at other times and in other places. We often think of cuckoos as 'our' birds that go to Africa for the winter. But their visit here to breed is brief, just a couple of months each year, and they spend most of their lives elsewhere. Their dramatic decline is a potent symbol of our diminishing natural world, and a stark reminder that events on this little patch of fen, and indeed everywhere, depend on the health of a wider world.

The season has turned. In the low winter light, colour drains from the fen and the landscape becomes silver as the fluffy seeds of the old reed tops blow in the wind. The soundscape is starker, too: the clacking of flocks of frosty fieldfares in the hawthorns and the whistling of wigeon from the grey waters of the mere.

My winter visits to the tower are often at dusk, and now I am marvelling at new wonders in the reeds as starlings fly in to roost. From all directions they come, and in silence except for the rush of wings as they speed past my hide. They arrive in small groups of a hundred or so, and then gradually the flocks begin to merge into one, so soon tens of thousands of individuals begin to wheel over the reed bed like a giant amoeba flowing gracefully across the sky in ever-changing shapes. They are reluctant to descend, and with good reason, for there are sparrowhawks waiting, hidden in the bushes below. Whenever a hawk dashes out towards the flock, starlings retreat from the point of attack and an invagination forms, as if the amoeba had been wounded. But it heals quickly as surrounding individuals also rise up, and the flock regroups to become a sphere. The starlings rise higher still, but as they gain safety from attack by surprise from below, they now face attacks by speed from above, as first a peregrine and then a merlin dive down towards them. Any starling on the edge of the flock that fails to keep up becomes an easy target. As individuals rush to escape and yet still maintain contact with the group, the flock constantly changes formation, elongating to a ribbon as it flows away in retreat, twisting and turning, before it re-forms and continues its sweeps across the sky.

As dusk falls, the starlings at last begin to descend, and they swoop lower over the reeds. Small groups begin to peel off and plunge down towards the roost, but if there are not sufficient followers the birds return in apparent panic to join the main group again. Eventually, sufficient voters begin their descent for all to follow, the momentum shifts suddenly, and for a thrilling few seconds the entire flock pours out of the sky, like liquid from a jug, into the safety of the reeds below.

Cuckoos and reed warblers play a game of hide-and-seek in their battle of trickery and defence. But in the open skies, as starlings fly in from the surrounding farmland, there is nowhere to hide. These murmurations before they roost are the outcome of another game, one of safety in numbers, and the scientific explanation, first suggested by Bill Hamilton in 1971, is beautiful in its simplicity. If there are birds of prey at large, an individual starling will be safer if it joins others, because this dilutes its risk of attack. If it is alone, clearly it is at risk if a predator comes along. If it is in a group of a thousand, it now has a one-in-a-thousand chance of being the victim. A larger group might attract more predators, but as long as a group of a thousand does not attract a thousand times more attacks – which is unlikely as there are usually far fewer predators than prey – an individual will still be safer in a group. Therefore individual prey should selfishly join others, in the hope that someone else gets attacked rather than them. The safest place is in the middle of the group, hiding behind a barrier of companions. So the flock is in constant motion as individuals jostle for the best places.

How can a large flock behave so synchronously, as if it was one organism? Early philosophers imagined that there must be a leader to orchestrate the movements, or perhaps such rapid changes in shape and direction involved 'thought transference' among individuals or other mystical powers. However, computer tracking of individuals has shown how waves of movements can spread rapidly through the group simply by local responses to neighbours. There can be sudden cascades of behavioural change in a group as just a few informed individuals flee and others follow.

Darwin likened the complexity and diversity of the natural world to an entangled bank where, even in a constant physical environment, natural selection forever leads to evolutionary change as individuals battle to beat their predators, parasites and social competitors. To human eyes, these games can lead to cruel outcomes, as female cuckoos plunder host nests and cuckoo chicks evict host eggs and young. But the dances of starling flocks against an evening sky remind us that the outcome of competition can seem extraordinarily beautiful, too. For me, watching the natural world is enriched by scientific wondering, and I hope to be inspired by many more spring dawns and winter dusks in this old tower hide.

TIPPING BUCKETS

Paul Farley

First, you need to Google 'tipping buckets' and 'Liverpool'. There. This'll make a lot more sense with an image to hand. In the last years before the invention of place, they built a fountain in the city, near the site where the old Goree Piazza and warehouses had once stood. It's a miracle it's survived. It was officially named Piazza Waterfall, but everybody I knew called it the Tipping Buckets, a piece of kinetic sound-sculpture designed by Richard Huws, which was installed in a small concrete square off Brunswick Street in 1967. If you happen upon it when it's working, the chances are you'll hear it first: the effect is of coming across an unexpected maritime sloshing and sluicing. The Mersey can be seen beyond the bottom of the street – all roads here lead down to the waterfront – but the sound still comes as a surprise: a little Atlantic enclosure, or the boom of a sea cove. When you see what's making the noise, the fountain's appearance sustains this maritime mood: in profile, there are echoes of topsails and mizzens, like in those diagrams of a ship's rigging. Each steel bucket fills slowly with water, the smaller ones upending when they reach their tipping points to empty into larger buckets, which in turn send a final excerpted waterfall crashing into the main pool. It's as automated as a set of traffic lights, and as mysterious as a machine from the *Book of Ingenious Devices*. I've seen it when it was new, as a child, from my father's shoulders. I've seen it derelict, the buckets seized up, its empty basin a pan of rusty silt littered with broken glass. I've seen it aged fifty, re-fitted and in full flow again. Because we're roughly the same age, it seems to abide, a thing that has always been there. It provides metaphor on tap. It's a living pool. It's a constant bailing-out, a spectacle of credit and debit. On parched and dusty city afternoons in summer, it's an oasis. On overcast days when it isn't switched on, it can ironise the drizzle. It's a piece of public art but a private curiosity, a rumour engine and unpredictable cascade in earshot of office blocks. One thing leads to another.

The A5036 dual carriageway cuts across the bottom of Brunswick Street, following the line of the old Dock Road, which along this section is still briefly known as the Goree. Or just Goree, like on the street sign at the base of the George's Dock Building, a huge, pale ventilating tower built so the Mersey Tunnel can breathe. That name fascinated me when I was younger. Maybe it was simply the homophone, the way 'gory' might catch the ear of a boy. I don't remember. Maybe I first heard my father say it. Or maybe I read the plaque, in the shape of an African shield, at the base of the Piazza Waterfall, and discovered how another place name was stowed away inside this place name. Gorée Island lies off the Senegalese coast near Dakar, and, as I came to understand it, was one point on the big Atlantic triangle that stretched between Liverpool, Africa and the Americas, home of the Maison des Esclaves, the House of Slaves, with its Dantean 'Door of No Return', a valve through which slaves passed on entering the 'Middle Passage', never to see Africa again. From then on, the word Goree filled me with a complicated dread. It was local and secretive, unwilling to come out into the light, or hiding in plain view: GOREE L2. It was shifty, losing an accent and taking or leaving the definite article. It was worse than gory. It became a dungeoned, shackled, bullwhipped, pustular, maggoty word, printed in slightly wonky eighteenth-century serif type on a colonial press. The Tipping Buckets become pails of seawater, washing down the decks of a Guineaman sailing west, rinsing the boards clean and running through gratings to fall into a dark, stifling hold where hundreds of human beings lay packed on plank beds.

Looking down Brunswick Street towards the river, I remember grasping the idea of offices, and being attracted to the sense of all that paper inside them, stacked right up to the water's edge. A few bills of lading and ledgers always managed to slope away to sea, but the vast and hidden paperscape of finance, insurance, investment and banking that the port relied upon seemed to increase in density and layers as it came closer to salt water, then stopped. The ecosystem of any city used to rely on paper: processed rag and cotton fibre, then wood pulp, circulating information around the whole biomass like xylem in the deepest forest. Even though the paperless office has never really (de)materialised, I like to think my father and I walked these streets in the twilight years of paper, an age that had begun when the earliest writing took shape next to water, the recording and control of material goods set down in hieroglyphs, made with plants of the water margin, the reeds and papyrus that grew along the fertile flood plain of a river. The Tipping Buckets become a fantasia on a theme of the shadoof or swape, one of the very earliest water-raising tools for irrigation.

One of the conditions of the new and rapidly expanding city was its gathered dryness, an environment for the stable storage of goods. Imagining all of this tindery space on the edge of salt water seems to be ignoring an element: fire. Much of today's square footage of office space was once bonded space, and many of Liverpool's warehouses went up in smoke. Even into the nineteenth century, plenty of storehouses were still being constructed using inflammable materials. The Albert Dock, towards the river beyond the Goree, was notable for its new-fangled fireproof construction. The Goree Warehouses themselves caught light in September 1802. Thomas De Quincey, frequent visitor to picturesque Everton Brow, described how

a prodigious fire occurred at Liverpool; the Goree, a vast pile of warehouses close to one of the docks, was burned to the ground. The huge edifice, eight or nine stories high, and laden with most combustible goods, many thousand bales of cotton, wheat and oats in thousands of quarters, tar, turpentine, rum, gunpowder, &c., continued through many hours of darkness to feed this tremendous fire. To aggravate the calamity, it blew a regular gale of wind; luckily for the shipping, it blew inland, that is, to the east; and all the way down to Warrington, 18 miles distant to the eastward, the whole air was illuminated by flakes of cotton, often saturated with rum, and by what seemed absolute worlds of blazing sparks, that lighted up all the upper chambers of the air.

The Tipping Buckets become an infernal human chain, drawing water from wellheads and standpipes and the river itself, an organised but frantic pumping and dowsing and dampening, an attempt to contain fire in the city.

My father occasionally smoked King Edward or Tom Thumb cigars, a quick and cheap machine-cut smoke in the dry Dutch style. If I catch the smell of one now – rarely these days – I think of him lighting up. He would dock the cigar with his teeth and spit away the end. After the whitewater of the Tipping Buckets would come the slowed-down, green-grey ancient river water, drawn from its mainstream and disappearing into huge arches and tunnels, trapped between sluice gates at the Canning Half-tide Dock, running in veinous gutters through deep silt at the Albert Dock. Visiting the latter was like being in a vast, gloomy mud bath for giants, a sump surrounded by brooding ruins. As an art student in the early 1980s, I came here to sketch it, a storehouse of the sublime that cried out to be rendered in charcoal. But I also imagined the inland sea of tea, the cloud forest of tobacco, the glacier of sugar that had passed through. I visited the Port of Rotterdam a few years ago, and was surprised by how you could tell which goods were being moved or stored, even in its closed steel world. To the eye, everything was a geometric Mondrian of stacked sea containers, but my nose knew when we'd entered the spice dock, pungent and unmistakable. In the ruins of the fireproof Albert Dock, even this weightless cargo of smells had long been dismantled, and all I can recall is the tang of salt water, the mud with its sheen of algal bloom, the cold damp of stone passageways, empty except for the odd tray of rat poison, and wafts of a Tom Thumb. My father has sparked up once more, making a shell of his hands to guard the flame, taking a few exploratory puffs to check it's caught. This isn't a film noir featuring a smoking man, collars pulled up against a biting river wind, keeping to the shadows of the derelict arcades. But my father is a complete mystery to me, and that waft of tobacco smoke in the huge and deserted dock rises like a memory, floating up from nowhere in a mind gone blank. The Tipping Buckets become synaptic, a cold firing sequence, a charge circulating through the closed system of a backwater.

These walks with my dad were bound to have happened on either a Saturday or Sunday. He worked as a window cleaner, and his firm was contracted to buildings and firms all over the city centre. The Piazza Waterfall might easily have fallen on one of his weekday rounds, its pool and concrete observation deck overlooked by workers in the office buildings that surround it. I find it difficult to imagine the Tipping Buckets on weekends in the past, toiling away with hardly anybody around to witness their display, especially on Sundays. Sundays in the past are switched off, closed and unbearable. Then again, the last time I visited the fountain, just a few days ago on a busy Monday afternoon, I found everything silent and still, the basin dry and empty except for a film of dark silt speckled here and there with wished-on coins (a meagre deposit compared to the deep coffers of Italian banking you'd find in the Trevi Fountain). I was standing in an enclave of Sundays, a concentrated emptiness, and I didn't hang around for long. In a bar round the corner, I considered who or what governs a fountain's operation, whether simple calendrical observances or occult lunar tables might be involved, and if some modern incarnation of the lamplighter or lighthouse keeper came to turn it on and off, somebody who carried a cruciform stopcock key about their person on a lanyard or belt loop; or if it was worked remotely, activated by a switch somewhere in a secret Bureau of Ornamental Street Furniture. The Tipping Buckets become the difference between life and death, day and night, Saturday and Sunday.

Because they're an early memory, the Tipping Buckets seem to loom over my childhood, but revisiting the Buckets now, I'm thinking it's entirely possible that my father might only have taken me on *one* walk, a single tour of the city around James Street, Brunswick Street and Water Street, the old Mann Island bus terminus and the Pier Head docks. Maybe I've replayed this scenario and gone over this ground so many times, it's crowded itself out, become a regular fixture, a place in the mind where me and my dead dad can meet and spend some quality time. The Tipping Buckets become a window cleaner's sculpture, a static pageant of ladders with pails of soapy water emptying and filling, a mechanical window cleaning round on the spot, just for show, a lathering of the air.

There's a way I can count the rings and carbon-date this memory, and that's by using the music that must have been in the air. When I hear 'Dedicated to the One I Love' by the Mamas and Papas, 'Can't Take My Eyes Off You' by Andy Williams, 'Do You Know the Way to San José?' by Dionne Warwick or – especially – 'Wonderful World' by Louis Armstrong, I'm transported very quickly to the greens of old Corporation buses, whitewashed shop windows, the sound of the ferry funnel being blown, doughnut oil at smoking point, rare earth smells (once common and abundant) like putty, solder, ozone in the underground station at James Street, the warm and vaguely electrical scents blowing up from street gratings choked with litter, and the Tipping Buckets' sea-spray generator ... So this is the late spring or summer of 1968. I'm three years old. Part of the recent mythology of Liverpool involves the entry of American Blues and R'n'B records into the city via these docks, but we all carry around our own iconographic hit parades. The Tipping Buckets are a bunch of strange instruments, a steel section, where water is lifted high into the air through valves and pistons that bring each gurgling metal calyx to life; then taking their final bows as the big drums empty, and everything falls to earth as white noise.

Nathaniel Hawthorne had an office nearby, in the old Washington Buildings overlooking Goree Piazza. Somewhere in the air above that dual carriageway, I'd guess. He was US Consul in Liverpool for a few years in the middle of the nineteenth century, and was visited here by a fellow American novelist, the younger Herman

Melville, passing through the city on his way to the Holy Land. His whale had stranded, and by this point Melville was also on his way to oblivion. There's a famous account of the two men – recorded by Hawthorne – taking a walk a few miles up the coast at Southport, where the Consul was living, and there in the desolate sand hills, wearing their stovepipe hats and smoking their cigars, Melville told Hawthorne he had 'pretty much made up his mind to be annihilated'. Whenever I take a walk around this waterfront patch, I think of Melville doing the same as a sailor on his first trip to Liverpool. In his partly autobiographical novel *Redburn*, the eponymous hero consults an old guidebook that his own father had used on an even earlier visit to the city, made long before he was 'included in the census of the universe'. The son finds an arch where he imagined his father had stood, the same bronze Nelson Memorial (still standing in Exchange Flags) whose four manacled figures round the pedestal remind him of four African slaves in the market-place. But in large part his father's guidebook only creates confusion. The Old Dock has vanished completely, long since filled in and built on. 'This world, my boy, is a moving world,' he reflects, 'and its sands are forever shifting.' Forget guidebooks: we might be better following our noses. In the way everything changes here, nothing has changed. This old city built on sandstone is still a work in progress, and I'm taken by surprise, blindsided or stopped in my tracks by something new or missing or unexpected every time I visit. A lot of my ancestral, familial Liverpool has been bulldozed, or changed beyond recognition, and cities, like language, don't stand still. Not even the Tipping Buckets, chugging away in their backwater. They now become an Arte Povera version of that Nelson monument, the water-bearing vessels themselves styled on the grabbing and digging heads of plant machinery, all mounted on a rig of scaffolding.

A couple of centuries ago, the river would have run a lot closer to where the Tipping Buckets now stand, its bank being nearer the bottom of Brunswick Street; the docks beyond stand on reclaimed land. The Pool that Liverpool takes its name from, the inlet that was turned into the Old Dock, would have lain just south of here, roughly where the new Liverpool One shopping development and Paradise Street stand today. But the whole thing was almost annihilated, reduced to nothing, in my father's lifetime. During the early years of the Second World War, Merseyside was heavily bombed. There's a photograph of the devastated city hereabouts, navigable only by the Victoria Monument that somehow remained standing at the top of James Street. As a teenager I crossed this debris field without realising it. In summer, we'd often take the Southport line up to Crosby or Freshfield, and walk through the turpentine scent of the pinewoods that stand on the approaches to the dunes along that coast. Once, I found the Brick Beach at Hightown, the shoreline underfoot suddenly and entirely made from rubble. This was where much of blitzed Liverpool had ended up, as infill to prevent erosion, a shattering of red Accrington 'bloods', floor tiles, grey masonry, ashlar, granite, sometimes a carved word or a numeral, smoothed and worn by the sea like soaps on the sink edge of the world. 'Sous les pavés, la plage!' the striking students over in Paris wrote on the walls when I was first brought to see the Tipping Buckets. Along the shoreline to the north of here, the cobbles and paving stones became a beach! But I didn't realise any of this as a teenager, clacking my way along the Brick Beach, and 'May 1968' was insignificant to me. I think now of something I would have known, something else from the same period, a film called *Planet of the Apes*, and that final scene where Charlton Heston – in loincloth, on horseback – finds the wreck of the Statue of Liberty on a beach, and realises he is not on some distant planet but has been here all along, at home, on a ruined Earth.

If this is only so much botanising on asphalt, or covering of waterfront, it still feels like returning to a source. Even within my timeframe, my lifespan, the ground has constantly shifted, flown even. Maybe I'm grateful for the Tipping Buckets, which stand for many things but remain rooted, plumbed-in, fixed to the same spot. I try to look in on them when I'm in town, to see how they're doing, to check the time on an old clepsydra. I can't be sure why I do it, and can only say it's something I've always done. They oxygenate me. I'm reminded that the imagination in early life doesn't need much, and can subsist on the simplest of things, and that even if my dad did only bring me here once, for a few minutes fifty years ago, something poured into me, and through me, and is still flowing.

A City Pastoral

Tessa Hadley

We moved to live in London five years ago, when I was in my mid fifties. I liked it that the move ran counter to imagining ageing as a centrifugal force – as you grow older you're supposed to move out from the humming centre to the calm periphery. There was a perversity in moving closer in. And I'm still besotted with the perversity. The air is filthy here, it's true – even though it's often clear and bright, because the pollution isn't as manifest as in the days of coal fires and fogs. And there aren't many stars in the London sky. Four or five, most nights? In Somerset the sky can seem almost dirty with its swathes of stars, like a sublime cosmic pollution. The metropolis has a compromised relationship with emptiness, or even openness. Everywhere you look, the vista is crowded beyond ever counting or knowing. You could never have been everywhere in London. You feel the absurdity of the weight of the built fabric pressing down, the pointless agglomeration of lives, the endless urgent movement replicating itself over and over and never ceasing, even at the lowest ebb of the night. Individuality drowns in the sheer mass, the impersonal huge politics and economics of the place. You're aware of yourself as an atom, carried along in great rivers of atoms. You can't be known here; the city can't know you.

But that's also a liberation. And a reality, anyway: you are an atom! All these people exist – they have to live somewhere! No point in pretending you're alone in a desert. And it's such a miracle of civilisation, a triumph of ingenuity and resourcefulness, that a vast city

93

functions at all. All those complex clunky systems, imperfect but functioning, delivering our nourishment and energy, carrying our communications, transporting us around, taking off our sewage and material waste, nursing us when we're sick, burying or cremating us when we're dead. Millions of people move around the arterial routes of London and mostly don't break out into violence, mostly don't kill one another, mostly even respect one another's property.

Our transience inhabits the shells of a built environment which changes at a slower speed than individual lives, so that we move around inside the forms of the past. In an old city like London tradition isn't an idea; it's in the shapes of our parks and streets and rooms, giving form to the shapelessness of our present. We redeem our ever-present collective stupidity through the persistence of the best things that have been made, the wisdoms of the past. Our built environment is the consequence of innumerable unrolling gestures of adaption and conservation, which are our version of ancestor worship. And we live, too, among monuments to our most complex art and thought and science. Not that the past was pretty. It was bloody – just like the bloody present, or worse. London is beautiful-ugly, heaped up with the leftover spoils of empire, brute power, ill-gotten greatness. It's as encrusted with history, as cumbersome with it, as – let's say – Rome or Istanbul or St Petersburg. And that's another miracle – that the new generations walking round inside the shapes of empire are also, so many of them, the children of the subjects of empire. Is it too romantic to think that London's population nowadays represents in its heterogeneousness some kind of redress, some rebalancing, from the days when the English deluded themselves that they lived inside a closed system all their own?

In the first months after we came I used to feel as if, through some sleight of hand, I'd been given two incompatible opportunities both at once. There was the chance to live somewhere exotic, with all the high colour and historical drama, the rich otherness, that one might move abroad for – to Istanbul or Rome or Barcelona. And yet at the same time, in the deep foundations of my imagination, this exotic place was home. I belonged in it; I wasn't an ex-pat. Perhaps in London no one's an ex-pat: that category simply isn't open. You might be displaced, exiled, marginalised, alienated, homesick – definitely. But not an ex-pat, not set apart – you're in the crowd, participating in the great global heterogeneous flow. My feeling of being at home must have something to do with language – my good luck that the first language of this world city is also my language: capacious, baggy English, which can be accented every which way and absorb every new idiom – a bastard creation in itself, out of the ancestral collision of its Teutonic and Romance origins.

There's more sleight of hand. We have got away with something. When we first moved to London – needless to say, selling a big family house in Cardiff only paid for half of our two-bedroomed London flat – we expected to be crowded, to have to put up with an intensification of the urban bleak environment. It was worth it, we thought. We were used to that; we were fine with it. In Cardiff the gardens tend to be small yards, so that our vistas were closed in by the fronts of the houses opposite, the backs of the houses in the next street. There wasn't much room for green, and the back garden next door had been concreted over by the housing association that owned it. The garden on the other side – the house rented to students – was concreted too, though at least the weeds grew through in that one. I was passionately attached in Cardiff, it's true, to the hornbeams that lined our street at the front, and to a massive rogue ash tree at the back which strewed its saplings bounteously across several gardens, filled our bedroom window with its grace. Last to get its leaves in spring, it was the first to shed them – they would lie like supplicant hands, palm upwards, on our mossy scrap of lawn. Because the ash was in the garden of a house of rented bedsits no one cherished it, and I was always afraid that it would be cut down; I said that I'd have to move away if it ever was. Our window without the tree filling it would have been too desolating, the scruffy house-backs opposite too rawly exposed, unmitigated. In the end, anyway, we went first: the tree outlasted us. I expect it's still there.

The irony is, living in the immediate environment of our new London home feels almost as if we've moved to the country, by contrast with that Cardiff street we came from, and where we'd lived for almost thirty years. London's a green city: you can see that when you fly into it – all those magnificent famous central parks saved somehow from past developers, all those scraps of lesser suburban ones – and all the private gardens, cherished and neglected, and the allotments, and the roof gardens, the little corners of wasteland and canalside. Our flat, only twenty minutes' Tube ride from the centre, two minutes' walk from the roiling A5 main road, takes up one half of the first floor of a red-brick detached Victorian villa, in an estate of such villas; the street at the front is very wide and lined with plane trees, and at the back the houses in the next street are almost remote, the distance of two very long gardens away. It's like looking out onto fields, or woods. Emotionally it's like that, like a country view. We don't have any garden ourselves, but that's fine with me: I'm not much of a gardener. I'd rather look out over gardens than be responsible for them.

And I do look out. We watch out of the windows sometimes with the same interest as if it were television, or art – call each other over to admire a sunset, or a cloud formation, or the moon, or a fox asleep on the back lawn, curled up like a cat, nose tucked into its tail. We survey this secret nook of nature's growth and respite, which seems to exist not in spite of the great thrumming brazen machinery of the city which lies all around it and never ceases from its striving, but because of it: it's the other side of the same life. People made these gardens as a conduit for all the rest of life, which isn't human. With big sash windows at front and back, and living elevated on the first floor, we feel as if we live inside the air. The sky takes up as much room inside our flat as the walls do, so that it matters: when we pull up the blinds in the morning and open the curtains, what's outside is such a presence, setting its mark on the day, colouring it. There's no such thing as ugly weather. You might not want to go out into the rain, but it always falls interestingly, differently. Earlier this afternoon there was a lemony-yellow watery sun and the watercolour clouds were flossy with light, smoke-grey against an effulgent, brilliant yellow-white. The slim silver pencil of a distant aeroplane drew its line, apparently noiselessly, across the tops of the roofs opposite; the winter trees seemed poised, in this late-January moment before spring begins, in extreme stillness. And the movement of the clouds was almost imperceptible at first, then giddying once you were aware of it – the slow inexorable drift of the whole sky towards us, then over our heads over the roof. Gleaming, the sun peeked through its veil of cloud, then withdrew and sulked, then burned through again.

The gardens stretch as far as we can see to right and left out of our back windows; our horizon is closed in with trees. We can see easily into the garden immediately below us and the ones adjacent. Between them these compose a comically varied spectrum of garden aesthetics. The one directly below isn't used much by our nice down-stairs neighbour – he's very busy. Someone comes to cut the grass and water things, and at some point a few ornamental trees and dumpy evergreen shrubs were planted uninspiringly down either side of the long strip of grass, half a villa wide, where the traces of old paths, and of what was perhaps once a fishpond, show up as yellower and mossier against the green. I'm grateful for its empty plainness, its polite non-statement, its absences ripe for filling up with thought. A ceanothus fills our view with its brilliantly vulgar blaze of blue in the spring. A fox pushes through the trees at the far end and scarcely bothers to check whether the coast is clear before he comes trotting casually down the middle of the strip as if he owns it, nose down, business-like, his haunches so superbly muscled and fluent, insolent. He does own it. He's out there far more often than our neighbour is. We've sometimes seen two or three foxes out there all at the same time. Once there were three of them curled up asleep. And then there are the grey squirrels, the dull wood pigeons browsing like fat cattle, jays, cats, rats, blackbirds, parakeets.

The other half-strip belonging to our house is prettier, with curvy vistas and seats and flowers, and the one next door again is positively the pampered baby among these gardens – planted, manicured, clipped, topiary-ed, adored, with solar-powered lights sunk in the beds and an extant fishpond. The man who owns it – a civil servant made redundant, someone said – is often out there at work: strimming and mowing, pruning and spraying, taping up tender shrubs and garden furniture in bubble-wrap for the winter. In summer he hosts an open-garden afternoon with a brass band and refreshments – we ought to have gone along, but we haven't yet. Something's touching in how that garden's cherished and he's put everything into it – but I'm so glad all the same that it's not underneath us, unsettling us, all that titivating and perfecting. That kind of garden is used up, exhausted, somehow, as a mental space. If you were a child, it wouldn't be any good for playing in – there's nowhere to hide, nowhere that hasn't been thought through already, nowhere not known. That conception of gardening is as an extension to interior decorating: the garden as another space to make-over, eliminating what's accidental, imposing a design.

He's out there now, using his noisy leaf blower. I loathe the leaf blowers – and the strimmers, for that matter. I grieve for the old swish of brooms, for rakes stuttering across wet grass, for the soothing, vacuous conversation of a pair of shears. It's because I'm not a labouring gardener hard at work, of course – only a watcher from the window. My favourite garden is the one next door the other way, to the left. It's generously wide – and it's almost a wild garden, but not quite. Apparently the flats in that house are social housing, or were, or some of them still are, and families seem to come and go: at present there's a Portuguese woman who comes out sometimes to talk on her phone, a man with long grey hair who potters with a plastic carrier, a Francophone African family with an angry teenage daughter who practises her singing. There's a municipal-sized trampoline, black rubber strung on a steel frame; girls lie on it to sunbathe, and whenever there are children in the house they love it. They talk companionably in pairs or threes while bouncing, or bounce in meditative solitude to the rhythmic accompaniment of the squeak of springs – which sound as sweet as the leaf blower is offensive.

No one who lives in those flats at the moment has taken any possession of the garden or has plans for it – although this must have happened periodically in the past, because there are three sheds in different corners, and in different stages of disrepair. Two vast pear trees have grown beyond the point where anyone could ever prune them: to the size of oaks, almost. In spring they're a bridal dream of white blossom, which blows across to our side like a spatter of snow; and in autumn the pears fall into the grass – I've never seen anyone pick them up, though I suppose they do. The beautiful grass in the garden grows waist-high and golden blonde and then droops its heavy seed-heads; two Polish men came at the end of last summer and cut it down with scythes, talking together in their language from time to time. I did not dream that episode of Mickiewicz pastoral: it actually happened. They also pulled down the dense bindweed which had grown over one of the sheds and down the side of the L-shaped back extension of the house, uncovering items we'd forgotten ever having seen before, because they'd been smothered for so long: an abandoned moped, a trailer for pulling a boat – minus the boat, with only an old garden umbrella in it. And a resplendent Victorian tiled floor, patterned in brown and black and cream, partly concreted over and partly grown with grass. Was it once the floor for a conservatory, perhaps? It's as eloquent of past grandeurs as a Roman mosaic.

The weather's changed again outside the windows while I've been writing. At the front of the flat now the clouds are slate-grey, and there's a lurid late light, almost coppery, on the thin young branches, straight and taut as whips, grown up from the knuckles of the plane trees pollarded by the council two years ago. The last single leaves clinging on in these trees look like small brown birds, only too still. Tiepolo clouds meanwhile are banked up at the end of the street, resplendent pink and gold against a pale blue. A magpie falls with drama, tail fanned out, through the tracery of a winter tree. I feel as if I belong here in this place, at this rich intersection between the made world and the found world, culture and nature: trying and failing to catch it in my language.

The Marsh and the Visitor

Alexandra Harris

Slip down between the general stores and the pet shop in Pulborough, West Sussex. Barn House Lane narrows from a track to a steep-sided path as it runs downhill. Then there's a gate, and you're out onto the Brooks, a great expanse of grazing marsh stretching away to where the Downs rise in the distance. The flood plain is flat, but the flatness is shaped and parcelled by raised banks and causeways. So the view in each direction is built up in strata: in summer there's the glint of water deep in a rush-lined ditch, reeds above it, the still, rough turf of a bank where a few clumps of ragwort stick up like bunches of shabby chrysanthemums, and meadow grass blowing in clouds beyond. A dark line of trees marks the point where the land turns from low clay to higher sandy heath. And then, always, smooth and spacious, steady parent of the land below, there is the long grand slope of the Downs.

The slope visible here is Amberley Mount: a yellow-green cliff, scalloped where it rounds into caves and swells out again, lime-bright in the sun, with a luminosity that comes of the chalk beneath. Woods grow up into the hollows, outlining the bareness between. And it's the bareness by which you know this Down, distinct from the hangers to either side, its turf closely nibbled by centuries of sheep. The few scattered trees have individual identity, each exaggerated by the shadow it throws. Sometimes they have a childish look: model trees stuck to felt; toys on a baize card table. Then the hill turns adult: muscle rounding over bone, flesh stretching and creasing. Mostly the Down is remote and ancient and impersonal. It loses its solidity as the evening fades, turning sage-grey to an elusive purple-blue. For a moment it is a low cloud on the horizon.

The path from the village follows the Arun as it runs between deep banks grown over with grasses, ragged robin, and meadowsweet in summer. From the east, the Stor comes to join it; where they meet, there's a clanging metal footbridge and a willow. Beyond the bridge, you can walk low down by the water, chin-high in grass, or up on the causeway built by the Romans to get across the marsh from the posting station at Hardham to the settlement with its bath house at Wiggonholt, which now lies under the nettles of a roadside verge.

From this high path, part of the Greensand Way, the network of drainage ditches and dykes becomes visible, cutting purposefully across the meadows. In summer, it's not the drains themselves you see, but the rushes that grow up from them. So there'll be purple clouds of fine-eared grass, and then a column of dense green. In autumn the ditches will be full, a kind of water-writing appearing on the flat. And then, as the floods rise, the humming grassland will become an inland sea. Most of the path is too wet to walk in winter, so I know the view only from a distance, from the village looking down over the pale floods reflecting low white skies. Even on summer days, when damselflies flap in the rushes and the high paths are cracked with dryness, the place holds the memory of winter like a basin. It is winter that makes it the shape it is.

This was the landscape I loved when I was growing up, and it's still my secret standard for understanding other places. There's nowhere like it; I've looked. But trying to describe it I feel a strain. I don't know the names of the sedges I thought I liked so much: why had I never looked them up? To describe a place you're meant to know it intimately, to have lived with it, to have kept vigil through seasons and through years; better, to have been its active cultivator and guardian. The tradition of English place-writing, which flourished in the eighteenth century, and which has today expanded beyond all bounds, espouses slow, patient looking. It projects an ideal: that the writer of a scene will be as familiar with it as Gilbert White was familiar with the hanger at Selborne, and that he or she will have an expert understanding of the ecology. It has little truck with holders of a return ticket via London. The nature writer does not go out with the Dorling Kindersley book of wild flowers in order to check that those big plants by the river are Himalayan balsam (invasive; disapproved of) and not a rare Sussex orchid. Quite right too in many respects, but not, perhaps, in all. It's a common thing to be a visitor in one's most loved places, and to learn about them has its own kind of value. My own way of looking has an urgency about it. I must stow away all I can in the short time before leaving again.

I grew up near Pulborough without knowing much about it in the naturalist's sense. The regular walk from home was over the golf course, a routine that seems to have left me with a lifelong aversion to gorse and sand. But going into the village was a pleasure. When we parked in the village car park, it was to go over the road for a prescription, or into the solicitors' to drop off an envelope at the polished front door with an equally shiny magnolia growing beside it. I knew every shop along Lower Street and the times of the trains that would take me to the shopping mall in Horsham, and these things were inseparable from the view of the Downs. The council tip came to the car park one week in four. The omni-guzzling machine alarmed me – its actions were so frighteningly irrevocable – but I liked to go along with my father so I could stand and look out over the Brooks. Behind me the lorry ate another box of defunct cassette tapes, and before me lay what seemed the very contours of peace.

I wasn't conscious of being 'in the country' until I came back to it in university vacations. I found a leaflet in Tesco's advertising the South Downs National Park and was astonished. There was a map showing all my familiar places marked as visitor attractions. Visitors! Never had it struck me that one might travel to the Arun Valley especially to see it. I had been for years a dedicated visitor to other places. My shelves were piled deep with saved-up leaflets from rural churches and guide-books from many hundred country houses. They were mostly from the

West Country, which was, as I knew from my family and from Daphne du Maurier novels, an area worth visiting. Sussex had always been the ordinary home we left behind on annual trips to real country, where there were red cliffs or moors. Now, suddenly, I wanted to look at the place from which we started.

As an adult, then, I became a visitor to this part of Sussex where the Arun cuts through the chalk. What had been background became foreground. The Downs acquired names and were sorted into scarp slopes and dip slopes. 'The path on the bank' became the Greensand Way. I sat making notes in churches, then put my coins in the slot for all the leaflets available, and postcards too. If there were no leaflets in the marked place on top of the prayer-book shelf by the door, I trespassed anxiously behind vestry curtains for further supplies.

I studied the Ordnance Survey map and saw with delight the profusion of italic lettering: Roman road (course of), priory (site of), Roman villa, cross-dyke, barrow, barrow, camp. I have never had much capacity for cynicism about italics on a map – not like Evelyn Waugh, for example, who was sceptical about old England in the 1920s. 'When I see Gothic lettering on the Ordnance Survey map,' he said, 'I set my steps in a contrary direction.' I am hopelessly unstylish in this regard. I can't accept that 'site of' means 'nothing to see here'; I'm stubbornly concerned to stand in the place, to look out from that spot. So I loiter on the verge among the ragged grass and pineapple weed as the cars go by on the A283, magnetised by the idea that somewhere under me, somewhere behind me, there's another language, a quite different way of life, and a frigidarium leads to a hot bath.

My shoe boxes of antiquarian knowledge are increasingly well stocked these days. Yet I'm still only a visitor. My work is in cities (Birmingham, London, Oxford) and, however vividly I dream of a small open window under a low tiled roof, I'm not in the market for second homes. How valid, then, is my feeling about Sussex? And in what possible capacity can I write about it?

I wonder about the difference in perception between an enthusiastic church visitor and an all-year-round parishioner. It's a difference much more pronounced if one shifts it back into the nineteenth century, or earlier, when a shepherd or the rector's wife, say, would know Wiggonholt church and two or three nearby, but nothing beyond that. I look at the font and recognise it as Sussex marble, I enjoy the plainness of the smooth arcades carved in low relief, and place it among the other eleventh- and twelfth-century fonts I know. I'm moved by its simplicity in contrast with grander carvings, its silence in comparison with the dragons and saints elsewhere. I touch its cool Norman sides with pleasure. But for the local farmer this is not one font in a whole inexhaustible language of fonts; it is *the* font. It is what a font is. Would I like it so much if I had no choice, if I could not – next month – be off to the great churches of North Norfolk where painted angels hold up gilded lyres in the rafters?

Then, and it feels related, there's the problem of cows. Cows have a tendency to bring things to a head for the visitor. Their giant stillness arouses a strong sense of permanence. The faint low sound of their munching, or moving over the grass, sharpens the ear to the quiet. Or in the evening, when sound carries, perhaps a cough is audible several fields away and reminds one of the herd still outside, and there for the night. But a footpath that leads into a busy grazing field is a worry. There is the possibility of turning back, but it is probably a long way, you will probably get caught out by the approaching dusk if you risk it, and you may well already have come through a field of cows, so that going back is on a par with going forward.

They look thoroughly absorbed and contented, the cows this afternoon. Most of the herd are grazing intently a little way to the left, but three cows have settled down around the stile which is the exit from the field. I set off calmly, and wait to catch the eye of a nearby grazer, not wanting to disturb her. I smile encouragingly, feeling ridiculous. She looks up and, very slowly, swinging her bulk from side to side, wanders towards me. Her movement is a show of both casualness and determination, which I return in kind – until I'm stopped short by disaster. There's a calf tucked into the hedge on my right, and its mother is on my left. I can't walk between them so must walk round, thereby going straight through the herd.

What matters about this typical incident, aside from the fact that I was not trampled or squashed that afternoon, is that it makes me feel so stupid. I bring myself to tell it only because I discover how many otherwise practical and competent people feel the same. The cow problem bars me from places I would otherwise love. It's worse than a 'Private Property: No Entry' sign: it's a no-entry sign put up by myself. My maternal ancestors were dairy farmers in Cornwall, continuously, hundreds of them, for about four centuries. And now I can barely walk across a field.

Then again, my ancestors didn't have a library card, and I don't think I'd relinquish mine for any level of familiarity with cows. All sorts of knowledge make a difference to the path down the side of the marsh, be it inherited or learned-up, gleaned through daily necessity or sporadic enthusiasm. So, for example, I'm starting to learn about local building stones. Lavant stone, Bargate stone, Wisborough sandstone, Upper Greensand: a whole new landscape. The names, which I read in long lists in conservation documents, suggest a geological tour of the area, some of it deep below ground and other parts shaping the familiar surface topography. The lists constitute a geological itinerary, but they are also a course in architecture. Reading the names I think of certain church walls and the differences in colour and erosion start to emerge, amazingly various, requiring attention. It's the overwhelming sharpness of new prescription glasses, which makes you feel giddy for a morning because there are so many bricks in the walls. Here, there are so many stones.

In the grand buildings not far away – Chichester Cathedral, Boxgrove Priory – the best materials were used for the job and no efforts spared. Fine-grained Caen stone was shipped over from Normandy – tonnes of it transported by human ingenuity and labour. It could be intricately carved, holding the true curve of a trefoil or a smooth ribbed vault. In the little hamlets on the edge of the marsh – Wiggonholt and Hardham – the churches were achieved with stones readily to hand. The Hardham walls are mostly rubble, which is not to say haphazard or made from rubbish (the word now suggests broken cement blocks piled into skips), but built from stones that had already been used elsewhere, shaped for the wall of a barn or a house. Particularly strong materials were reserved for the church quoins, and there they still are. One of the big quoin blocks is a group of Roman clay tiles, set into Roman cement that dried around them two millennia ago. A later builder thought – why not? And with a good slathering of his own fresh-made mortar, he set the whole lot of tiles into the wall. He must have known a bit about those old Roman people who had left their remains all over the land; he gleaned odd bits of knowledge, like rubble. There's an Anglo-Saxon poem about a Roman wall, which refers to proud builders, long lost, now held in the earth. The medieval builder knew there was a long history of life around these marshes.

Over at Wiggonholt I peer at the church walls, trying to identify the stones for myself. It's like looking for clues in a painting to identify the hand – a connoisseurial kind of looking that moves from hunch to analysis, from a first impression to an up-close reading of an inky line. Except that here it's nothing like that, for me, as yet. I don't know nearly enough about stones for the grain and the ridge lines and the kinds of lichen to be meaningful. Resorting to the internet, and the excellent *Building Stone Atlas* produced by Historic England, I discover that I am looking at Pulborough sandrock. To know your stones you have to know the character of every quarry ever dug within in a radius of a hundred miles. I am content to realise that, though I'll never know those quarries, there is a common store of hard-won knowledge to which I can turn.

For the first time, I see the dials on the south wall. There's a rough dial incised into a high quoin stone, and a finer, larger dial a few blocks below. All the twenty-four-hour lines and numerals are just about legible. Since the sun is out, I rummage for a biro and hold it in place as a gnomon. The shadow falls, and yes it falls precisely: seven o'clock. The sun hasn't changed its orbit and the dial hasn't moved, so on this bright evening the dial still tells the right time.

Seven o'clock in a crowded café on the Cowley Road in Oxford and I readjust my earplugs as two small boys wail distractedly into their milkshakes. The tall man next to me is reading Cervantes while swaying his crossed feet to music I can't hear; the glossily dressed student on the other side is explaining her thesis to her laptop camera with professional confidence. I can see the shadow falling on a dial scratched in sandstone on a church wall a hundred miles away.

Holding my coffee cup, I'm cross-legged in the long grass by the river. The sun is lowering behind me, sending a raking light over the meadow and the willows. It picks out bronze in the rusting spires of curly dock. Every hummock of grass casts a shadow. Yard by yard, as the sun moves, fields are lit up for examination. The light gives substance to each ear of grass and measures the thickness of sedge. For a moment the meadowsweet is luminously bright: creamy lace curling above red stems. Sappy buds move against hairy nettles.

The light begins to be more forgiving; the examination has been passed. Evening walkers come out along the path from the village in ones and twos, their dogs racing round me and then bounding into the water. The bare Down in the distance is smoothly aloof from it all.

Behind me, the roofs of Pulborough have joined together. The estate on the hill and the retirement flats and the old barns and the controversially prominent village hall are now all one, an ancient settlement on the edge of the flatland. There's a light coming on here and there. Later the wind will rise as the temperature drops; in the houses up the hillside people will look out at the black trees moving and pull their windows to on the way to bed. The marsh, now, is the visitor. It's come to Oxford. I'm glad of it here.

THE UNFINISHED WORLD

Philip Hoare

For part of my childhood – a rather conflicted part – I shared the three-bedroom, semi-detached, suburban house in which I grew up with eight other people. My personal space was reduced to the width and length of a bunk bed. There was no common ground; or perhaps, there was too much of it. I felt like the peeled potatoes in the huge pan of water my mother had to prepare: bare, bobbing there, crowded like carp in a pool.

To escape, I lived in one long fantasy. I imagined, as I walked to school on dark winter mornings, the layers of other worlds beneath my feet, the strata of histories laid down below. I invested the reliquary green space of a strange, semi-village area that had been swallowed by the greater city of Southampton with the power that confinement lends. Everything was heightened by normality; nothing was what it seemed.

Our suburb was where the city petered out; that which the city had yet to drown. It was gravelly, hilly and drained, built on a former soft-fruit-growing area; but also one where troops had trained since medieval times, and where travellers had traded. There was a sense of no-man's-land to it. Gypsies lived in caravans in a sub-section known as Botany Bay, separated from our quiet road by a residual wooded valley, muddy and dark and traversed by a narrow overgrown path that dipped up and down, crossing a desultory stream, usually embellished with an upturned supermarket trolley.

On other sites around here, pockets of green that the developers had somehow overlooked, Victorian houses stood empty, gently crumbling into the Hampshire heathland, where gorse and bracken still sprouted, given half the chance, re-appropriating, as if they'd been there all the time and were only waiting to take their chance. These were the places where I dawdled. They scared and excited me, because of the freedom that they offered.

This eastern side of Southampton Water was nicknamed Spike Island – a reference, I would later discover, to the vast convict depot on Inis Pic in Cork Harbour where men made criminal by the Great Famine were deposited in what was the largest prison of its time. The epithet presumably imputed that the Irish navvies and dockers who were here, in exile, in Southampton were themselves prison fodder. (Spike Island in Bristol – a city physically connected to Cork by steamer – may have been similarly named.) It was a migratory pattern which, had I but known it, also applied to my own family: my father's ancestors had come over from Dublin and Limerick to the north of England, as strangers in a strange land. Their identities too were regarded as suspect and other, until they learned to conform.

The openness of the heaths on which our 1920s semi-detached house was built – just one of many that marched across the heath-land – was associated in my mind with some archaic image of dolorous transportees chained up ready for prison hulks and their transition to other penal colonies. Now dull-eyed ponies chained to concrete blocks grazed these left-over fields. Herons perched over a forgotten mill pond that froze solid in winter. I remembered a story my mother had told me, about a boy who had walked out on the ice and never came back.

Returning to my childhood home after an adult life spent in London, I found myself reclaiming those spaces, even as they ran out. A housing estate now occupies the gravel pit where I used to play, and from where I'd occasionally see a badger lumbering across the path like a stubbly tank. Front gardens yield to the tyranny of the car; you can barely see the houses now. Even walking on suburban streets now seems a kind of subversion.

I opted out of that process. I do not drive. I don't operate a mobile phone, or wear a watch. I cycle, like the boy I was, negotiating streets I could (and do) ride in the pitch-dark, I know them so well. They are part of my neural network, just as my body is hard-wired to my bike. These are my escape routes, and wherever I go, they lead me to the sea.

I can't see the sea from my house. But I can see, through the trees and over the roofs, the red lights that stud the power-station chimney which stands sentinel over the waterway. It is a piece of modernist industrial architecture, solid and block-like. But peregrines circle its summit, and it summons me.

In the winter I find myself drawn there even in the middle of the night, rising with the full moon at spring tide at 2 or 3 a.m., riding down the streets with my arms open wide like a bird, daring the traffic lights not to change. Skidding through the shingle down at the shore, I watch roe deer launch out of the undergrowth; rabbits run in my lights. I prop up my bike by a sea wall reduced to rubble by the storm surges that have ravaged this soft southern coastline in recent years, a physical casualty of the 'managed retreat' of bureaucrats' terminology. A testament to our abandonment of nature. The future.

Then I tip myself into the inky black water, align myself to Orion's grid as it wheels over the vast refinery on the far side of the shore; its spires and silos are lit up as a simulacrum of some future city. Once the space station prowled overhead as a shooting star fell in the other direction. In the darkness, the cold becomes comforting, a reassurance of my physical self and intimation of my mortality. Climbing out, I cling to my hot-water bottle, shivering like a dog as I tug my clothes back on.

My love of the water – that most fluid of common grounds, the thing that connects us even as it separates us – has always been problematic. Although I grew up within sound of dolorous fog horns, and although I felt the sea close by, its presence intimidated me. Not least because I could not swim, and had no way of engaging with or entering the alien element. I'd look at the birds that scrabbled their living out of the blackened wasteland at low tide – Southampton Water has a remarkably *full* relationship to the swell and sway of the moon-tugged tides, its daily double tide a result of the Atlantic Pulse that surges up and down the English Channel – and I'd wonder at their loyalty to this scrubby shore.

The oystercatchers and the brent geese that occupied the suburban beach; the crows that hovered and flickered in the nearby car park; the gulls that overflew it all like a white blur: they didn't feel part of my world, any more than I felt part of theirs. They made their space, negotiated it; occupied their liminal place. I didn't even register them, then.

But as I grew up and felt more of a stranger in the human world – informed by that world that I was *unnatural* – so the natural world seemed more of a solace, since nature itself is queer. Its solitude and escape has always attracted the other, to those who claimed the common ground for its utopian prospects, proposing a future world in which their desires, like those of the rest of creation, were not proscribed. During the nineteenth century, Walt Whitman and Edward Carpenter realigned their lives to different rhythms, at a time before their desires had been diagnosed or pathologised. Their otherness and their 'back-to-nature' impulses – partly invested with the sensuality of the noble savage – would earn them the scornful and euphemistic epithet, 'nature-lovers'; partly because no one else had a name for them yet. In the same way that, as it has been observed, a blackbird doesn't know it is a blackbird, so their identities were not defined by human judiciaries and the relentless categories of capitalism, imposed to sustain its own brutal progress.

Perhaps that's what drew me, aesthetically and emotionally, to the shore: some non-genetic memory, a subvert culture, passed from hand to hand. The porous, shifting shingle of Southampton Water, overlooked by its industrial installations – petro-chemical simulacra of the New Forest on whose edge it stood – also reflected the way that Derek Jarman colonised his Dungeness beach, repurposing its stones, plants and debris in a post-nuclear vision of a garden-wilderness. For Jarman, nature elided with sensuality: for him common grounds were cruising grounds, like Hampstead Heath, another city-contained wilderness.

Like some contemporary Thoreau – his tar-painted seaside hut set, not like Thoreau's Walden next to the new railroad, but in the shadow of a nuclear reactor – Jarman recorded his sojourn in *Modern Nature*, his ironically titled journals, alongside the development of the virus that would soon take his life. His shore proposed another kind of mortality. His writing spoke to a queer nature, as well as being a natural history of his infection in the way that Kathleen Jamie's essay 'Pathologies' treats cancer cells under a microscope in a Dundee hospital as an equally valid subject for 'nature writing'. Questioning what is natural, and frustrated by 'the foreshortened definition of "nature"' ('It's not all primroses and otters'), Jamie looks to 'our own intimate, inner natural world', a mirror of ourselves.

I thought too of Denton Welch's writing, which I discovered in a copy of his novel-memoir, *A Voice Through a Cloud*, that I found in a local jumble sale when I was a teenager. Welch had the same visionary ability to evoke queer suburbia and the southern England of the 1940s, and to observe so minutely the mix of the natural and human history with which most of us live. When I picked up the book, I knew nothing of the author. I just liked the slender feel of it in my hand, the putty-grey-green cloth cover – the same colour, I imagined, as Welch's greenish tweed suit – blocked with what Wilde would call 'tired' bronze lettering.

Even more enticing were the endpapers and drawings inside, spiky illustrations of semi-human, semi-animal, semi-botanical images: curling shells and blank-eyed statues, spouting cornucopia and moonish faces, all done in spidery, scratchy ink, precise and inter-nalised, like his words. They were mythic and naturalistic in the style of other neo-romantic artists of the period; both contemporary yet retrospective, referring to a land which had already been lost. For me, Denton's writing provided a counter-version of the mid century into which I was born; another history, pages passed from hand to hand.

In *A Voice Through a Cloud*, Welch is injured in a serious bike crash while riding from Greenwich to his uncle's house in Surrey. Chronically ill, he is taken from his London hospital to the desultory resort of Broadstairs, at southern England's most easterly edge, to recuperate within sight and sound of the beach. His bed is pulled up to the window, looking out to sea; he describes feeling surrounded on three sides by sea and sky, and how his bay window shakes in the high winds.

The expanse of sea becomes an extension of his terror and loneliness, its emptiness 'the negation of everything living. The suck and mumble of the waves on the beach, licking and slithering and eating, filled me with a wry, fearful pleasure.' He invents words to echo its relentless rhythm, its 'everlastingly industrious, hopeless music', singing to himself not so much in consolation as in despair. At night he resigns himself to the 'washing and whining' waves, which had by now become an extension of his own body: 'the wonderful, booming, wriggling skin of the sea', a phrase which recalls Melville's image of 'the ocean's skin' – the sea as a body of water, a transgressive place, in its own fluid state.

Later, as a semi-invalid, Welch lived in a kind of blur of rural-suburbia, contained by war and fitful peace. England, always a place of ruins, had been ruined anew, destroyed to save itself. In the spaces the destruction created, Welch's imagination flourished like opportunistic weeds on a bombsite, in the shocking pink and purple of buddleia and rosebay willowherb. A place in which beauty might be preserved, and yet slowly decay; where what one used to be and what one had become were one and the same thing. When he watches, voyeuristically, young men with pale flesh diving in the river and lying on the grass, the scene might come from Ovid, or a Powell–Pressburger film, while his description has the distance of anthropology and the intense observation of a 'nature-lover':

The first boy lay flat on his back and half shut his eyes. He looked charmingly coarse and young-animalish now, with thick brown neck, smooth arms and hairs round each brown-red nipple ... 'He dives too deep,' I said to the friend.

Welch's writing gave me a new way to look at suburbia. A generation after him, I lived in the lee of the Second World War. Common ground, in a blitzed city such as Southampton, was what the bombs had left behind. Like Welch, the neo-romantics of the 1940s such as John Piper or Graham Sutherland (with his 'unfinished world', as seen by George Shaw, the great contemporary artist of abandoned spaces of modern Britain) created sublime landscapes out of this destruction, just as their predecessors – from Turner to Constable and Palmer to writers such as Horace Walpole and Thomas Gray – had romanticised ruined Gothic abbeys and overgrown ancient sites as a reaction to the lumbering inevitability of the Industrial Revolution and the enclosures that John Clare protested, a slower sort of destruction.

It was another way of reconfiguring common ground with the other; the recreation of an imaginative or even an imagined landscape. In those lonely, dark places, the natural world of plants and animals inevitably adopted – or were invested with – anthropomorphic identities, assimilated by the human need for narrative. Another kind of imposition.

That is exactly what I, in my teenage manner, did to the empty spaces where I lived, the unfinished world in which my imagination could thrive.

One of the wildest places I knew was the cut that ran along the end of our garden, ostensibly connecting the backs of the semi-detached houses. About three foot wide, it had long since lost its navigability, like some overgrown jungle path into the heart of the suburban darkness. In the process it became a conduit for wildlife, a runway for foxes, hedgehogs and grass snakes that crept and crawled and slithered, protected by a tangle of high privet hedges and haphazard brambles. George Shaw's paintings, created using the ultimate teenage medium, Humbrol paint usually reserved for model kits, encapsulate that sense of the reliquary world in which he and I both grew up. To an imagined soundtrack from Joy Division or the Smiths, his work – superficially glossy, three-dimensionally dark with the adolescent imagination – sees what is at stake in the edges of things. The end of the twentieth century. What the future had left behind.

If common ground means anything, it means freedom. And yet to some what they regard as common *good* reduces the individual to a body in pursuit of political or even totalitarian aims. In his book, *What a Fish Knows*, Jonathan Balcombe refuses to call his subjects 'fish', collectively, since the plural is reductive of what he regards as sentient, social animals; rather, he insists on calling them 'fishes'. Anyone accused of turning their back on the human world, the better in order to study the natural, can, in these times, retort that the abuse of the animal is directly analogous to, and intimately connected with, the abuse of the human.

The ultimate denial of common ground – the control of everything, the development of all land and even sea towards total human dominion – is the terrible future dream which we must resist and subvert as it denies our identities. Our common ground is our commonwealth: the shared resource of a fragile planet. In the microcosmic is the macrocosmic. To Thoreau, Walden Pond was an ocean. Whitman, walking with his 'electric self' on the beach at night alone, saw 'All souls, all living bodies though they be ever so different, or in different worlds / ... / All identities that have existed or may exist on this globe, or any globe'.

I learned to swim in a dank, echoing Victorian baths in east London when I'd washed up in the city unemployed. And when my widowed mother needed me, and I needed to escape, I came back to this shore, substituting my life in underground nightclubs for the nocturnal allure of this interzone. The darkness, far from an absence, is itself a reclamation: an intimation of what was, a seceding to primeval rhythms. Even though the sodium street lights prompt blackbirds to sing through the night.

Now I feel more at home here than I do almost anywhere else; unless that anywhere else is the sea. Shifting, shaping the land, constantly re-inventing itself, the sea doesn't care about me. It leaves me behind, even as it bears me up. But it, and this grubby, desolate, lovely shore, overlooked by a petro-chemical refinery, by container ships and the rumbling of the docks, has become my common ground. It is everything and nothing.

And I like it here.

An Elemental Education

Richard Holmes

1

There is a brass outdoor tap in our garden in the little village of St Hippolyte de Caton, on the edge of the Cévennes hills. It is mounted in a circular metal casing, die-cut in the shape of a heraldic southern sun, and screwed into the back of the small stone arbour at the foot of a mulberry tree. When first installed, this tap was bright, sharp-edged and industrial, with gleaming threads that could cut the thumb. But it is now oxidised to a soft, blurred verdigris green, as if it had somehow grown directly out of the mulberry. The tips of its butterfly handle have been re-polished to a dull glow by seventeen years of human use. They remind me of the bright brass toes of the bronze goddess at the entrance to the Hofgarten in Munich, which are traditionally touched for good luck by passers-by on the way to work. That is how I have come to feel about the water tap.

On some days the tap has a slight drip, beloved of lounging wasps and beetles. Here we keep a green 15-litre watering can, and our three-year-old grandson, who can only just reach the top, grips the sides and peers down into it with intense concentration, as if he were examining a new world.

He reaches down into the dark of the can, and grabs the water with one hand as if it were an animal, making it splash and swirl, and then bursting into puzzled laughter. More laughter when we attach the lawn sprinkler, *le tourniquet*. It is a powerful agricultural one, made of metal, and sits on triangular legs, throwing out a high, turning helix of water. The child dances in and out of this ever-shifting rain-storm, trying to judge its approach and retreat, leaping in and out with shrieks of delight. I have seen the same water-dance in pre-war photographs of children in London's East End, or the Bronx in New York, or the back streets of Calcutta.

Here water is a universal cause of laughter, as well as mock terror and secret reverence. It is also a cause of early metaphysics, when later that evening, tucked up in bed, the boy compares the flying water spray to ordinary falling rain in England. After a long pause he asks, 'And does it *know* it's raining?' I thought I could answer that question easily, but now I'm not so sure.

2

At the western end of the garden, by the herb and tomato bed, is the stone well. It is a monument to water: an impressive, looming beehive shape of Cévenol limestone, about two and a half metres tall, with a waist-high sill and an iron grille made by a local *ferronier*. The grille takes the form of a Gothic gateway, with two wings and bars like arrowheads, which can be swung open like an altar piece, and then shut and locked again with a central bolt. Obviously this grille is to keep live creatures, and notably children, *out*; but I sometimes wonder if it is also to keep other things *in*.

Inside, a tin bucket waits on its chain in its niche. It suggests rituals, offerings, immersions, not always benevolent. My face, looking back up from the reflection thirty feet below often startles me, especially at midday when the sun casts *contrajour* shadows. There is an M. R. James ghost story, 'The Treasure of Abbot Thomas', which involves something hidden in the walls of a deep medieval well, down which the innocent treasure-hunter looks, only to find the face reflected in the water at the bottom is not his own.

My measuring rope, with its iron plummet, indicates that the well water itself goes down another two or three metres, but its blackness and its echo suggests unfathomable depths. It reminds me of all the great underwater beasts slumbering in the abyss: Tennyson's Kraken, Melville's Moby-Dick, Spielberg's Jaws, Ted Hughes's pike …

The bucket can be hard on the hands, when trying to water the nearby herb garden. So we have installed a submerged electric pump, with a black hosepipe that kicks like a snake when it's turned on, and spews a thick rope of water over five metres as far as the two olive trees. This hissing curve of water, stippled with air-bubbles, is itself curiously alive and snake-like, and seems to attack the ground where it lands with a sudden white thump, and slithers away.

The actual snake I met there one morning, slithering out of the wall and along under the ivy, I assumed had appointed itself as the guardian of the water hole. We have since established an uneasy relationship, and I think of D. H. Lawrence's Sicilian poem, 'Snake':

> A snake came to my water-trough
> On a hot, hot day, and I in pyjamas for the heat,
> To drink there ... And truly I was afraid, I was most afraid,
> But even so, honoured still more
> That he should seek my hospitality
> From out the dark door of the secret earth ...

There is also a small black scorpion that likes to live in the cool space under the flat Roman brick, where I keep the key to the well grille. Every time I pick up the brick it is waiting for me, a black tattoo on the stone, and I briskly crush it with a special cube of rock kept there for the purpose. But it is always back there the next time I pick up the key, the small black triangle of menace. I assume its malevolence, but in fact it has never done me harm, and I wonder why we have not yet found a ground for peaceful co-existence.

So the well seems both sacred and sinister. Here in the Cévennes one is never far from the history of the early eighteenth-century Camisards, the Protestant peasants who in spring 1702 revolted against the authority of the French Catholic king, and murdered the local bishop who had been persecuting them for heresy. They expected help from a British fleet commanded by Sir Cloudsley Shovel, but it never arrived. They were eventually suppressed with much cruelty by squadrons of the Royal Dragoons sent down from Paris. The standard punishment for a captured Camisard was simply to throw him – or her, or their child – down the nearest well.

3

Beyond the garden wall to the east, is a small stream, the Troubadour. It gushes a foot deep over the stone ford leading into the vine fields where the farmer grows merlot grapes. Further down the valley, beneath the small hill known as Le Caton, it feeds into a larger stream called La Droude, which in turn runs into a real river, called Le Gardon. The Troubadour has a silver crown of foam in April, then suddenly dries up overnight, usually in the first three days of May.

Severe summer droughts in July and August have always been indigenous to the region, but they have got steadily worse. Temperatures can reach forty-two degrees Centigrade, and when a *canicule* is officially declared, drought regulations are strict: no hose pipes, no *tourniquets*, no car-washing, no hand-watering of the garden between 8 a.m. and 8 p.m. The bans are announced on the board in front of the Mairie. Our grass becomes straw. The big soft leaves of the tomato plants droop. The fields of sunflowers go from yellow to black. Even the water in the well slowly drops away. Up in the Cévennes, above Le Martinet, the rivers shrink inside their white sleeves of shingle.

The sudden summer storms and downpours are received sceptically by Monsieur Hugues, the vine farmer next door: '*Celà suffit pour arroser la poussière,*' he will say after an hour's driving rain – just enough to settle the dust. (*Arroser* is the same word used for drinking wine with a meal. There is no good English translation of it – 'washed down with' will do for beer, but not for wine.) Nature's brief waterings can give endless pleasure during drought. Sitting on two white wooden chairs, side by side in the stone arch above our front door, we indulge in the great St Hippo spectator sport of simply watching the rain fall, and smelling that strangely exotic perfume which rises from hot flagstones.

The winter floods (*les crues*) of the Cévennes are infamous, and go back to ancient times. Major inundations are recorded from the thirteenth century onwards, about once every fifty to seventy years, with catastrophic ones occurring in 1403, 1604, 1768 and 1846. But they have become more severe. The most recent ones occurred in 1958 and 2002, the latter causing 1.2 billion euros of damage and leading to the building of a new raised motor road, the A106 between Alès and Nîmes. On its way this flood reached knee-high in our kitchen, carried our fridge out into the garden, and the wooden gate out into the vine field.

To this day the bridges on the country D-roads and narrow lanes around us carry a warning sign: *'Attention! Pont Submersible'*. The surrounding vine fields are classed as *'innondable'*, floodable, and consequently they cannot be built on by law. To celebrate this fact we formed a society known as 'Les Innondables', and families from the other five houses at this end of the village (the whole village consists of some two hundred souls) used to have an open-air lunch together every August. Beatrice, the *maire-adjoint*, wrote a song to celebrate this. The *déjeuner* began at midday and ended about 6 p.m., by which time we were all ready to sing. Very little water was consumed.

When he lived at nearby Uzès as a young man in the 1650s, the poet Jean Racine wrote a chant against flooding. It begins roughly along these lines: 'Let no wild waters come unto these pastures, let every stream lie quiet in its bed, let the lovely Naiads be pleasant and peaceful, let the torrents of springtime abstain from the flood ...' One day we are going to have it carved on a tablet and set on the front of the well.

It was the Romans in the first century AD who first seriously addressed the regulating of the flood/drought problem in the Gard department. They planned, surveyed and built in a mere twenty years a fifty-kilometer canal from the springs at nearby Uzès to their regional capital Nîmes. Their engineering genius included six aqueducts to carry the water, of which the huge Pont du Gard is still standing. It is built of local limestone, in three tiers of fifty-two arches, standing 160 feet high. The canal itself, often underground, is little more than a stone conduit a metre wide and two metres deep, but it is a miracle of civil engineering. To flow smoothly and steadily, relying on the force of gravity alone, it had to have a precise fall of thirty centimetres every kilometre, over its whole fifty-kilometre length, and to move at an average speed of two kilometres an hour. Once successfully completed, it delivered 200,000 cubic metres of fresh water every day to the fountains, public baths and private houses of Nîmes, and remained in working order for over 300 years. Yet no one knows the names of the engineers who designed and built it.

Today, the rivers are being managed by a newly created regional water board, sometimes known as 'Le Petit Parliament de l'Eau'. This operates a policy known by the convenient acronym of SAGE (Scheme for the Improvement and Management of Water Resources (*Aménagement et Gestion des Eaux*). It declares with a flourish five main aims: balanced water consumption, prevention of flooding, control of water quality, improvement of river banks and the study of underground water reserves. It publishes a small campaigning magazine, *Le Journal des Gardons*, and has certainly cleared many sections of overgrown riverbank and blocked riverbed, and encourages the trout.

But not all these water policies are popular. Over the last decade there have been rumours of a plan to construct a huge reservoir up in the Cévennes hills, somewhere above Saint-Jean-du-Gard. This was a project on a Roman scale, and with a Roman logic, intended to control and preserve the winter flood-water with a huge dam in one of the valleys somewhere near the beautifully named village of Saint-Etienne-Vallée-Française. With the vast inland lake thus created, it would be possible to release a steady supply of fresh water during the parched summer months to the thirsty towns and villages on the plains below. But the mountain spirit of the eighteenth-century Camisards is still alive in those remote communities. Popular village protests against the flooding of any Cévenol valley, with its remote wild life symbolised by the golden eagle, have been stiffened by visiting environmentalists and ornithologists, preaching like the illuminated *pasteurs du Désert* three centuries before them. Whether it has been their objections, or technical engineering problems, or simply shortage of regional cash funds, no reservoir has yet appeared in these wild hills. Up there the old water gods (and the Naiads) still exercise their ancient powers.

4

I'm not sure the Naiads don't also influence the swimming pool at the eastern end of the garden, with its remarkable transformations. At dawn it has a placid, unbroken, gleaming presence: a Zen statement of calm. But its appearance alters at different times of day with infinitely subtle reactions to changes in wind and weather and the angle of the sunlight. It has sudden evaporations (often caused by the drying wind of the Mistral), or mysterious pollutions and 'turnings', from lucid turquoise to hazy green. It has brown dustings from the vine fields, and occasional red dustings from the sands of the Sahara. And then there are all its visitors: the wasps, dragonflies, butter-flies, snakes, flying ants, beetles, hornets, a mouse (saved), a wild boar (rumoured), and the heartbreaking swallows, with their cries and aerobatics overhead, and their sudden dramatic dives downwards to drink on the wing.

No one can observe the dynamic life of a swimming pool without beginning to take its measurements, and learn some of its physics. Though the basin is comparatively small, some seven metres by nine, it contains about eighty cubic metres which take over twenty hours to fill from scratch with a hose. This only has to be done once every three or four years, but in summer, because of evaporation, it has to be topped up weekly, sometimes with about 250 litres (three bathfuls of 85 litres), but sometimes, when the Mistral blows, as much as twice that. I started to record these figures from the household water meter, and this first made me aware of domestic water consumption figures in general.

Most European households consume 150 litres of fresh water per head per day, and surprisingly 30 per cent of this goes on flushing toilets. Showers can of course be more economical than baths, but brushing your teeth while the tap runs can consume six litres, as also running the cold tap to produce acceptably cool drinking water. Washing machines with their new eco-cycles have become less spendthrift, but then most European households wash clothes more often than before. In the eighteenth century most well-to-do households had only one 'washday' a month – as for example in the memorable opening chapter of Penelope Fitzgerald's masterpiece, *The Blue Flower*. Water consumption around the world has also become a measure of comparative wealth. American East Coast households can consume up to 300 litres per head per day, though restrictions are starting to operate on the West Coast, since the great Californian drought began in 2015. Meanwhile many Third World households still do not use – or have access to – more than ten litres of fresh water a day.[1]

Prompted by these thought-provoking statistics, I began to wonder what water actually consists of. The H_2O we all learned in school chemistry sounds familiar and reassuring: two hydrogen atoms arm in arm with an oxygen atom, thus forming a single friendly water molecule. Yet the necessary bonding or ganging-up of many water molecules, to form the continuous flowing stuff we all recognise, depends upon a quite strange and complicated five-part structure, and this too changes when it hardens into ice, or expands into vapour. I learned some of this theory from Philip Ball's wonderful science classic, H_2O: *A Biography of Water*, and also the fact that water has a history.[2]

It was the eighteenth-century French chemist Antoine Lavoisier who first showed experimentally that water is not a 'prime element', any more than earth, air or fire. He proved that in reality it is an elastic compound of hydrogen and oxygen, in a public demonstration performed in Paris in 1783, also attended by Charles Blagden of the Royal Society, and published in his *Traité élémentaire de Chimie* of 1789. He showed that it is an unique substance which occurs naturally in three different states; liquid, solid (crystalline as ice) or gas (water vapour) out of which fog, frost and snowflakes are all formed. This was followed in 1800 by William Nicolson's experiment in London, using the newly invented voltaic battery, proving that the hydrogen–oxygen chemical bond could be broken with an electric charge (electrolysis). Yet to this day its structure and bonding remain ultimately mysterious, producing such anomalies as 'surface tension'.

The complex content of water is also surprising, even in its supposedly purified state. On the side of a bottle of San Pellegrino there is a list of minerals and sulphates: 'Silico, Nitrate, Strontium, Potassium, Fluoride, Sulphate, Bicarbonate, Calcium, Magnesium, Chloride and Sodium'. The pool also shows me that its acid level is permanently fluctuating. The human tear drop has an acid pH of 7.6, which is thought to be a perfect environmental balance. But the misapplication of 'purification chemicals' to pools can raise this by ten per cent, and around the globe so-called 'acid rain', caused by man-made pollution of sulphur dioxide and nitrogen oxide (mostly from burning coal), can rise to levels high enough to begin to destroy such vast and ancient structures as the Great Barrier Reef.

When it comes to water even physics has its limitation. Philip Ball writes at the close of his strictly scientific study that he has not covered everything, and notably he has omitted the magic: 'In the end it seems to me that the "magical" properties attributed to water – an inexhaustible fuel, a universal remedy – derive from psychological and emotional correspondences.'[3] I wonder about these.

The problem of water 'magic' is illustrated by Richard Dawkins's critique of the parable of the Marriage Feast at Cana. This is the New Testament story of how 'a wandering Jewish preacher called Jesus' (as Dawkins puts it) miraculously turns the jugs of water prepared for the wedding guests into delicious wine. In his study for young people, The Magic of Reality, Dawkins points out that on the molecular level this transformation from water to wine is simply not possible. 'Molecules of pure water would have to have been transformed into a complex mixture of molecules, including alcohol, tannins, sugars of various kinds, and lots of others.'[4] The 'miracle', he concludes, was either simply 'a conjuring trick' or, more likely, 'a piece of fiction that somebody made up'. In short, it is nothing more than a piece of religious nonsense, comparable to the fairy tale of 'the pumpkin being turned into a coach'.[5]

Yet this supposedly scientific analysis completely overlooks the possible meaning and symbolism of such a parable of water. Why should somebody make up such a story? Clearly, it is intended to express a universal truth about the need for human generosity and hospitality, and these are not nonsense or superstition. The marriage feast represents a transformation of human lives into something richer and more fruitful. What happens is just 'like' water being transformed into wine. The 'miracle' is not a trick, but a metaphor, a parable of generosity and communal hospitality ('the best wine until last', as Dawkins remarks). Moreover, the parable has universal roots in folk tales from many other cultures, telling of bottomless urns or 'unemptiable' jugs of water, wine or oil, all celebrating the vital principle of generosity and largesse.

5

The physics of water leads naturally on to its poetry. I have begun to collect a little anthology of water, as a sort of poetical reservoir or prayer book, for times of dry inspiration. It begins with D. H. Lawrence's 'Snake', then Philip Larkin's brief and enigmatic 'Water', in which he considers how 'to construct a religion' from a liturgy of fording and sousing, and a 'furious devout drench'. Both these poems find, in their own way, the sacred element in water, though from quite different sources. With Lawrence the snake-god is drinking from a dark pagan subterranean one, 'from the burning bowels of this earth'. While in Larkin the sacred is located in a bright, sunlit space, as simple as a clear glass of water, raised ceremoniously towards the east, 'Where any-angled light/Would congregate endlessly', a brilliant joyful image of a whole worshiping community of dancing water molecules.

My anthology has become especially rich in the Romantics poets, who make use of images of water in so many different ways. Who can forget Wordsworth's lakes, or Shelley's clouds, or Coleridge's rivers and seas?

Water always had magic powers for Coleridge, and often connected with memory. The whole of 'The Rime of the Ancient Mariner' can be seen as a study in the effects of water, and also the traumatic memories it can release. By contrast, in his beautiful early poem on his own native river, 'Sonnet to the River Otter', he transforms water into blessed memories of childhood:

> Dear native brook! wild streamlet of the West!
> How many various-fated years have passed,
> What happy and what mournful hours, since last
> I skimmed the smooth thin stone along thy breast,
> Numbering its light leaps! Yet so deep impressed
> Sink the sweet scenes of childhood, that mine eyes
> I never shut amid the sunny ray,
> But straight with all their tints thy waters rise,
> Thy crossing plank, thy marge with willows grey,
> And bedded sand that, veined with various dyes,

Gleamed through thy bright transparence! On my way,
Visions of childhood! oft have ye beguiled
Lone manhood's cares, yet waking fondest sighs:
Ah! that once more I were a careless child!

Here 'bright transparency' is both the peculiar, bright, magnifying clarity of water, and also that of earliest memories and recollections. Coleridge's Notebooks are full of such water observations, drawing constantly unexpected similes and metaphors from both its appearance and its movement. In the Lake District he found 'a whole new world of Images in the water!' He wrote detailed prose studies of the water-falls at Moss Force, Scale Force and Lodore, and compared the latter at twilight to 'a vast crowd of huge white Bears rushing, one over the other, against the wind – their long white hair shattering abroad in the wind'.

In the stripling River Greta, behind his future house, he spotted a tiny whirlpool of water forming and re-forming in the lee of a large flat rock in the midst of the fast-flowing current, and made it first into a flower, and then into a metaphysical image of recurrence and human hope itself: 'The white Eddy-rose that blossom'd up against the stream in the scallop, by fits and starts, obstinate in resurrection – It is the *Life* that we live.'[6]

By contrast, Shelley's poem 'The Cloud' turns out to be based on an accurate meteorological description of the workings of the convec-tion cycle. Yet its form is dazzlingly musical, light and rapid, carried on dancing dactyls and quick internal rhymes, making it seem more like a child's song than a scientific treatise. Throughout the Cloud itself (herself?) speaks, another kind of pagan sprite, full of laughter and mischief. In the last stanza the identity of the Cloud takes on a series of surreal transformations, becoming a pure pagan symbol of death and resurrection, endlessly repeated or recycled.

... I am the daughter of Earth and Water,
And the nursling of the Sky;
I pass through the pores of the ocean and shores;
I change, but I cannot die.

For after the rain when with never a stain
The pavilion of Heaven is bare,
And the winds and sunbeams with their convex gleams
Build up the blue dome of air,
I silently laugh at my own cenotaph,
And out of the caverns of rain,
Like a child from the womb, like a ghost from the tomb,
I arise and unbuild it again.

6

For me, too, water has many ghosts, and has become associated with my early dreams of freedom and adventure in France. I have never forgotten the primal mountainside spring from which I drank, fifty years ago, as a lonely eighteen-year-old walking with an ex-army backpack and sleeping bag, over Mount Lozère, as later described in my book *Footsteps*. I now see how many other 'furious drenchings' there are in that secret autobiography.

For instance, there was a memorable starlight swig from my metal water flask when I woke during my first night '*à la belle étoile*' on a remote Lozère hillside following Robert Louis Stevenson's walk and, looking up into the glimmering southern night, felt 'I was falling upwards into someone's arms'. But whose arms? I now wonder. Then there was my endless search for fresh water in each tiny Cévenol village I came down to out of the hills, sweating. My first question would always be: '*Bonjour, où est la fontaine qui coule?*'

This was a pilgrim's question, which is not remotely rendered by the English version: 'Excuse me, is there a fresh-water supply somewhere in this village?' In those days there always was one. Usually it was a simple brass or iron spigot, coming directly out of a piece of stone, either in the main square (if there was such a grand place), or sometimes on a roadside bank at the entrance or exit to the village. I would often hear this water tinkling long before I could find it. No tap or switch, simply a thin steady stream of continuous water from some local spring, always icy cold and clear and free.

Sometimes, but not always, there would be a plaque: *'Eau potable'*. I think I read this as: 'Holy water', and all my Catholic childhood would rush back to me as I drank and drank. Now these blessed little fountains are mostly disused and silent. Although there is a restored one in Uzès, in the little square above the Hôtel d'Entraigues, not far from that original Roman spring which fed the distant city of Nîmes. I last used it fifty-two years ago, in summer 1964.

In those days I invented many brief water chants as I went along. But more recently I wrote a song – or rather, what Byron used to call 'a versicle' – about the shrinking of the River Gardon in high summer: 'Song for the Thirsty Gardon'. It was originally dedicated to the farmer's teenage son Maxim, a passionate fisherman in the local pools with his grandfather, until he was sent off to train as an accountant in distant Montpellier. It was partly designed as a farewell gift, and also to remind Maxim of some English words. The only two French words included in the poem were local ones – *apéro* and *pression*, meaning the evening drinks hour (aperitif), and a cold lager drawn from the keg in a café – which were words he naturally honoured.

Chanson pour le Gardon Assoiffé

Deep beneath the shingle
And hidden from all eyes
The Water Gods are working
And another river lies.

Silently and swiftly
A current dark and strong
Wells up from distant Lozère
And southwards snakes along.

Where Gardon lies a-gasping
As dry and white as bones
His subterranean sister
Uncoils beneath his stones.

She rises up at Alès
And makes the fountains leap,
Then sinks again for ages
As if she's gone to sleep.

At Pont de Ners she wakens
When *apéro*'s on hand,
And bubbles up like *pression*
And quenches all the land.

7

There is an old white wooden seat under the cherry tree in the centre of the garden, which we have christened the Philosopher's Bench. Sitting here over many evenings, as the shadows lengthened, I found myself trying to formulate an inclusive and hopeful philosophy of water. This became 'le philo d'eau'. It was eventually condensed, or crystallised, into this formulation: 'All things would go much better in the world if we had three elements that were both cheap and universally available: *education, solar power and water*.' I haven't greatly improved on this formulation since.

A genuine philosopher, the ancient Greek Thales of Miletus, who 'flourished' in the fifth century BC, said simply that everything in the world came from water. It was the foundation of all matter, the beginning and end of all life on earth. It strikes me that this beautiful naïve theory would now make complete sense to modern cosmologists who, in their search for any signs of life on the exoplanets (the first only discovered in 1997), are looking essentially for signs of water.

Water would be the unique cosmological signature of extra-terrestrial life anywhere in the universe (or at least in this universe). Hence the excitement about the new exoplanet recently discovered by a telescope in Chile in August 2016 orbiting Proxima Centauri, the closest star to our sun, a mere 4.24 light years away. This planet, not yet named, is thought to be small and rocky, like the Earth, and in the 'Goldilocks position', that is, neither too hot nor too cold, where liquid water – and therefore life – may be possible, and what's more, discoverable. I hope there may be a garden like ours up there.

Notes

1. See WaterAid *www.wateraid.org.uk*
2. Philip Ball, *H₂O: A Biography of Water*, Phoenix, 2000, pp. 134–5
3. Philip Ball, p. 310
4. Richard Dawkins, *The Magic of Reality: How we know what's really true*, Bantam, 2011, p. 253
5. Richard Dawkins, p. 239
6. *The Notebooks of Samuel Taylor Coleridge*, edited by Kathleen Colburn, Routledge, 1957, vol. 1, entry 496 (1799)

SOMEWHERE IN NORTHERN KARELIA

Tim Ingold

Somewhere in the woods of northern Karelia there lies a huge boulder. If you could count such boulders, it would be one of thousands. But my boulder cannot be counted. I do not know whether it is one, two, three or four. Once it rode a glacier as a wandering erratic, having been torn from granite bedrock by the force of moving ice. Then, when the ice melted, it was unceremoniously dumped on a steep incline. It has remained there ever since, ever about to roll down the hill but never quite doing so, as soil, moss, lichen, shrubs and trees have grown up all around it. The boulder has become its own environment, providing shade and shelter for plants on the lower side, and surfaces for other plants to grow; there is even a pine sapling rooted in a fissure near the top. Deep in the forest, you have to pick your way over rocks and wade through a carpet of vegetation to find it. Standing some four metres tall, with an equivalent girth in all directions, what meets your eyes is about 200 tonnes of rock, not settled flat on the ground but falling down the slope with a velocity of zero. Only a precarious balance of forces holds it there.

But at some time in the past – possibly thousands of years ago – it was rent asunder. It is likely that water penetrated a crack, expanded when it froze and, with immense force, split the boulder from top to bottom, breaking off a massive slab that at the same time shifted some seventy centimetres to the side. The wedge-shaped crack remains open at the top, and a small block of stone has fallen into it, where it remains jammed, about a third of the way down. Another shard of rock has slid from the cracked face and rests on the block exactly as it fell, supported on its sharp edge. All this must have happened in a split second, and in the stillness of the forest I try to imagine the explosive sound it must have made, and how it must have echoed through the landscape. Looking at the precariously balanced assembly, of shard on block, of block in crack, of crack in boulder, of boulder on incline, I have the feeling that I inhabit a silence on the inside of the explosion. It is as if nature, in this boulder, were forever holding its breath. One day it will give way, and the boulder will tumble down. We cannot know when that will be. Best not to be beneath it when it comes!

Somewhere in these woods is a special tree. If you could count trees, it would be one of millions. But my tree cannot be counted. It is not large, nor has it grown to any great height. At its foot, its roots are tightly wrapped around an outcrop of glacier-smoothed rock, from which a thick, gnarled trunk coils out like a snake, eventually inclining towards the vertical as it thins into more recent growth, dissolving into a spray of needle-covered branches and twigs. The tree is a pine and, thanks to its location on the shore of a great lake, it has known extremes of wind and cold from which its larger inland cousins are somewhat protected. Its twisted trunk bears witness to early years of struggle against the elements, when once it was but a young and slender sapling. Deep inside, that sapling is still there, buried beneath decades of further growth and accretion. Within every tree hides a younger version of itself. Now hardened and gnarled with age, my tree can hold out against anything that nature might throw at it.

What for me is so special about this tree, however, is the way it seems to establish a sort of conversation between rock and air. At base the wood has all but turned to stone. The roots, following the contours of the outcrop and penetrating its crevasses, hold the rock in an iron grip. But up above, delicate needles vibrate to the merest puff of wind and play host to tiny geometrid caterpillars that measure out the twigs in their peculiar looping gait. How is it possible for such ageless solidity and ephemeral volatility to be brought into unison? This is the miracle of my tree. Through it, the rock opens up to meet the sky, while the

133

annual passage of seasons nestles within what seems like an eternity. To spend time with this tree, as I have done, is at once to be of the moment and to sink back into a reverie of agelessness.

Here in these woods, forest ants are at work, building their nest. From a distance the nest reveals itself as a perfectly formed mound, circular in plan and bell-shaped in elevation. Observe it closely, however, and it turns out to be seething with movement as legions of ants jostle with one another and with the materials they have brought back – mostly grains of sand and pine needles. From the centre, ant-roads fan out in all directions. You have to peer at the ground to see them. Often they are more like tunnels, boring their way through the dense carpet of mosses and lichens that covers the earth. If you were the size of an ant, the challenges of the passage would be formidable, as what to us are mere pebbles would present precipitous climbs and vertical drops, while tree roots would be mountain ranges. Yet nothing seems to deter the traffic as thousands upon thousands of ants march out and back, the outward goers often colliding with returnees laden with materials of some sort to add to the heap. Wandering alone in the forest, it is odd to think that beneath one's feet are miniature insect imperia, populated by millions, of unimaginable strangeness and complexity.

In the woods the wind is blowing. If you could count gusts, you would never finish, as fresh ones always come along. But the wind cannot be counted. You can hear it coming from a long way off, especially through the aspen trees. Each tree hands it on to the next until, for a moment, their leaves are all singing to the same tune. Every leaf is aquiver, even though the trunks sway only a little. Then all is quiet again. The gust has moved on. On the waters of the lake the surface is disturbed into ripples which focus the reflected light into little suns that flash first double and then single. As the ripples reach the lake shore the reeds bend over, rustling in unison, until they in turn fall silent. Do trees create the gust of wind by waving their leaf-draped limbs? Does water create wind by rippling? Do reeds create wind by rustling? Of course not! Yet surely the clarinettist needs a reed to turn his breath into music. So if, by wind, we mean it's music to our ears, or it's sun-dance to our eyes, then yes – leaves, ripples and reeds do make the wind. For when I say I hear the wind, or see it in the surface of the lake, the sounds I hear are made by leaves just as much as is the light I see made by ripples.

Once I was flying a kite out on the field, where the grass had recently been cut. As I played on the string, it seemed to me that my kite, like the leaves of the trees, was also an instrument for turning aerial gusts into music in motion. However, the string, often entangled on previous flights, had been repaired at many points by cutting and retying. An unusually strong gust overwhelmed one of the knots and my kite broke loose. Off it went, sailing over the treetops, buoyed up by the wind. I imagine the kite having relished its new-found freedom. 'Watch me,' it would have crowed. 'I am a creature of the sky. Field and forest, they are all the same to me!' But its dreams were to come to an ignominious end as it drifted down to earth. Most likely it was snagged on an angling tree branch as it fell. I never found it again. But I am sure it is there, somewhere in the woods, draped forlornly from the branch, utterly lost.

I too, in straying from field to forest, have risked becoming lost. I know an old path that runs through the woods, though I am not sure where it begins, and it ends in the middle of nowhere. Long ago, however, it was made by the passage of many feet as people, year in year out, would go with rakes, scythes and pitchforks from the farms around the lake to cut the hay in far-flung meadows. The hay would be stored in field barns and brought in by horse and sledge over the winter to feed the cattle in their stalls. But that was in the past. First the horses went, as every farm acquired a tractor. Then the outfields were abandoned, as forestry became more profitable than dairy production. Then the cows were sold off, and finally the people left. Few farms remain inhabited year-round.

And so the path fell out of use and is gradually fading. In places it has completely disappeared. Trees have fallen across it or are even growing in its midst. I can tell the path is there only by following a line of subtle variation in the leaf mould on the ground, a gap in lichen cover, a thinning of soil on rock. So long as I am on it, I can discern the path by running my eye along the line. But I know that if I move to one side or the other, the line will disappear. Indeed, this has happened to me on more than one occasion: having deviated from the path in one direction – my attention drawn by an anthill or by luscious bilberries to pick – I have crossed right over it on the return without even noticing, and strayed too far in the opposite direction. How then should we think of this path, which is visible only as you go along it? It is a line made by walking; an inscription of human activity on the land. Yet while one can distinguish the path from the ground in which it is inscribed – albeit only faintly, and with an eye already tuned to its presence – it is not possible to distinguish the ground from the path. For the ground is not a base upon which every feature is mounted like scenery on a stage set. It is rather a surface that is multiply folded and crumpled. The path is like a fold in the ground.

Somewhere in northern Karelia there are still cows. But here there are none. The fields fell silent many years ago. Once we would row across the lake with a churn to fetch milk, warm and fresh, from the dairy. But these days, it doesn't pay to look after a few head, and anyway, who will do the milking when the old folk retire? No girl wants to follow her mother into the cowshed; no boy aspires to what has always been seen as women's work. Nowadays cattle are concentrated in big production facilities, whose managers rent the fields once used for grazing to provide a year-round supply of fodder. Sometimes I imagine that the cows are still there, wandering the fields like ghosts. I think I see them staring asquint with their doleful moon-eyes, and hear them lowing, chewing the cud, crashing through undergrowth. Then silence falls again, pierced only by the wistful cry of the curlew. Where the cows once lingered, strange white oval forms can be seen scattered here and there over the meadows, or lined up on their trackside perimeters. People call them 'dinosaur eggs'. Really, they are gigantic rolls of machine-cut hay. The machine rolls the hay as it cuts, and as each roll is completed it is automatically wrapped in white plastic sheeting and laid – like a great egg – on the ground. Later, the 'eggs' will be collected and taken far away, to the place where all the cows are now.

Amidst fields bordered by woods and lake stands an old timber-built cottage. As a family, we have often spent our summers here. The cottage has a living room, two small bedrooms, a porch and a little veranda.

Outside, a set of wooden steps leads up to the front door. I can tell you exactly how many steps there are. Every morning I sit on the steps and think. I think about all the life that has passed there, from when our children were taking their first steps to now when they have families of their own. I listen to the birds, watch the bees as they pollinate the flowers, follow the sun as it passes between the trees and drink a mug of tea. And I think about what I am going to write that day. If the weather is fine I write outside at a small wooden table, seated on a bench hewn from a log, and look across the yard to the trees on the other side. The table is covered by a plastic-coated cloth, which is bare apart from a tin on which I mount a spiral of insect repellent. I light one end and it burns very slowly, giving off a sweetly aromatic smoke that is alleged to drive away the mosquitoes that might otherwise invade my writing space. With fewer mosquitoes these days – an effect of climate change, perhaps – it is hardly needed, and I'm not even sure that the mosquitoes take much notice of the smoke. But I burn it anyway, as I quite like the smell. It is a sign that I am thinking. As the spiral of repellent is slowly consumed it seems to me that my thoughts curl up, like the smoke, and waft into air.

For the rest of the year, when I am not here, I dream about my bench and table and about the steps to the cottage. Nowhere is there a more tranquil place to be. Nowhere is more conducive to intense reflection, for my mind can withstand the stress of churning thought only when it is otherwise at peace. And nowhere are the multiple rhythms of the world, from the glacial to the atmospheric, so perfectly nested. The cracked boulder, the twisted tree, the empire of the ants, the sighing wind and the suns that reflect from ripples on the lake, the memory of a lost kite, the fading path and absent cows, the dinosaur eggs, the steps on which I sit and the table at which I write these lines: these are among the many stories woven into the fabric of my favourite place. I won't tell you exactly where it is, as this would give away my secret. But it is somewhere in northern Karelia.

CHILDHOOD GROUND
ABIDING PLACES

Richard Long

The cliff ledge den
The look-out tree
The bicycle racing track in the wood
The dumps
The long grass place for stalking
The cave in the cliff
The slide
The footpath where we dug a trap
The smoking cane place
The place of the secret grave on the scree
The tobogganing zig-zag
The place where we dug quartz with hammers
The place of some soot behind a wall
The swampy place

City of Bristol The Downs and the Avon Gorge 1983

A Wood Over One's Head

Richard Mabey

It was pinned to a beech tree in the lane like a poster announcing the circus was in town. 'WOOD FOR SALE'! Bold letters, no stated price. A path tumbled down into a dry valley, then up again, statuesque beeches to the right, frayed ashes trapezing to the left. Through their trunks the haze of bluebells looked liked dry ice. The prospect made me giddy. What was I doing, dreaming of buying a wood when I didn't even own a house? The reasons I gave my friends were sociable and sensible. I wanted to see if a modern community could go back to the woods, if all I'd read about woodland history and management could be put into practice in the twentieth century. But thirty years on I recognise that there were other kinds of neediness at work. I was almost forty years old and single. I think I wanted to make something, leave a legacy, maybe have a place where I could go feral among the trees again as I had when I was a kid. What I hadn't anticipated was that I was to become embroiled in implicit debates about the privileges and abuses of ownership, and about woods as autonomous ecosystem as against managed artefacts.

One problem was that to dis-own a wood, so to speak, to take it out of the province of the functional and commercial, you first had to own it, and play the property game. You had to be prepared to deal with fences and planning law and the insidious pressure to *do* something. I did not accept this frame of mind with much grace, even at the very beginning. In the months I was negotiating with the agent, I mooned about in Hardings Wood (as it was called), hiding in the undergrowth when yet another bidder with a Norfolk jacket and a clipboard hove into view and made me wretched with gloom and frustration. In the end I sealed the deal by contacting the vendor directly, and being emotional about my romantic plans for the place. I would have to pay the same rate as a forestry company, so it was no skin off his nose.

Even objectively it was a more promising site for me than a commercial operation. The wood was slung like a hammock over a dry valley half a mile from the village of Wigginton, and in the north corner there was a patch of some commercial value – a beech plantation established in the 1890s. But most of the tree cover was natural regrowth after the place had been gutted of timber during the Second World War. There was ash and cherry in the valley, oak and holly on the clay plateau, all worthless as timber. And some time during the 1960s the last owner, an absentee wood merchant over-excited by an ephemeral subsidy scheme, had over-planted the whole site with matchwood poplars. They became infected by honey fungus and were dying on their feet. The wood was dark from the dense regrowth, but full of ferns and flowers that relished the shade. I wandered about among its strange and unremarked tuftings – beeches shaped like candelabras, dynastic badger setts, orchids glimmering in the deepest shade – and wondered what I could make of it. I was full of hubris then, expert in suppressing the fact that in the long term the wood would survive and flourish even if I did absolutely nothing. But I was passionate to get engaged, to let in some light (in more than a literal sense), to make the place wilder, woodier, more beautiful in some ill-defined way, to feel I had enhanced the earth's growth a mite before I was added to the leaf litter myself.

The novelist E. M. Forster owned a wood in Sussex in the 1930s, and confessed that he too was troubled by this compulsion to intervene. Possessing Piney Copse, he wrote in an essay entitled 'My Wood',

makes me feel heavy. Property does have this effect ... [it also] makes its owner feel that he ought to do something to it. Yet he isn't sure what. Restlessness comes over him, a vague sense that he has a personality to express – the same sense that, without any vagueness, leads the artist to an act of creation.

I never felt that kind of grand creative impulse towards Hardings, but there was no vagueness about my idealistic fantasy of restoring one small plot of the Greenwood to the People. I declared my ambition to establish a 'parish wood' by cutting the fence across the entrance.

And then, with the help of local friends and allies, I canvassed the village, asked for memories of the place, invited the inhabitants to come and help with the 'work', whatever that might turn out to be. The response was mixed, revealing the different declensions of possessiveness people can feel about places. A taxidermist, bizarrely, was the one soul to express outright hostility, protesting that activity in the wood might disturb his illicit trapping vigils. The Master of the local foxhounds imagined that sharing a few whiskies might persuade me to open the wood to the hunt. A handful of villagers fretted that the phrase 'community wood' presaged coach parties from Islington. Not that they seemed engaged as a community themselves. When I talked about our scheme to the local primary school I was shocked to find that not a single child had ever slipped into the wood, despite its comparative closeness. No dens, no bike scrambles, no dirty games in the deep ditches. Things had been different half a century before. The oldest villagers could remember the 1930s, when the local woods were worked by cross-cut-saw teams, and kids gathered up the debris in shopping bags as fuel for home. One woman showed us a basket plaited from willow and hazel by the Italian POWs who had looked after Hardings Wood during the war.

It was no great surprise that on our first working day locals were outnumbered by friends and fellow woodland enthusiasts. A score of us assembled one autumn Sunday with the beech leaves turning golden and the bracken tipped by frost, and realised we hadn't a clue what to do. There was little evidence of any ancient management practices we might carry on, certainly no preening 'heritage' model to live up to. That morning all my nebulous visions about the place collapsed at the stark prospect of making the first cut. Why do *anything?*

So, a little nervously, we talked. Those present shared their feelings about the place, and how they felt it might be enhanced. Tree identities and the merits of space versus shade were debated. There were different

142

points of view, but in the end we seemed to agree what might be done. We happened to have met by a woodland pond, a very dark and overshadowed body of water, and clearing a glade around it so the sun could get in seemed uncontentious. Pardons were granted to characterful oaks and hollies whose case was argued before this impromptu forest court. At the end of the day we found we had a created a curious but pleasant miniature landscape, like a patch of savanna around a waterhole.

And that was pretty much how work would proceed over the next few years. It would be fanciful to call it on-site democracy, yet it wasn't some rigid pre-established management plan either. What gave our actions a kind of coherence was that we were all responding to the prompts the place gave us as much as to our personal visions. The network of footpaths (there were none at the start) were trodden out by people following animal tracks and natural contours and the magnetic pulls of viewpoints and big trees. Everyone felt that letting in light was a priority, so thinning dense stands of ash and sycamore and poplar soon became routine.

For the first time in half a century villagers came to enjoy the wood. I once chanced upon a couple of watercolourists seated among the bluebells in straw hats and looking much more a part of the place than I was. There were new customs established too. On Ascension Day the children from the village school tramped over the fields, and in a clearing among the freshly leafed beeches sang hymns to new life and the mysteries of transubstantiation. In summer, after exams were over, there were secular rites and woodland sleepovers.

Some part of my own dream of ushering a parish woodland into existence had happened. But with hindsight I was driving the agenda much more than I admitted to myself at the time. On one occasion I acted as an outright commercial forester. The big beeches which had been planted on a field adjacent to the wood at the start of the twentieth century were, on a forester's time sheet, ready for thinning. But of course they didn't *need* thinning. They would have survived as a group of trees perfectly well for another two centuries. Nonetheless, they had been planted for timber, and thinning them would contribute to our philosophy of enlightenment and, I reasoned defensively, help pay for a pick-up truck to fetch our cut wood ... I salved my conscience with the high-minded phrase 'continuity of intention'. And one November day I found myself progressing through the wood with a professional surveyor, deciding trees' destiny and the future interior landscape of this part of the wood with the help of cans of different-coloured aerosol paint. My mentor would choose those trees that might eventually make fine timber. I could pick those that were picturesque or promising dead wood habitats, or just tickled my sentimental fancy. Between these, and marked with red dots, were the trees that could comprise an immediate money-making harvest, mostly close to the chosen ones, so that their removal would give these more space to flourish. I was pleased to learn that the whole process is known in forestry jargon as 'selection'. It sounded as if we were preparing a Tree Show for the Royal Academy.

It was in my private time in the wood that I came closest to understanding my complicated and sometimes contradictory relationship with it. From spring to autumn I spent time just mooching about the place. Walking the same tracks two or three times a week I could spot the tiniest changes: which ash seedlings had put on an inch in height; where windfall branches had dropped from; how our minimalist experiments with the light were affecting the rhythms of growth. When I return to the wood now, fifteen years after I moved away from the Chilterns, I find those two decades of intense memory are still there – 'like a peat core drawn from my mind', I jotted in my diary.

I paid obsessive attention to the flora of the place, which was shifting partly because of the work we were doing, partly from its own cryptic cycles. One May, working on my hands and knees, I counted eighteen colour variants in the bluebells, from pure white and white stripes on pastel blue to dark indigo. I had volunteered to survey the wood for the Hertfordshire County Flora, and a generalised ecstasy over the spring florilegium wouldn't do. So I learned to evaluate glumes and lemma in the woodland grasses (our single tuft of the rare wood barley was a conspicuous bearded oddity among the crisp anemones). I tracked the migrations of supposedly immobile ferns from their redoubts on the medieval woodbanks to nondescript addresses among the planted beeches. I realised that our exquisite wood-vetch – sweet-pea-scented, liquorice-striped and the only colony in the county – depended for its survival on the disturbance we created along the tracks. After ten years Hardings had the highest score in the county, relative to its size, of what ecologists call 'ancient woodland indicator species'.

In winter my relationship with the wood became more physical. The mid nineties were an exceptionally rainy time. Often I'd go there after a downpour and hear an unfamiliar sound: the lap and gurgle of water running over stone. The current of rainfall pouring down the lane had found an easy left turn at the wood's entrance and made off down the hill. It fingered its way into every track and rabbit run. It carved out runnels down to the bare flint, piling up dams of woodland flotsam – beechmast, dead leaves, a leavening of fine gravel – and laid out terraces with miniature pools and rapids. For a few hours most rainy days I had an upland stream on my patch.

The heaviest downpours sent flash floods rasping through the wood. Everywhere the water took short cuts, dashing down badger trails, bursting through hedges from the fields next door. In the valley one day it built up to a torrent that tore clumps of fern out by the root. It snapped off a branch from a fallen tree and drove it forward like a snow plough wiping a swathe of ground ten yards long clean of vegetation.

It occurred to me that this might be a prompt for a piece of beneficial landscaping. Why not facilitate moving water in the dry valley? It is what would have been there in post-glacial times, and would have helped form the topography of the place. Re-introducing it is what the earthmover Capability Brown would doubtless have done. And there had been a watery motion in the valley more recently. In the 1930s, when the Rothschild family owned the wood and many of the houses in the village, they'd lain sewage pipes from the cottages down the hill to evacuate their contents among the cherry trees. Fifty years on trees would still not grow in the eutrophic midden that resulted, and insisting that this unwholesome traffic was stopped was the first action I took after buying Hardings. Joining up the pipes with the village gutters in the hope of rather more splendid flows during storms might have been theoretically possible, but it would have been an absurd and unnatural artifice. The valley had been dry for thousands of years. It was part of the identity of the place, not something to be tinkered with as if it were a gardener's plaything.

Sometimes I would work in the wood by myself in winter, sawing up logs from thinnings we had generated on a working weekend. More often I would saunter round the place with a pair of heavy-duty loppers doing just the sort of tinkering I despised. I clipped the brambles round my favourite primrose patches, so they would make a better show. I lopped sycamores that were shading ashes, and ashes shading young beeches, as if I had certain knowledge of the proper hierarchy in trees. As for the pesky poplars, I was in the habit of looking for ones about to topple and nudging them into a position where they would take other poplar branches with them when they fell. And I remember the excuses I made to myself for this finicky primping in a place I liked to think of as halfway wild. I was doing something no less natural than the local badgers or a tribe of bark-beetles might do, making corners of the wood commodious for themselves. I reckoned I deserved a niche along with the rest of creation.

But William Wordsworth's admonitions to presumptuous land-owners nagged me. In 1811 he had visited Foxley in Herefordshire, seat of the philosophical high priest of the Picturesque movement, Uvedale Price. Wordsworth admired the estate, but not the owner's habit of lopping branches to open up a view, or levering a few rocks into the splash of a stream. '[A] man little by little,' he chided, 'becomes so delicate and fastidious with respect to forms in scenery: where he has a power to exercise control over them and if they do not exactly please him, in all mood, and every point of view, his power becomes his law.' Foxley 'lacked the relish of humanity' of a 'country left more to itself'.

The odd thing is that I experienced not a mite of the tinkering instinct outside my wood. Everywhere else I was delighted by muddles, by the glint of obscured flowers, by views from, not views of. Wordsworth was right. It was the licence given by ownership and power that encouraged gratuitous intervention.

In 2002 I moved to Norfolk and, with no wish to become an absentee landlord, sold Hardings Wood to a village trust – a sadness for me, but a boon for the wood, which now had a written constitution and a guarantee of open access in perpetuity. When I go back I think I have been too hard on myself. The wood does have Wordsworth's 'relish of humanity', but an obstinate, self-willed temperament too. In response to what we did there during my tenancy, it's been generous. The foot-paths we trod out have firmed up, but not dogmatically, and wander pleasantly wherever a fallen tree or a new badger digging intervenes. The gaps in the beech plantation have filled with spectacular natural regeneration, of more than ten species of tree. The whole wood has been a dramatic demonstration of the fact that trees can start their lives perfectly well without being stuck in the ground by humans. We did plant a few saplings, mostly gifts it would have been churlish to refuse, but their weedy growth was a caution by the side of the self-sprung wildings. New species arrived – wild daffodil, nesting buzzard, fallow deer. And I suppose one could add to that list a benign strain of *Homo*, not overbearing or presumptuously stewardly, just making a space for themselves alongside their fellow creatures.

Tekels Park

Helen Macdonald

I shouldn't do the thing I do, because motorway driving requires you to keep your eyes on the road. I shouldn't do it also because pulling at one's heart on purpose is a compulsion as particular and disconcerting as pressing on a healing bruise. But I do it anyway, and it's safer to do it these days, because this stretch is being transformed into a smart motorway, so the long slope of the M3 as it falls towards Camberley is packed with speed cameras and 50 mph signs, and when I'm driving there on my way somewhere else I can slide my car into the outside lane to bring me closer and slower to the section of fence I'm searching for, running west and high under skies white as old ice.

Perhaps a hundred thousand vehicles pass this place each day. Back in the mid 1970s I could lie awake in the small hours and hear a single motorbike speeding west or east: a long, yawning burr that Dopplered into memory and replayed itself in dreams. But like snow, traffic noise thickens with time. By the time I was ten I could stand by Europe's second largest waterfall, listen to it roar, and think, *it sounds like the motorway when it's raining.*

I shouldn't look. I always look. My eyes catch on the place where the zoetrope flicker of pines behind the fence gives way to a patch of sky with the black peak of a redwood tree against it and the cradled mathematical branches of a monkey puzzle, and my head blooms with an apprehension of lost space, because I know *exactly* all the land around those trees, or at least what it was like thirty years ago. And then the place has passed, and I drive on, letting out the breath I'd been holding for the last thousand feet or so, as if by not breathing I could still everything, movement, time, all of the dust and feet that rise and fall in a life.

Here's an early memory. A ridiculous one, but true. I learned to speed-read by trying to decipher military warning signs that bordered the roadside on my way to primary school. KEEP OUT was simple, but DANGER – UNEXPLODED ORDNANCE took me months. I needed to read the words *all at once*, because my mother's car was moving and the signs were very close. Each weekday morning I'd stare out of the window as the army land approached and wait for the words to appear so I'd have another chance at them. The feeling I had then, of wanting to apprehend something important that was passing by me very fast is the feeling I have now when I look for the place behind the motorway fence where I grew up.

I was five in my first summer in the Park. It was 1976. Cape daisies bloomed and died in the flowerbeds and pine cones in the trees behind the house crackled and split through endless indigo afternoons. Standpipes, orange squash, dry lawns, and a conversation in which the matter of *drought* was explained to me. That's when I realised for the first time that not every year was the same, or perhaps that there were such things as years at all. My parents had bought this little white house in Camberley, Surrey, on a fifty-acre walled estate owned by the Theosophical Society. Mum and Dad knew nothing about Theosophy but they liked the house, and they liked the estate too. There'd been a castle here once, or Squire Tekel's early nineteenth-century approximation of one, all faux-Gothic battlements and arrow slits, peacocks and carriages. After it burned down the Theosophists bought the grounds in 1929 for £2,600 and set about turning it into a place for them to live and work. Residing here was *a privilege*, the residents were told. *A privilege for service*. Members built their own houses, bought tents and a second-hand Nissen hut for a newly-created campsite. They grew food in the walled kitchen garden; opened a vegetarian guesthouse. In the 1960s, after leaseholders were granted the right to purchase the freeholds of their properties, outsiders like us began to populate the place.

Theosophy had been banned in Nazi Germany, so many of our neighbours were refugees from the war, and others were the black sheep of good families: elderly women, mostly, who had refused the roles society had reserved for them: the quiet Lolly Willowes of Surrey Heath. One wore ancient Egyptian jewellery she'd been given by Howard Carter; another kept a great auk egg in a drawer. Spies, scientists, concert pianists, members of the Esoteric Society, the Round Table, the Liberal Catholic Church, the Co-Masonic Order. One resident sent his beard clippings back from Nepal to be burned on the estate bonfire. On discovering that I had gone to Cambridge, another, years later, inquired of me where I had stabled my horse – for he'd had dreadful trouble finding livery for his hunter while a student there in the 1930s. Everyone had lives and pasts of such luminous eccentricity that my notion of what was, and wasn't, normal took a battering from which it's never recovered. I am thankful for that, and for the women in particular, for giving me models for living a life.

But most of all I'm thankful for the other freedoms I had there. After school I'd make a sandwich, grab my Zeiss Jena 8x30 Jenoptem binoculars and strike out for my favourite places. There were ivy-covered walls and specimen trees, redwoods planted to commemorate the death of Lord Wellington – they called them Wellingtonias back then, of course they did – and creosoted summer houses with fly-specked windows. 'Arthur Conan Doyle liked to sit here,' I was told, of the smallest summer house beneath the sparse shade of a balsam poplar, the one with original prints of the Cottingley Fairies hanging on its cream-washed walls. There was a round, shallow pond on the Italianate terraces that held an intermittently broken fountain, smooth newts and great diving beetles, and from which vespertilionid bats dipped to drink at night; there was a nine-acre meadow with decaying stables on one side, acres and acres of Scots pine, and damp paths obscured by bracken, rhododendrons, swamp laurels with piped-icing flowerbuds; and there were roads that went nowhere, for when the motorway was built on land compulsorily purchased from the Theosophists in the 1950s, it cut the estate in two. I loved those roads. Bare feet on the rotting tarmac down by the straight avenue of sessile oaks that ended in drifts of leaves and a new desire path that curved right to trace the perimeter of the motorway fence. One dead-end lane at the back of the Park had ten-foot sandy banks I'd scramble up to get to the vast grey beech carved with hearts and dates and initials above, and I was awed by the notion that anyone had found this tree, because I'd never seen anyone near it, *ever*, and one afternoon I dug up a rotted leather drawstring bag from the humus beneath it that spilled threepenny bits into my hands. There had been glow-worms here, and snipe, and ponds, before the motorway came, I was told. Everything on the other side was already houses.

I was permitted to roam unchallenged because everyone here knew me – though they'd have quiet words with my parents after they'd yet again spotted me knee-deep in the middle of the pond looking for newts, or walking past the guesthouse with a big grass snake, two feet of supple khaki and gold twined about my arms. Reg the gardener took me for rides on his tractor-trailer, and we'd putter down the road singing music-hall songs he'd taught me:

> It's the same the whole world over
> It's the poor what gets the blame
> It's the rich what gets the pleasure
> Ain't it all a bloomin' shame?

And while Reg rolled a cigarette I'd race off to explore the bracken and scrub in the back woods, where rhododendrons had grown to near-trees with branches shaped by ancient prunings. They were *superb* to climb when I was small: frames of right-angled kinks and acute wooden curves I could hoist myself into and up, and sit inside a canopy of dark leaves that clicked and pattered with tiny rhododendron leaf hoppers that on closer inspection resembled the brightest of bestiary dragons. In the back woods too was the wood ants' nest, that glittering, shifting particulate mound which moved from year to year and reeked of formic acid. You could turn blue flowers pink if you tossed them on the top before the ants carried them away, and for a while I'd prepare skeletons of the dead birds I found by folding them carefully in little cages of wire mesh and lodging them on top of the nest. When I pulled them free weeks

151

later they'd been reduced to clean white bone that never quite stopped smelling of ants.

Almost by accident I'd been granted this childhood of freedom and privilege, partly through a quirk of location, partly through my parents' trust in the safety of this place, and I lived in the familiar setting of so many of my children's books, from *The Secret Garden* to *Mistress Masham's Repose*, though I wasn't half as posh as their protagonists. I was a state-school kid running free in crumbling formal parkland that might have been written on paper as a metaphor for the contracting empire, or a wilder life, or social transgression, or any number of dreams of escape forged in the imagination of writers years before I was born.

I didn't know how unusual my freedom was, but I knew what it had given me. It had turned me into a naturalist. And for a new naturalist like me, the nine-acre meadow was the best place of all. So much of what was there must have arrived in hay brought for long-dead horses, as seeds from lowland meadows: scabious, knapweed, trefoil, harebell, lady's bedstraw, quaking grass, vetches, diverse other grasses and herbage. And butterflies, too, marooned in this small patch of the nineteenth century: common blues, small skippers, grizzled skippers, marbled whites, small coppers, and grasshoppers that sang all summer and pinged away from my feet. The other side of the meadow was different, and more what you'd expect on acidic soil: a low sea of sheep's sorrel, stars of heath bedstraw, white moths, small heaths, anthills and wavy hair grass brushed with fog by the sun. I knew that meadow intimately. It was richer, more interesting, had more stories to tell than any other environment in my life. I'd press my face in the grass to watch insects the size of the dot over an 'i' moving in the earthy tangle where the difference between stems and roots grew obscure. Or turn over and prospect for birds in the thick cumulus rubble of the sky.

So many of our stories about nature are about testing ourselves against it, setting ourselves against it, defining our humanity against it. But this was nothing like that. It was a child's way of looking at nature: one seeking intimacy and companionship. When I learned the names of these creatures from field guides it was because I needed to know them the same way I had to know the names of my classmates at school. Their diverse lives expanded what I considered home far beyond the walls of my house. They made the natural world seem a place of complex and beautiful safety. They felt like family.

When you are small, the things you see around you promise you they'll continue as they are forever, and you measure life in days and weeks, not years. So when the mowers came one day in early August to cut the meadow as they had done every year since the meadow was made, and I saw what was happening, I burned with terrified outrage. There was no time to think about what I was doing. I ran. I stumbled. I sat in front of the mower to make it stop, then mutely, passively, held my ground in front of the bewildered driver, who came down to quite reasonably ask me what the hell I was doing, and I ran home crying. I didn't understand how hay meadows work. All I saw was destruction. How could I know that the mower's job was to hold history in suspension, keeping the meadow exactly where it was against the encroachment of heather and birch and time?

Every year the meadow grew back and thrived and was as rich as ever, right up until we left the Park in the 1990s. A decade later, I returned on a summer afternoon. Driving up Tekels Avenue the passing scenery possessed the disconcerting, diffuse, off-scale and uncanny closeness of things in dreams. I was frightened of what I might find when the car crested the curve down to the field. But there the meadow was: impossible, miraculous, still crowded with life.

Then I went back in my forties, less scared now, more certain of myself and what I would find there. But I was wrong. Someone who thought meadows should look like football pitches had treated it like a lawn and mowed it repeatedly for several years until the exuberant moving life I'd known and loved was gone. The meadow now looked how that man thought it should look: blank and neat and flat and easy to walk upon. I cried when I saw it: a woman weeping not for her childhood, not really, but for everything that had been erased from this place.

Losing the meadow is not like losing the other things that have gone from my childhood: MacFisheries, Vesta paella, Spacehoppers, school lunches, Magic Roundabout toys, boiled sugar lollipops when

I'd finished my meals in roadside café chains on holiday trunk roads. You can mourn the casualties of fast capitalism for your own generation, but you know they've merely been replaced with other programmes, other media, other things to see and buy. I can't do that with the meadow. I can't reduce it to nostalgia *simpliciter*. When habitats are destroyed what is lost are exquisite ecological complexities and all the lives that make them what they are. Their loss is not about us, even though when that meadow disappeared, part of me disappeared, too, or rather, passed from existence into a memory that even now batters inside my chest. Look, I can't say to anyone. Look at the beauty here. Look at everything that is. I can only write about what it was.

When Henry Green started writing his autobiography in the late 1930s it was because he expected to die in the oncoming war, and felt he did not have the luxury of time to write a novel. 'That is my excuse,' he wrote: 'that we who may not have time to write anything else must do what we now can.' He said more. He said, 'We should be taking stock.' I take stock. During this sixth extinction we who may not have time to do anything else must write what we now can, to take stock. When I sat on the verge that day and wept I told myself over and over again that he was a nice man, that perhaps he had simply not known what was there. Had not known what was there. And I thought of something that I was talking about with a friend just the other day: that the world is full of people busily making things into how they think the world ought to be, and burning huge parts of it to the ground without even knowing they are doing it, utterly, and in the process accidentally destroying things. And that any of us might be doing that without knowing it, any of us, all the time.

A few years ago the Park was sold to a property developer. Today when I drive past the fence the pull on my heart is partly a wrench of recognition when I see those trees, knowing they are the standing ghosts of my childhood. But it's also the knowledge that with care, attention, and a modicum of love and skill, the meadow could be incorporated into the site plan and turned into something very like it had been only a few years ago. The pull on my heart is also the pain of knowing that this is possible, but that it is very unlikely. Centuries of habitat loss and the slow attenuation of our lived, everyday knowledge of the natural world make it harder and harder to have faith that the way things are going can ever be reversed.

We so often think of the past as a something like a nature reserve: a discrete, bounded place we can visit in our imaginations to make us feel better. I wonder how we could learn to recognise that the past is always working on us and through us, and that diversity in all its forms, human and natural, is strength. That messy stretches of species-rich vegetation with all their attendant invertebrate life are better, just *better*, than the eerie, impoverished silence of modern planting schemes and fields. I wonder how we might learn to align our aesthetic and moral landscapes to fit that intuition. I wonder. I think of the meadow. Those clouds of butterflies have met with local extinction, but held in that soil is a bank of seeds that will hang on. They will hang on for a very long time. And when I drive past the fence these days, staring out at 50 mph, I know that what I am looking for, beyond the fence, is a place that draws me because it exists neither wholly in the past, nor in the present, but is caught in a space in between, and that space is a place which gestures towards the future and whose little hurts are hope.

CLIFTON SUSPENSION BRIDGE

Patrick McGuinness

Beside the school is a suspension bridge. To get to the playing fields across the gorge, the boys have to cross it. They do this three times a week, rain or shine. It has to be pretty wet for any match, even the crummiest remedial game, to be cancelled. 'It's *corpore* fucking *sano* time,' says Mr McT***, the heavy-smoking, whisky-perfumed form teacher who talks to the boys like mates from the pub, and discusses historical figures as if he'd known them personally. They like him, though he's tetchy and unpredictable, and when he's angry he's feral and looks like he'll bite. He's big and barrel-shaped, and wheezes like an old accordion when he bends over to tie his laces or pick up some chalk or a dropped cigarette. He remembers nothing, mixes up their names, turns up late and leaves early, but the boys think he tells good jokes. What they mean is that he tells dirty jokes. Some of the older boys go to his house at night to smoke and drink and watch films. When they come back they smell of adults.

They all have their reasons for going to the bridge: mostly it's to smoke or drink; later it will be to meet girls or just for the view. One boy, now a successful entrepreneur in Bristol, collects the pages of porn magazines from around the bridge, and from the caves and crags near the observatory, that have been thrown out by passing cars or hedgerow masturbators. Unless he's very lucky, they're usually damp and dew-soggy, so he takes them back and dries them on the school radiator. When they're dry he sells them. There is a price list: the whole pages are expensive, and there are discounts for the shredded or lopped-off partials. They are available to rent, too.

On windy days the bridge can sway, and lorries and buses have to make the detour down and along the gorge and then back up to the other side. In really bad weather it shuts. The temptation to look down into the brown sludge of estuary, the glistering oyster grit and the silt, the little drain-ditch of trickling water, thin as rain coursing down guttering, is hard to resist. In the sunshine the mud flexes and ripples. It doesn't need much light to look alive. And inviting – a cushion of shimmering brown silk. It's tempting to jump.

The schoolboy is struck first by the smell that rises and catches on the wind. It's the smell of estuaries: on the one hand, drains, and on the other, the open sea. They should clash, but here they seem to go well together, like sweet-and-sour cuisine: the one is blockage and rot and stasis, the other escape and freedom and drift.

And you can always jump. You can jump any time you want. Mostly it's curiosity rather than suffering that makes you look down and find yourself wanting it, sending your mind up ahead to imagine what it's like to fall; to fall and fall and fall. The boy often feels hypnotised by the view, by its completeness. Not many things feel so total as what he sees when he looks down here. It's not dying in itself that's attractive – he's nowhere near unhappy enough for that, though he likes to imagine precisely *how* unhappy he'd need to be: what sort of dosage, millilitre by millilitre of unhappiness climbing the notches of the desolation-syringe, degree by degree in the sorrow-thermometer ... No, not dying so much as its hypothetical nature. It's the idea of seeing yourself afterwards that draws you in: lifting off, peeling away from your body like a pen nib rising from the letters it leaves on the page, then looking down at your shell as you leave it, then at the people in the distance. Though really it's you in the distance: you *are* the distance; dead, you've become it.

He imagines death as one of those aerial shots in a war movie they show in school, where they leave the soldiers behind and rise in their helicopter, and the soldiers run but can't catch up and they shout and cry out and stretch out their hands for their comrades, fingers meet and grip and hold on and then are prised part; and the helicopter rises, shakily at first, and then steadies and pulls away, sticky and reluctant, and the soldiers get smaller and the enemy catch up or mow them down, and everyone becomes a dot and then everyone is gone; then it's all jungle and then all just sky.

And, well, there's also the advantage of just not having to drag this beast of a body around with you, no longer being shackled to the burning animal you are.

There's a legend of a Victorian woman who jumped from Clifton Bridge and lived, as the saying goes, *to tell the tale*, thanks to her big dress ballooning out into a crinoline parachute. There's little possibility anyone would survive the fall today, the boy knows, since, one, the velocity at which you hit the water would kill you outright; two, your heart would explode from fear long before, the way dormice burst inside when you pick them up, or, three, you'd hurtle so deep into the mud that you'd suffocate. It's the lady's image the boy has in mind when he and his friends peer down, or drop balls of paper, sweet wrappers, handkerchiefs or penny pieces over the edge and try to time their descent.

A few feet up, water is hospitable. It opens up and lets you in. After about seventy it is like stone. It will break you as if you'd hit a quarry floor. They learned that in physics.

Another reason it's tempting to let the mind play with the idea of falling is that it's so banally possible: the parapet only a little over five feet high. For most of the boys that means barely shoulder-level. One modest high-jump, using the wood of the handrail for leverage, and you'd be up and over, over and down, down and dead. Maybe then the fall would feel endless, though it would take just a few seconds. You could live a whole lifetime backwards in those seconds: back to birth, as the myth goes, the dying watching their lives unwind before them in reverse. You're interested in whether the same story told backwards is the same story at all. It's the 1980s, so your reference points for backwards and forwards are different from what they are today: they're the fast-forward or the rewind button on a cassette player or a video recorder, or perhaps the lifted needle of a record player dropped approximately between songs. Much later, with the arrival of CDs, you'll hear the old tunes again, like your parents' Jacques Brel or Beatles songs, but on a CD. And for the rest of your life, with a small tug of disorientation, you'll listen out for, and fail to hear, the scratches in the songs that made them yours, and without which you had never until now heard them.

Back then, back in the then, back on the bridge, you think it'll take a few seconds and a whole lifetime to reach the estuary silt; the cool, shiny, hourglass-fine sand. Maybe you could change a few things too, second time around – who knows? Make corrections.

He sometimes takes his introspection, which, like the rest of him, needs exercise, for a walk there. It's probably the only part of him, even in that sporty school, that gets any genuine exercise. There's always someone else on the bridge and, though he thinks of it as a place of extreme loneliness, he realises, years later, that never once was he actually alone on it. There were always others, sometimes as many as half a dozen, all doing the same thing: looking out and over and down. Once he saw someone writing the number for the Samaritans, whose notice is posted at each end of the bridge, on the back of his hand with a biro. For now, he leans over, dangling his arms, the handrail wedged in his armpits. His grandmother is a dressmaker, and she made him his school suit. The way the wind nips and tucks at his clothes like a tailor reminds him of being measured for it. He's being measured for a suit of air, so he can be sleeved in the rush of falling.

Years later, he comes back to the bridge. The Samaritans number used to be local; now it's an 0845 number – like insurance companies, mobile phone companies, telesales. The parapet is the same height, but now it has been supplemented by a four-foot grille of steel that turns inwards at the top. To jump off now, you'd need a ladder.

He's an adult, and has his own children, but when he's back on Clifton bridge, he realises he has his child self on an inner thermostat: always on low, but never quite off. There is a photograph, long-lost materially-speaking, but still intact in his head: it's of his aunt and uncle from a small town in Belgium, who have come to visit him here in Bristol. It's the first and only time anyone from there came here. The three of them are on the Clifton side, at the mouth of the bridge, in autumn sunlight. They must have asked someone to take the picture, because everyone who should be in the picture is in it.

Going back in time is like climbing into an old photograph. He remembers it in sepia tone; remote as an old postcard. But it's a postcard of his life: the treacly air, the heavy school furniture, the gelatinous glaze of things seen through a syrup of time and tears. If he dived into the photograph now, or ran his fingers along its surface, it would be the texture of cream, not the hard floor of water below the bridge. He thinks of the school, a few hundred yards away, and remembers the smell of the place, the universal boys'-school aroma: floor polish, over-applied deodorant and badly wiped arse.

He remembers, too, the wooden desks with their – even then, even in his day – long-disused inkwells, rims impregnated with black and blue spillages. Cocks carved with compass-points and fuckwords etched into the grain, past the varnish and into the pulpy meat of the wood. All that stuff looks a little prehistoric today, as faraway and tribal as bison on cave walls. You can get the desks now on eBay – 'Complete with graffiti', the sellers announce, by way of authenticating them.

But the bridge is always there: tonnes of iron and steel but looking, in the distance, delicate as lace, the cables taut as the strings of a harp. Sometimes you can hear the wind pluck them and fancy you hear a song. It is the song of the air, which is the sound of falling. The boy thinks he'd like to hear that song through to the end, that he'd like a long, long fall so he can hear it over and over and never hit the ground.

We think of haunting as a people thing: something essentially sociable, however unnerving. Ghosts are domesticated creatures, because we have invented them to replicate our actions, which they repeat – repetition is important to the ghost-life: like pets and children they need routine – slowly but often with surprising exactness. They are spectral replays of our matches, won or lost, and we impute to them something of ourselves we do not like to see: an inability to move on, a hunger for return.

As a child I found ghosts disappointing for these reasons: how constructed they were, how made up they were of us. It was our lack of ambition for ghosts that disappointed me; as if, with all we knew about the unknown, we couldn't imagine something better for them than repositories of our unfinished business. I'd have liked them to pull away a little more, to peel off from us, but no: they were hemmed in by their patterns, which were our patterns. A lost opportunity, I thought; for us in our imaginations and for them in their imagined reality. There are rules and regulations for ghosts, and the primary one is that you can't haunt somewhere you've never been, not properly at least, and though there have been ghosts who erred into other stories, other hauntings not their own, the effect there is comical, of actors stumbling into the wrong play.

Three bridges haunt me, though really I'm the one haunting them because I keep returning, and keep remembering the overlaying selves I see and feel whenever I cross them, or look up at them, or stand on one or other of the shores they connect. I explain to my students, early on in the first year of their studies, that the difference between a simile and a metaphor is like the difference between a bridge and an estuary: the bridge links two bits of land, and reminds you that they aren't linked at all. Like a bridge, the simile connects two things at the cost of reminding you that they aren't really connected. The metaphor is the estuary, in which two elements, earth and water, infuse and overlap and merge without its being clear which is which. At the right time of day, you can cross it safely, and at the wrong time of day you can sink into the silt or be swept away by the mad tides and the intricate, unpredictable currents.

The bridges I haunt and am in turn haunted by have something in common: that they are thrown (that is the verb for a bridge: you *throw* it) across estuaries. I remember being offended to hear, back in school, about time's forward flow – the old Heracleitan river you never step into twice. This seemed a satisfactory way of thinking about world events, battles and victories and some (but not all) politics; but as an account of human beings and their relation to Time, it seemed pretty cursory and left a great deal out. From Clifton bridge, looking over the parapet, it also seemed wrong: up there you could imagine Time more as an estuary – with its constant land/water level-shifts, its intermingled elements, its rises and falls, its drain-and-glut, its cross-currents and backstitching, its mud and silt and overlapping in-betweenness – than Heracleitus's river. At some point early on in my life, I must have fixed on that – and back then, not even consciously – as my metaphor for time and memory.

My three bridges are these: the Humber Bridge, which we caught sight of coming from Belgium, where I was brought up, to England; Clifton Suspension Bridge, which loomed over my schooldays at Clifton College, where I was from the age of nine to the age of eighteen; and the Severn Bridge, which welcomed me to Wales, the country that became my first and (I hope) final home – though I had had many houses.

When I arrived in Bristol, my English was piecemeal and full of holes. It sounded faraway in my mouth, not quite mine. Far away, but also someone else's. I felt like a ghost who had broken the revenant rule: a ghost in the wrong haunting, an actor in the wrong play. Speaking English was like wearing a dead relative's clothes, which is not such a dramatic analogy, since my father's Irish-Geordie family were either all dead or nearly so. The ones who were alive seemed already to be turning in like leaves, crisping at the edges. They lived in Newcastle, Doncaster, Bradford, Cullercoats. I always had the sense of somehow trying the language on for size. It had the feel of folded things. When, as a teenager in Bristol, I started buying trendy second-hand clothes – this was in the period, the mid 1980s, when the charity shop was seguing into the vintage clothes shop – I felt I'd known that smell for years, that I finally recognised it: it was the smell of English, and of my English self. Someone had died in it and it had been washed and pressed and put on a hanger in the Salvation Army store on Whiteladies Road for me to come and buy and climb into. As my Belgian grandmother was a dressmaker, and I spent a lot of my childhood with her while she worked, I took and still take many of my metaphors for fitting and *fitting in* from the world of *couture*. So I knew right from the start when things fitted and when they didn't.

When I was doing my O levels, I found, in a shop on Park Street that specialised in dapper, dressy second-hand clothes, a grey single-breasted linen jacket with a blue-and-green threaded piping, and a lining that was the colour of shallow water over estuary mud: a silvery-brown silk-shimmer that tugged at the light and drew it in. It fitted me perfectly, but had been tailor-made for someone else. Whoever it was must have been exactly like me in every physical respect, and really it was I who fitted it. It was bespoke, just not for me, which is how I thought of English, and how I still think of it: made for someone exactly like me, but not me. I associated it too with a betrayal of my grandmother, who used to make me my clothes and took huge pride in them. That I should now be buying them from others, and tailor-made at that, albeit at one ghostly remove, was treachery. Finding that jacket coincided, for me, with getting my English right, with feeling that I finally *had* it, that I'd mastered it and made it mine. That was an illusion – in fact, it had mastered me, just as I fitted the jacket rather than vice versa. I started to find holes in my French where once there had been holes in my English. The *mot juste* still came to me, just not any longer in French. Now I could say more than I felt in English, but in French I felt more than I could express. In tailoring terms, French had become the lining, and English the jacket.

I wore that jacket for our post-O-level party, an amateurish rave on the rocks near the bridge, with ghetto blasters, newsagent-sourced booze and ineptly-rolled joints. Two years later I wore it for my university interview – to study English – and kept it until my early thirties.

Wherever I am, I still haunt the bus stops around the bridge, and the benches where the foxes scavenge by the bins, and when I leaf through the portfolio of regrets that is my adolescence, I always meet myself in the vicinity of Clifton bridge, a clumsy shade in a sharp jacket, taking his melancholy for a walk across a gorge. But the estuary has everything I want and everything my ghost wants, because it is the opposite of Heracleitus and his river: it is water that hasn't yet flowed and sand that hasn't yet passed through the hourglass. Together they make a clay that hasn't yet been fired.

There's still time to change everything.

HERE AND THERE: OR, THE PLOT

Andrew McNeillie

The deadline for this piece threatens like a sudden warning of late frost, one that should take me hurrying across the way to do what I can, to unfurl gauzes, cloudy bundles and unravel them over the tender broad-bean plants, like ribbons of heavy mist in the half-light.

The blackbird on her nest there watches me sharply but holds her nerve. Home I go, leaving her to sleep under the hard night sky that will, or will not, for nothing is certain, form a stiff and blanching frost come morning, winter's Pyrrhic victory if I don't look out – if the blackbird's unlucky and misfortune befalls her new-hatched nestlings in the bitter night. I must nurse my crop as best I can, as the blackbird nurses her new brood.

I was surprised to find her nest, in the corner of an upended wooden pallet through which some fingers of ivy and thorn had taken hold in the past year. Once I knew the nest was there it seemed too obvious, too exposed, but I never noticed it building, and the blackbird was three eggs in before I realised she was there. Safe in plain sight for now. Somehow I feel she's in my care, or that we share something, the spirit of a place, perhaps.

But it is December now, not spring. Now I must dig here, dig in, with my pen and black ink towards my deadline. 'Here' is a far cry, though only a short step, from my physical or material plot out 'there', on the nearby allotment, my only common ground (to speak unmetaphorically) in my retirement, and only hope of any. How I would love a field's-worth or two, a whole Sabine farm, but too late. I will never have the means for it. A token tenancy, it has become a special place to me nonetheless, though it is not strictly 'common' ground, but rented by our Society from the local landlord, owner of a vast demesne north of the Chilterns.

Some of us come and go, unable to keep on top of things, or else throw in the trowel, disillusioned by the reality of keeping Nature at bay with spade or hoe or potato fork. But those of us who hold out cling with some passion to our allotted portions of God's earth, small though they be, our feudal strips that might at any time be sold off to make room for a housing development. Upon which the outcry would be great but unlikely to stay execution. We form a loose but supportive community, respectful of each other's need for solitude, ready enough to help each other out, all within bounds. The powers-that-be are face-less. We are pawns whose protestations, when push comes to shove, will be bulldozed aside by a cabal of other interests. New housing is creeping up, encroaching along a nearby arc of the ring-road, in fields beyond the town's pale. The houses are jammed together without anything you might call a garden between them. My plot is little more than fifty yards out from the ring-road. Rumour is rife that developers are working in our direction, with their eyes on the allotments. I am not sure how much substance there is to them. There may be none, at least for now.

Our tenancy is ever a brief affair, you say. But until this year we were protected by our immediate neighbour. Call him Alexander. It is not his real name. He had a ramshackle barn and a couple of small crooked fields on our westerly border under the terms of an old-fashioned agricultural lease. He kept chickens, a few sheep, a cow and a calf, two or three bullocks or heifers to fatten, and likewise lambs, a pig now and then. The lie of his land was such that it would hamper development. The nature of his lease would make it troublesome to obtain planning permission. The lease ran and could not be cancelled while there was an heir ready and willing to take it on.

Alexander had no heir. He died. He was a rare breed, all but extinct now across the land. He'd left school at fourteen, perhaps earlier, and gone to work for a local farmer until he came into his lease. He kept farmer's hours, late and early, driving up in his white van at dawn, day in, day out, from his nearby council house, a loaded .410 shotgun across his lap, the window down, the vehicle scarcely moving along the lane as he looked to take a magpie or wood pigeon by surprise. He didn't like killing things. But the magpies stole his new-laid eggs by the dozen, given half a chance, and the wood pigeons cropped away at anything they fancied from winter brassicas to summer lettuce.

That Nature is red in tooth and claw he knew by second nature, but he was a thoughtful man too, though some doubted it; and you could see his caring nature in the character of his stock. They were calm and steady, and they flourished, his poultry bold and inquisitive, not easily put to flight. He maintained upwards of a dozen semi-feral cats. Some complained that the cats fouled their plots, especially when newly dug and planted. But they overlooked the benefits the cats brought, at least to Alexander's immediate neighbours. There were no mice to steal our newly planted peas or beans, no rats to do what rats do, to anything they fancy, and no rabbits either.

My plot is just across from his old holding. I often spoke with him. We became friends in a way. There was nothing he didn't know about growing vegetables, and he would advise me often but always in a round-about manner, acknowledging the vagaries of the seasons, and that he too got things wrong. After all, we are all at the unpredictable mercy of the weather. He succeeded and subsisted, however, and loved his way of life and knew he loved it. It was based on a primitive belief system. If you nurture the soil, and plant and sow, then you will reap and harvest. Along the way your faith must survive many trials by plague and blight.

Alexander was a local, a native, a kind of English crofter. It meant everything to him, to belong in his native heath. Sometimes he philosophised about the nature of Nature and, like the country mouse contemplating the town mouse, mocked both DEFRA's civil servants and campaigning environmentalists alike, for what he saw as their red-tape interferences, their ill-informed alarmism, their want of hard-won, hands-on experience. The spirit of place, however degraded his holding, however far from being a rural idyll, the target of thieves and of fly-tippers, haunted him in a way that can only be called mystical.

Never a smoker, he developed what used to be called 'farmer's lung', caused, he thought, in his case, by exposure to chemical dips rather than the bloom and mould in old hay. Latterly he would struggle for breath, especially on warm days. Sometimes I would see him standing stock-still, head bent, one hand resting on a fence post or anything else sturdy enough to support him (he was a big barrel-chested man) while a crisis passed.

Eventually it brought him down. He was buried in a field a quarter of a mile away, a small field he did own, by the sewage works, where he once kept a horse, and where he was interred, as was his wish, in 'a green coffin'. Thereupon the lease on his holding reverted to the landlord. Some people said he was a rogue. When things went missing, some pointed a finger at him, in a kind of reflex way. He did not enjoy the respect of everyone. But to my mind we were diminished by his passing. He was a reminder of a harsher reality, of what it was to scrape a living, hand-to-mouth, the lot of the poor the world over. What's more, we were weakened on what until now was our surest flank against the developers.

I think at first Alexander had me down as a middle-class dreamer, with New Age or Green tendencies: an educated fool, perhaps, persuaded I was doing my bit for self-sufficiency towards saving the planet. But little by little, in the first two years of my tenancy, he seemed to understand I was a lesser kind of mortal, a more down-to-earth specimen, for all my so-called education, with a taste for labouring and fresh vegetables. And I suppose, like him, I have some little scorn for humanity, in the spirit of Henry David Thoreau. I am surprised when I discover among friends and acquaintances individuals who claim either not to know what to do with fresh vegetables, or to have no time to spare for their preparation. But I don't see what I am doing as virtuous.

I was somewhat put out the other day when an old friend, a metro-politan man, praised my virtue for 'growing my own'.

Virtue is its own reward, I said. I am merely a materialist, in love with the flavour of vegetables cooked within minutes of harvest, pleased to readjust the balance in my mind–body equation by labouring out of doors. I cannot save the planet, nor contribute significantly to doing so. It is too late for that, and the scale of the problem too vast. If the recording angel thinks otherwise, then that's her business. I just enjoy my contact with the soil, the processes of nourishing and nursing it, and the dance the seasons lead me, a wilder dance by the year, it seems, these days, thanks to climate change, as we all go rattling off to hell in the proverbial handcart. I love to labour. I am eternally grateful that Adam and Eve were evicted via the little wicket gate from Eden. Or how boring life would be, deprived of knowledge and work.

My approach to things is, I suppose, to a degree existential. Knowing that something is the case is never enough without know-how. Labour teaches me know-how. Husbandry teaches me know-how. I dig. I have a mantra. 'Expect nothing, hope for nothing. Dig. Toil …' I sometimes say it to myself as I dig. I often say it to myself as I write. I sometimes call myself a lapsed Zen-Protestant. I feel more like a tramp in the pages of Samuel Beckett than a so-called transcendentalist à la Thoreau. (Notwithstanding my granddaughter's delightful way, when just two years old, of referring to my plot as 'the aloftment'.)

I am strongly aware in all this that to the town mouse I am more than faintly risible. I suppose I have Romanticism in my bones. What else is our appreciation of place and local habitation? I disappear before my own eyes into the rhythms of work. I will work in the cold. I will work in the rain. I like it when it is inclement once I am under way. But I do not like the carcinogenic sun on my head, the scorching sun de nos jours.

There is always work of one kind or another to do. I am living my dream or the compromised version of an old one, with which I've made my peace. No matter the thunder of traffic nearby, the violent clatter of tailboards as vehicles shudder to a halt, the hiss of air brakes, the boom of rappers and others blasting by in low-slung cars with full-bore exhausts growling, thundering there at a halt, with only a scraggy hawthorn hedge between us. Forget the pollutants that, to one degree or another, settle on my soil and plants.

A man at seventy is lucky if he can afford to live any version of his dream. He is lucky if his body will allow him to labour, as I have done now for at least eight years. He is lucky if his name comes up on the Society's waiting list before it is too late, and he has already left for a very different plot.

Not only do I love to labour, it's almost as if I need to, and not simply to preserve my sanity, or my version of sanity, in the face of the world as it is, in its 24/7 news-feed madness, its technocratic plutocracy, its deafening opinion (instant opinion), its abuses of language (going forward), its terrible politics, its violent upheavals. Its ... its ... its ... morose old men.

Digging and husbandry clear my head and keep me going, not least by speaking back to other places and times, time in my youth above all, when I toiled and moiled for my father, in the days when we were more than self-sufficient, from bean-row to bee-loud glade, and honey, on our patch of rough land above the Irish Sea in north Wales. Where we also had apple trees and sometimes, though rarely, a serpent, a grass snake. This ground I have now, this little bit of God's earth at the heart of Middle England, may be all compromise (it is not even third-best), but nonetheless it grounds me and frees me into reverie. Every place is unique. Did Thoreau say that? I seem to think so, but I can't remember where and perhaps I am mistaken.

It isn't new or alien for me to travel between place and page. For almost as long as I can remember, from late youth at least, it's been essential to me, as reader as much as aspiring writer. But the proportions and exchanges have altered, between there and here, here and there, and they keep altering, as now I am entered on my older age. I have just had my biblical three-score-years-and-ten birthday. No use you telling me it's the new sixty. Ask my aching limbs after a damp winter's afternoon's labour wheelbarrowing a dozen and a half loads of manure 200 yards to my plot from the communal midden. Or after as much time digging, or a-lugging water fifty yards from the standing tap, in summer drought, on a warm evening.

What I go to and return with in my mind is of a markedly different kind from even a few years ago. My orbits are more curtailed, my circuits shorter, my pace slower (though I rarely realise it is), my concerns different. But if anything I'm haunted more intensely day by day. 'There' looms and lingers longer, unbidden. It's not perhaps so much that I bring it back with me as that it follows me home like a stalker, and stays with me and tumbles in my head as I fall asleep, more intensely than ever, planning and scheming and taking pleasure in work done and things seen and felt, ushering me into oblivion. I think it has something to do with wear and tear in synapses and circuitry. No doubt toiling and moiling keep me fitter in mind and body than I might otherwise be if I sat reading all day, but a fifteen-mile walk staggers me now far more than ever a twenty-mile one used to.

I still walk out round the local farmlands, a latter-day Loony Dick, mooching about. They are my plot's hinterlands, vast swathes of them owned by the same peer of the realm that owns the allotment land. The efficacy of walking is thoroughly known and long established by philosophers. Sublime scenery might infuse thought with drama but I think, as in labouring, it is the motion that matters above all. Motion and emotion are only separated by a single vowel, as has often been observed.

The landscape just north of the Chilterns is of weald and otherwise lacks uplifting contours. The arable agriculture is highly mechanical and chemical. Birdlife here is frugally distributed (I will not speak of red kites) and little varied, despite the token extra widths of headland, set aside for grant money. In winter I will see large flocks of fieldfares and, most years, redwings. Once in a way I hear a curlew to my west, strayed over from the edge of Otmoor. It will always make my heart beat faster when I do. Sometimes there are clouds of lapwings. They nest here in some number. In spring I might see wheatears passing through, heading north-west; or on a dreary day in March catch sight of a merlin harrying a lark. When I first saw such species in these parts I was taken aback, and taken back, too, to Welsh mountains and moorlands and boyhood. I travelled between here and there and back, with their unexpected help.

Momentary correspondences are present anywhere and everywhere in all kinds of forms and particulars. It depends on how and where you were made. They seem to suggest themselves, but we meet them at least halfway, ministering to them. They cry out to be brought to book, caught in words, like that balloon steered by Yeats's poem into a shed. I tell myself this regularly. I tell myself to keep my feet on the ground. As if it might help me to do so, I went up to my plot the other day and, with a six-foot cane, surveyed and measured it.

It is the first plot you come upon as you leave the short lane, a byway between an A-road and the rugby club beyond.

Spin the wheels in the padlock to the right code and step through the wicket gate. Re-run Adam and Eve. My plot is the one on the right-hand side of the path. It occupies a corner. It is a corner of land and runs in something of a crescent where the path begins. In its main body it is neither square nor rectangular. This year I have acquired the greater part of a neighbouring plot, one run to neglect by a friend. He is in full-time employment and in his passion took on too much.

The Society measures things in perches or rods. That means little to me. So to make account of my now expanded ground I measured it all out with my cane. Thoreau, a land surveyor by profession, would have laughed to see me or to read my figures. He knew a perch or rod = 5.5 yards or 0.25 of a surveyor's chain. Looked at one way, I have more than 3.5 perches or rods by about 3. It still makes no sense to me when I work that out and round it up to equal 1/20th of an acre. Don't trust me. I am innumerate. The exercise fails to bring me down to earth but hoists me back into speculation. How can I describe and define my plot? There is no equivalent to being 'there'. Being 'here' I think runs it close, as a form of cultivation. Or what can we say of the world? Though I am not sure Alexander would not have made much sense of such a question. Rather it would probably have confirmed him in his original suspicions as to the kind of man I am.

Coda: Hedge Fund

In the last three or four years my walks have not always been ends in themselves, at least not in the autumn and spring. These walks have had only my plot in mind, or I should say its new hedge. Along the lane, to the right or broadly the south of my plot, is a fence, a few strands of wire and a stretch of sheep netting, supported by posts and angle irons. Nettles grow through the wire, at the top of the bank that drops at an easy gradient to the edge of my plot. I grew a chestnut from a conker and planted it on the bank. It flourished quickly but had to be lopped at about four or five feet. I began to poke chestnuts, hazelnuts, acorns, berries into the bank at quite close intervals. Some took root but it was hit or miss.

Then in my wanderings one soggy day at the back end of winter, sheltering from heavy rain, I found in a coppice a leafy floor through which sprouted scores of saplings – chiefly ash, some hawthorn – and I found that with a firm grip and sharp tug they would come out, bringing their root systems with them. I would take them in their dozens and replant them along my bank. I found a similar stretch of sycamore wood and brought back dozens of sycamore saplings, and the same for blackthorn and hawthorn elsewhere.

On a recent trip to my native heath I gathered a bag of sessile acorns and planted them in giant flowerpots. I still have to see how many Welsh oaks I can add to my hedge. At times this hedge takes over. I think of it first and my plot second. I have found that you can't just put saplings in the earth and leave them. You must clear the weeds and grasses from their stems and from around their roots; you must water them in times of dry weather. They can be strangled by other growth and perish.

At this stage in its development the hedge has a long way to grow, but already I see something of it, in two or three hawthorns that have put on a spurt of growth; already I can see how I will begin to lop and to weave one whip or miniature trunk, one branch with another, to create a shapely tangle, something with a nod in the direction of David Nash to it; to create in the end a high barrier to the world, a thing of wonder, full of light in winter, and of tender green foliage in spring, with cover for the blackbird to build her nest and other species too. I call it my hedge fund. I am hedging my bets in the hope I'll see it fully grown there, as I see it here, in my mind's eye, a thing of great wonder, a windbreak to my plot, a thin line of mixed wood, a conservation area in little, beyond which my plot will continue to thicken long after the new housing stock round the corner has grown to look outdated and generations of blackbirds have gone forth and multiplied.

A couple of weeks after I sent this piece off, I went up to the plot to find Alexander's smallholding demolished and a giant JCB scooping the assorted rubble into a truck. By the end of the week everything had been cleared to resemble a ploughed field down as far as the orchard where Alexander used to keep his hen huts and sometimes graze a beast or a few sheep. Our tenancy is ever a brief affair. Where are the nows of yesteryear? – as Tim Robinson once asked.

You might think it the beginning of the end. But not so. The event led to a meeting between representatives of our Society and the land-lord's agent, at which a startling reassurance was given: the Estate will *never* sell the allotment area for housing or anything else. The cleared ground will become a wildflower meadow. Dare I revise my mantra to: 'Expect the best, hope for the best' – keep digging and toiling, here and there, as if for all eternity?

EMBARKING

Philip Marsden

I turned off the ferry road into the woods. Sunlight flickered through the windscreen and over the dashboard. The trees were oak mainly, sessile oak, which long ago had been coppiced and now grew as thin and twisting figures, stunted by sea-salt. It was late September and the leaves still showed green; only in patches of open ground, where the light fell on rust-coloured ferns, was there any sign that summer was over.

Through the trees, just visible now as the road dipped and swung to the left, was a ship. I could make out its white superstructure and its radar antennae and the low stern deck. It was an ocean-going research ship laid up between commissions; the name painted on the bow made me chuckle: *Deep Investigator*.

There was something odd about the road itself. It had been constructed half a century past, in five-yard squares of concrete. Where they joined, along the seams, were green lines of moss and grass. The road also was much too wide for a cul-de-sac and the single waterside cottage where it led; in places two or three trucks could pass each other without slowing. In the last section a cutting some thirty feet deep had been blasted through the killas. It was a ghost road.

I left the car in the cutting and walked on through a gate into the sun. I was in a large apron of concrete, made from the same squares as the road. Here was the river, the Fal, deep-watered and steep-sided and no more than a couple of hundred yards across. The single cottage lay off to one side, cutely thatched and small-windowed. Visible upstream was a V of wooded slopes and a distant bend in the valley. The oaks all dropped their skirts to the same level – the level of the spring tide. There was the gap too where the Truro river joined the Fal and, high above the confluence, with its scooped-out parkland and antler-like chimneys, stood Tregothnan, Cornwall's largest private house.

Right in front of me, just twenty yards offshore, was my boat – a white-hulled 1960s sloop, thirty-one foot long, with a solid-looking mast and a canvas cover tenting over its cockpit.

I had bought it in June, for a book project. I was going to sail it up to Ireland and Scotland, and write about it. Because the boat's wooden, I needed to keep it on a mooring through the winter to prevent the boards drying out and opening up, and because boat ownership brings with it a certain anxiety – going to check it was still there, undamaged during the season's storms, and not half submerged because the automatic pump had failed – the road leading down to the moorings became intensely familiar to me.

Until a few years ago the thatched cottage had been a seasonal pub: the Smugglers at Tolverne (*Teas, lunches, bar meals*). In winter it was always a hidden-away place, but in summer a great many visitors drove down to it, following the too-wide road through the woods. Since the pub closed, the route has sunk back into sylvan obscurity, its pitted surface edged by a mulch of leaves, its dodder-hung oaks unseen by passing cars. Only the young couple who live in the cottage, and a few boat owners like me, use the road.

That winter, driving down it once or twice a week, as the trees dropped their leaves and revealed more of the *Deep Investigator*, I found the broad road filled with expectation. It built to a peak before the reveal of the last corner: *would the boat still be there?* Such a sharpening of the senses stirred a sediment of deep memory – not just my own half-forgotten visits to Smugglers as a child – but a host of historical connections that came tumbling out as soon as I started looking into its past. With each new story, I noticed the appearance of the land beginning to alter – as if meaning could somehow affect topography, rather than the other way round.

In his 1955 *The Making of the English Landscape*, W. G. Hoskins suggested that what we see of the country's land surface is now almost entirely man-made. Rather than viewing it as something spoilt, a vulgarised version of pure Nature, he presented it instead as endlessly revealing, a story-book, a storehouse of memory, an archive waiting to be dusted off and read. Hoskins's approach – which has enlivened faculties of geographers, archaeologists and historians ever since – encourages a localisation of study, a move away from the regional and the abstract to the immediate, to that scale of territory that is not just more visible but more closely related to human experience. Uncover the past of particular places and history can break free of the textbook, come alive in the open air.

'The view from this room where I write these last pages is small,' concludes Hoskins. As if pulling from his pocket a gate-fold map, he then reveals the centuries. He points to the traces of bankside buildings recorded in the Domesday Book, to the Saxon name for the river, a twelfth-century charter proposing the fishpond, eighteenth-century hedges, the distant chimneys of a Victorian 'big house'. 'Here in this room one is reaching back, in a view embracing a few hundred acres at the most, through ten centuries of English life, and discerning shadows beyond that again.'

Some years ago, I began researching the story of Falmouth. I never imagined it would yield enough for a book; personal interest only. But I soon found myself immersed. County archives, state papers and records offices turned up a glittering hoard of stories and individuals. I was amazed that a not-very-large town could produce so much material. But it wasn't just that: put together, those lives and their locale began to tell a much bigger narrative, of an entire nation, an entire era. It left me with the heady feeling that you could take any small town, any field or woodland, and discern the whole – in the way that each microscopic strip of DNA contains the genome for a complete organism.

The initial zeal calmed, as zeal does, and revealed something more interesting. Hoskins concedes that his own window is particularly rewarding: 'Not every small view in England is so full of details as this.'

Rather than significance being equally distributed, certain pockets of land become hotspots of history. Arbitrary features like river crossings, prominent hills or natural harbours concentrate human activity, or accrue significance: when you come to them, you cannot help but be aware of some strange quality, the sum perhaps of all those others who have passed through, and all they have felt and all that they have done and thought in that particular locale.

Such a place is Tolverne and its road. Several things combine to give it an advantage. The estuary is very deep. It turns a ninety-degree bend. It gives both shelter and a certain discretion for those like the free-traders of old who required it. There was always a ferry here. Before it was a pub, the cottage was the ferryman's cottage, and had been for 500 years; countless people stood on the shore waiting to cross, or disembarked here with the expectations of return or reunion. Such is the geography of the long tidal fingers pushing into Cornwall that ferries have always been needed; less than half a mile from Tolverne is another, King Harry Ferry, still in use today with a thirty-car chain-powered craft, running six times an hour.

On the hill above the cottage is the ancient barton of Tolverne. The Arundel family who lived there grew rich from the ferries, and by the sixteenth century had begun to expand their horizons. In the 1580s John Arundel left Tolverne to take part in Grenville's expedition to set up a colony in Virginia (or rather a nest of privateers to prey on the Spanish silver trade). Arundel was the commander of the first ship back and was knighted by the 'pirate queen' herself, Elizabeth I. Emboldened by the spirit of the age, Sir John then left Tolverne again, this time to search for the mythical island of Hy-Brasil. He lost all his money, the estate was sold and the family permanently impoverished. Even now, four centuries later, when you approach the house, with its ivy-clad walls and its missing windows, trying to work out whether it's inhabited or not, it's easy to imagine the reckless days of the early nation-state.

Below the house, not fifty yards from the road itself, is a thicket. One day I pulled up the car next to it and, pushing aside brambles and holly, came to a place of flattened ground and half-collapsed walls.

In the handwritten notes of the historian Charles Henderson, I had read of the chapel: dedicated to Henry VI, whose canonisation was thwarted only by England's estrangement from Rome during the Reformation. On down the road, the thatched cottage of Smugglers itself dates from the 1400s. All alone beneath wooded slopes, it too looks ageless.

Then there are the ships. This stretch of the Fal river makes a handy boat-park for spare cargo capacity. The number of ships is said to be an indicator of the global economy. After the banking crisis of 2008, more than half a dozen were laid up here. The oil crisis of the mid-1970s had brought thirty-six. Now it was just the research ship *Deep Investigator*; in February she left to do some deep investigating in the Baltic.

One winter, years earlier, an old Soviet factory ship ended up here. The *Kommunar* had spent two decades trawling and buying up fish stocks from the world's oceans. But what worked for the planned economy failed when it collapsed. By 1995, with a string of unpaid harbour dues behind her, the *Kommunar* had a writ from the Admiralty taped to her radio mast; she was legally under arrest. Having just returned from six months in Russia, I used to visit the men who remained on board, taking them supplies. The skipper was of Chechen origin and told stories from seafaring in West Africa and the Far East, and his crew of seventy-five who heaved fish in over the stern, processed and canned it. Now he presided over just two, and a ship that no longer had power. Off Tolverne, in the ship's chilly companionways, its empty hold and the rubbish-filled decks, the last stages of the Soviet Union were being acted out. In March the three men left, unpaid, for St Petersburg. The *Kommunar* was towed off to Turkey for scrap.

And then there's the road itself: why so wide?

For tanks, for troop trucks, for staff cars, for the men of the 29th Infantry, of the US 5th Corps who, in June 1944, embarked at Tolverne for Normandy and the horrors of Omaha Beach. The thatched cottage and the steep wooded slopes were the last piece of friendly territory many of those men ever saw.

As early as 1942, plans were being made for an Allied invasion of the continent; officials were hunted along the south coast of England for suitable sites. With its deep waters and narrow sides, the Fal at Tolverne fitted the bill. First came teams to widen the ancient ferry track. They cut into the rock to level the last section. They felled trees at the shoreline and built an artificial beach with blocks of granite and shingle. They suggested pulling down the thatched cottage to make room. But it had a phone line, so became a coordination centre.

US forces arrived in Cornwall early in 1944. At Tolverne they felled more trees, they dug latrines, built storage huts and cookhouses. They piped in fresh water from a source a mile away and held it in a tank above the shore. A checkpoint and barrier were placed on the road and its surface was widened further, to accommodate rows of Sherman tanks. Down on the water a pontoon of wood and steel pushed a third of the way across the river, to the edge of the channel. The shoreline was covered to create a hard, but the concrete dried white and had to be tarmacked to be less visible from the air. Secrecy surrounded everything.

Through May 1944, barges and landing craft began to assemble in the narrows above King Harry Ferry. The troops themselves were based in sausage camps around Cornwall, so called because of their shape, stretched out along the edge of the county's roads. At the end of the month, the camps were sealed, the roads closed to the public and hundreds of trucks transported the men to the coast. At Tolverne, General Eisenhower drove down the widened road, past the tanks and armoured cars. Thousands of troops gathered, along the shore and on the decks of numerous ships, to hear his eve-of-battle address.

The noise of the preparations was something local people commented on; they just weren't used to the clang and hiss of traffic. After the Americans had gone, in landing craft along the English Channel to meet up with other groups, then south to the bloody beaches of Normandy and the largest invasion in human history, it was said that at Tolverne 'you could hear a pin drop'.

Seventy years later, Tolverne is again a backwater. The old pontoon has gone, and a new one put in – shorter, designed for leisure craft. On still afternoons, on board my boat, I would go up and stand in the bows to check the mooring line. The tide brushed past the hull and made ripples against the buoy. The only sounds then were curlew, the squawk of a heron or the rasp of a black-headed gull.

At the time of D-Day, the cottage at Tolverne was the home of the Newman family, and remained so for years afterwards. Only in 2010 did they finally leave. I had come to know Peter and Elizabeth Newman a little while visiting the *Kommunar* in the mid 1990s; I still saw them once a year when they came back to the village show to judge the dog-racing. They had retired to Truro and a flat in a large Victorian house.

In April, shortly before I was due to sail to Ireland, I went to see them. The house had high ceilings and a wide communal staircase. A ship's figurehead stood outside their apartment door. On the walls of the sitting room hung early charts of the river around Tolverne, aerial photographs of Tolverne, a watercolour of Smugglers Cottage fronted by marigolds. There were photos of the ships that ended up at Tolverne – the SS *Uganda* which had served as a hospital ship in the Falklands War, and the *Windsor Castle*, which looked like a small freighter but was a gentleman's yacht.

'People always said to me – Peter, you'll never leave Tolverne. They'll carry you out of there in a box. But in the end, we were ready to retire.'

He looked to Elizabeth, who agreed: 'Forty years of cooking in the pub seemed about enough, really.'

It was Peter's father who first took the family to Tolverne. In the early 1930s, before Peter was born, Rodney Newman was living downstream at Devoran working as an engineer. He used to go up the river in his boat. Seeing the cottage at Tolverne always made him daydream of living there. But it was the home of the ferryman and always had been.

Then one evening, in 1933, there was an accident. Returning late from Truro, the ferryman's punt struck a rock in the darkness and sank. He drowned. Rodney Newman went to the Tregothnan estate office soon afterwards and, to his surprise, was given the keys. He loaded his boat with furniture, a piano and with his young family motored up to the cottage. You're mad, his neighbours told him, going to live up there, all isolated and alone. But by the time war broke out, the place to them was the centre of the world. Rodney was running passengers up and down the river, and his wife was letting out rooms for B&B. He remained there throughout the war, joining the river patrol, towing dummy ships up to the deserted stretches of river to draw the bombs. When Eisenhower came, Mabel Newman served him tea and biscuits.

With the GIs gone and war over, the Newmans resumed their pleasure-boat business and the B&Bs. They opened the pub and tea room. They became a much-loved part of river life, with their blue-and-white Tolverne ferries running from Falmouth to Truro and back again. Large ships came and went, spending months in front of the cottage, dwarfing it with their bulk. Their skeleton crews used the US Navy hard to receive supplies. Over the years the bar filled with ships' memorabilia.

When Rodney Newman died in the late 1950s, his son George took over. He ran the ferries while his mother continued with the B&Bs. The waters of the Fal might look benign, but water's water; one evening, mooring the ferry, George fell overboard and drowned. Mabel carried on alone until her younger son Peter was ready to take over.

Peter and Elizabeth ran Smugglers for the next forty years. Each summer, US veterans came to visit; each summer they grew fewer, slower of limb and stockier. In the woods, Peter cleared the scrub around the traces of the 29th Infantry's brief passage through the site – the Nissen huts, the sheds and latrines. In 1994, half a century on from D-Day, a small group of vets visited Tolverne to unveil a bronze panel set into a lump of granite on the foreshore:

The plaque commemorates the fiftieth anniversary of the departure of thousands of American troops from this beach in landing craft bound for Omaha on the Normandy coast for the invasion of Europe.

Above it was engraved an entwining of the Union Jack and Stars and Stripes.

'I arranged for that plaque,' explained Peter, just as he had arranged for the handwritten signs showing the remains of the D-Day preparations. Most of the signs have now gone. His collection of memorabilia was offered to the Tregothnan estate. Without the pub, without the visitors, it had little appeal. In 2012, the whole lot was put up for auction in Penzance.

That afternoon, after visiting the Newmans, I returned home by the car ferry. I turned off to Tolverne, towards Smugglers. Spring sun flickered in the windscreen and over the dashboard. Last autumn's leaves were still pasted to the fringes of the road; the woods were stirring from the floor up, with bluebells and white ransomes scattered beneath a tangle of bare-branched oaks.

I was preparing to leave. In Truro I had bought some new lanyard for the boat's jack-lines and some chrome polish for the coach-roof windows. I had picked up the mainsail from the sailmakers, repaired and cleaned. I loaded them all onto the dinghy and rowed out. The wind was blowing hard from the west but the cloud was high and broken. I let my gaze rest on Smugglers Cottage, thinking of what it had witnessed. It looked, if not actually bigger, somehow more substantial.

During those final days, toing and froing to Tolverne, my mind was abuzz with boaty dilemmas – thinking how best to stow the Zodiac on board, and the outboard, what food to take, which charts to buy, which books to put in the saloon. I'd had the sea-cocks serviced, and the engine, and ironed out one or two problems with the rigging. I'd rolled on the self-furling headsail. I'd recruited a friend from Falmouth to help with the passage to County Kerry; after that, going on up to the Western Isles, I'd be on my own. It was not something I'd ever done before.

One afternoon in mid April, I took the last of the gear aboard and, with the lockers full of food, and the tanks full of fresh water and diesel, I was as ready as I'd ever be. I sat in the cockpit. For the umpteenth time I checked the weather on my phone. Another twelve hours of easterly meant a nasty swell going down to Land's End, but from then on, for the two days it would take to Dingle, it looked not too bad.

On board that afternoon, it was hard not to think of that other embarking, in 1944, and the part the weather played then, delaying the invasion by a day or two. It was hard not to think of the thousands of young Americans who boarded the landing craft here at Tolverne, and the apprehension they felt crouched on the boxed-in decks, and the much greater danger they faced, and the history they made when their boots splashed onto Omaha Beach. It was hard too not to think of John Arundel, setting off to Virginia and then for Hy-Brasil; and those who had drowned here – Peter's brother George, and the ferryman in 1933.

Then too, as Hoskins put it, you could gaze over the same site, the same view, through many centuries of activity, 'and discern shadows beyond that again'. Half a millennium of ferries crossing the river, and the numberless passengers and, before that, the traffic of small craft that passed along this slim stretch of water for hundreds, perhaps thousands, of years: medieval pilgrims boarding ships at Tregony – now several miles inland – bound for Compostela (the amount of silver and the dedication of the vanished church of St James's testament to their number and their destination); the early missionaries from Wales and Ireland, who sailed up these creeks to establish monastic cells, and whose names survive in the shoreside villages of Kea, Lamorna and Ruan Lanihorne; and those ships before that with their cargo of alluvial tin bound for the Mediterranean, where it was forged into the bronze weapons that shaped the ancient world. And beyond that, even less recorded, the seafaring groups who spread megaliths and early agriculture along the Atlantic seaboard, and for whom the Fal's long and safe navigable waters provided easy passage to higher ground.

I stood and looked ashore. In the cottage now lived a family who ran the moorings and had a charter boat of their own. I could see Colin crossing the hard to the pontoon. His three-year-old son was running before him, plump and tottering in his all-in-one waterproof suit. He reached the water and stopped, then he heaved a rock into the shallows. The splash made him yelp with joy. He stood there for some time, watching the ripples as they spread and disappeared, and the place where the rock had vanished.

SEAVIEW: THE ANTHROPOSCENIC

David Matless

Anthroposcenic: Landscape emblematic of processes
marking the Anthropocene

Breezy summer nights roar. Surf and undertow cradle sleep. Ten feet
to the cliff edge from salted glass, sound washes inside; over the two
steps, the slippery mat, the kitchen corner, the banquette and bedrooms.
Seaview caravans, the constant sea.

And on a winter's night, sleep in trepidation. Unseasonal clinging
as sea surges, banked up with northerlies, water lifting to low pressure.

Atmosphere's release, valves open, vans wobbling; metal gale-tested, rust salted. That which never ends proceeds regardless, to a possible fall.

Cliffs of till undercut, sodden soil slipping, trapped flints and bones seeing first light for an epoch. The caravan shudders, lists, slips a little, then some more. Fencing descends with the cliff-edge long grass, the trimmed grass follows, the van tilts to topple. A one-way rollercoaster to the beach. Cupboards fly, windows and waves break. Unrivalled sea views.

Things have fallen since things have been built on soft cliffs. Turn the lining of England's east coast to find ex-places offshore. Boats net odd human remnants, ears claim phantom chimes. Melancholy gathers on the shore, haunting hubris. Treasure hunters rummage the wake.

And so human misery, and beachcombing joy, proceeds as it has proceeded. Yet the shore gathers new freight, other stories colonising floods and falls. Coast signals climate, seas rising for reasons other than their own. Humble tumbling vans catch in larger nets. As new epochs are labelled, the world becoming Anthropocene, sea views turn Anthroposcenic, their landscapes emblematic.

Labels enable, yet stain. Beaches colour with abstraction, miniature gaieties tainted by epoch. In seaside amusement, the penny drops. So enjoy it while you can, and don't let it spoil the holiday. Keep choking on lolly-stick gags: the sand was wet, and the sea weed.

Holidays at East Runton; forty years ago, with predictions of a new ice age, and in newer hotting times. A beach mile from Cromer, rock pools and sand, the wave-cut platform and forest bed. A minute from door to paddle, cliff's topping to North Sea summer icing; always a chill.

Once upon a horizon, seascape showed day ships and night lights; at anchor, or giving warning. Now turbine blades turn from shallows, nocturnal red twinklings. Ships and birds evade, seascapes filled to mitigate rising seas. Atmospheres dance in the cool night air.

The sewage outflow, marine direct, is gone. The bobbing turds of memory pass. Paddle with assurance in improved waters. Descend the beach from soft to firm, tentative over shingle and flints, to revealed sand, and sea collapsing on the ebb. Firm enough for a bowl.

Inshore craft beach with the catch, hauled by tractor to the slip; bathers descend, sea creatures ascend. Boxed crustaceans pique young curiosity, marine still life. Tides fall to platform chalk, miniature canyons for sea streams. Weed and whelks wait twice daily, crabs strand, anemones wave. Young fingers, nipped and sucked, touch knowingly.

Along the shore, exposed by retreat, mammoths emerge, laid down 600 millennia. Cohabiters of the ancient human poke from till. On this 'Deep History Coast', mammoth back and coastal bulge merged in logo, past surprises project, in Anthropocene resonance. Strollers glean relics.

Before descent, check the sea timers. The public served via provision of tide clocks: plan your day for high and low fun. Kites flown, castles moated, waters damned. Beach burial helps sharpen sense; sandy and damp, up to the apple, the vivid scenery of the stuck.

So diurnal turns accumulate, epochs meet through a fall, odd storms renew. Horizons fill, structures fall, words mark. Views become Anthroposcenes, emblematic prospects, as soft cliffs toast: 'to the sea'.

Waders

Andrew Motion

1

After the accident, when summer brings
slow afternoons with nothing left to do,
I take what used to be your garden chair
and park it underneath the wayward ash
that sidles forward where the garden swerves
and hides the house from view. In secret then
I conjure up the notebook I have found
among your bedside things and open it.
Blank pages. Thoughts you never had, or had
but could not bring yourself to say. Should I
imagine them or write my own instead?
I close my eyes and scrutinise the white
that also lies inside me while the ash
rattles its pale green keys above my head.

2

The milk float with its thin mosquito whine
straining through larch and elder from the lane,
the nervous bottles in their metal basket
intent on music but without a tune,
the milkman in his doctor's stubby coat
and sailor's rakish dark blue canvas cap

are all invisible, imagined/dreamed
beyond my curtains in the early light,
along with tissue footprints in the frost,
our rinsed-out empties, and the rolled-up note
exchanged for bottles with their silver tops
the blue tits have already broken through
to sip the stiffened plugs of cream before
we come downstairs and bring our order in.

3

To think the world is endless, prodigal,
to part the hedgerow-leaves and see the eggs
like planets in a crowded galaxy,
to hear my mother's voice advising me
the mother-bird herself will never mind
if I take only one and leave the rest,
means nothing more than showing interest.
As does the careful slow walk home, the ritual
of pin-pricks through both ends, the steady breath
that blows the yolk and albumen clean out
but keeps the pretty shell intact, the nest
of crumpled paper in the cedar drawer,
the darkness falling then, the hush, and me
bringing the weight of my warm mind to bear.

4

Beyond the grazing and the bramble bank
where on another day I might lie down
and press my ear against the trampled earth
to hear the rabbits scuffling underground,
a headland round the Ashgrove leads me on
past wheat fields which still show the buffeting
of last night's storm, towards the Blackwater.
The stream has long since burst inside my head,

the banks collapsed, the water-meadows drowned,
the mesh of overhanging branches bowed
with plastic voodoo junk and hanks of wool.
Then I arrive and see things as they are:
a settled surface with a clearing sky,
and shining gravel drifting inside clouds.

5

My father with no explanation stays
behind at home; my mother drives away
and takes me with her to the Suffolk coast
where I lie down all day on rounded stones
and will the sun to thaw my frozen brain
while she … I've no idea what she does,
until the evening she manhandles me
to stand beside her in the cypress shade
which makes a double-darkness on the lawn
and watch the round moon roll into our sky
as Neil Armstrong takes his one small step
and pokes his flag into the silver dust
although we cannot see him, nor he us
except in ways I think my father might.

6

Before our time they used my room to store
apples collected from those crooked trees
now wading waist-deep at the garden end
in frilly white-capped waves of cow parsley,
and laid them out in rows not touching quite.
I know all this because the floorboards show
wherever they had missed one as it turned
to mush and left a round stain on the wood.
My bed stands over them and when at night
my eyes grow used to darkness they appear:

the Coxes, Bramleys, Blenheim Oranges
whose names alone can fill the empty air
with branches weighted down by next year's crop
and turn its scent half-sickly and half-sweet.

7

That lead tank like a coffin with no lid
lying between the cooler greenhouse-room
my mother uses for her cuttings-trays,
and one as steamy as the rainforest
with air so thickened by tomato plants
it lies like moist green velvet on my tongue –
that lead tank, that disgusting (almost)
store of syrupy black water is where Kit
my brother slipped, or threw himself to see
if that would make our father like him more,
and where, as I look down to see myself
alive and sensible, I envy him
his moment in a time outside our time,
free from the earth and all its appetites.

8

The low tent-tunnel of the laurel walk,
where no one but a child can stand today
encloses me but keeps the world in view
in sudden supple leaps and starts of light.
Here out of sight I wait to meet myself
with no idea of what myself might be.
I drink the musty air and bide my time.
I shake the sullen shadows from my head.
I feel the deep earth rising in my bones.
I make believe the shivering small flies
beside me on the leaves, the sparrow gang
that flusters in its shallow bowl of dust,

suppose that I want nothing more from them
except to stay here and not mean a thing.

9

I try my father's waders on for size
then take, with him encouraging, his rod
and wading-stick, his canvas bag, his cap
rigid beneath its crown of favourite flies,
and step into the river. From the bank
he says I look like him. As for myself
I only think of how to stand upright
with water hardening one second round
my ankles, and the next uprooting me
as though I have no purchase on the world.
My father shouts, Don't fight it. I obey.
I let the deluge settle round my heart
then lay me on my back and carry me
round the long sweep beyond my father's sight.

10

Those roofless kennels where the nettles shake
their fine-haired leaves and tiny bright green buds.
That almost-buried path of blood-red bricks
confined both sides by tiles shaped like rope.
The ruined square of cracked disrupted blocks
where once a summer house had turned and stared.
These are the former glories of the house
although I like their fall and brokenness
much more than grieving for a time I missed.
As also I like walking with the ghosts
that wander through the garden everywhere –
the mother and her son whose footsteps leave
no prints beside us in the grass as though
our selves are all the company we keep.

THESE ARE MY CHANGES

Adam Nicolson

When I look out of the window, almost everything I see – the stone wall on the edge of the garden, the already-craggy hawthorns beyond it, the track they shade between them, the chestnut fence and hedge the far side of that, the beeches and hornbeams just now gesturing in the wind from the west, lining the little valley below the farm that was first noticed in an Anglo-Saxon charter 1,100 years ago, plus the slightly gappy mixed thorn and hazel hedge of the field beyond it – all of these things, and their gates and fences, are there because I have put them there. Or, to be more honest, because I have asked and paid people to put them there.

These are my changes. In the twenty-five years since we came to live here on this ninety-acre grass farm in the Sussex Weald, Sarah and I have wanted it to look and be like this. When we arrived, no trees were growing on the ancient parish boundary: they had been taken out. A sort of stark, driven, impoverished wreckage of abused grazing and broken-down buildings filled the farm. There was no hedge dividing the Cottage Field from the orchard, nor Jim's Field from Great Flemings, or Beech Meadow from Way Field. No gates worked. The grazing was, in wide pools, so thick with thistles no dog would enter it. Stone walls had been buried in concrete. The whole place – a small dairy farm which had been unable to keep up with the demands of modern life – was crusted in poverty and failure. The big oaks around the farmhouse had been cut down to make way for new corrugated sheds. Ponds had been filled in. The farm had reached a crisis when inspectors found that the milk it was sending out had been diluted with water.

Perch Hill wasn't entirely lovely then, but we thought we could see loveliness in it: in its modesty and ancientness; precisely in its lack of *bien soigné*, silk-lined gravel; in its *echtness* – the word I loved at the time, its sense of being true to itself. The farm may have reached the end of a long road since it was first cut out of the Wealden oakwood in the sixteenth century, and it may have suffered all the abuse of the twentieth-century industrialisation of agriculture, but something supremely valuable seemed detectable beneath all that: the interfolding of human enterprise with the natural world, a beauty whose materials were oak and tile, brick and grass, cuckoos and finches, hay and hay barns, calves and lambs, with the promise of a summer ease whose memory would sustain us in the long soul-clamping, clayey winters.

That sense of implicit, concealed value – and the hope of redemption – was what was alluring here, and in service of that idea we quite deliberately, over two and a half decades, began to change this micro-slice of the world. We wanted to restore its virtues, looking to the old forms, the old hedge lines, the old arrangement of lanes and paths, the old materials, and in doing so have made something that does now seem beautiful: soft, divided, a Wealden farm in the shape Wealden farms are meant to be in, wooded, grassed, butterflied and dragonflied, the Sussex cattle grazing in the low meadows this summer, the sheep on the valley sides above them, the long grass shut up and soon to be made into hay, the cords of ash and hornbeam now lying, drying in the coppices where they were cut for firewood last winter. If a man from the mid-to late-sixteenth century came here now and was led blindfold past the house and yard where the cars are parked, and then walked these twelve fields and modest, slopy woods, the Wealden shaws filled in midsummer with their collapsed, drowned-out bluebells, he would see little difference from the moment he was last here. And he would, I hope, think it good.

But is that right? Quite often, I walk across these lovely fields and think we are faking it. Have we actually returned this farm to itself, or have we dumped ourselves all over it, requiring it to be what we wanted it to be, using those historical cues only in the way someone would do up a bathroom: scrape a beam or two, slap in some tongue-and-groove, get out the Farrow & Ball? The farm, like nearly every small farm in the Kent and Sussex Weald, is no longer providing a family's income. It is essentially a huge garden, mown and fertilised by beautiful conker-red cattle, with the simplest of aesthetics governing its look and pattern: nothing too showy, a kind of looseness in every part, so that nothing seems over-driven, but washed over with an Arcadian contentment that looks disconnected from any hint of getting or spending. This, it says, is a theatre of how things are. Or at least of how things would be if we lived in a good world.

Christopher Lloyd liked to say that a garden, to be its best, should seem as if the owner had died three weeks previously. That is the condition Perch Hill now mimics: not the thistledown chaos it was when we arrived, but in the relaxed form of order called by Renaissance theorists *sprezzatura*: a self-control so deeply absorbed and ingested that there need be no outward sign of it. Just as young men in Veronese frescoes loll in their satins against the pillars of their Palladian halls, so this little Sussex farm, which would never have known anything of the kind, is now being forced into the mould of expensive, laid-back contentment, a fantasy of Horatian beauty imposed by owners who earn their keep in other ways and elsewhere. What a fate: a real farm with real lives, real triumphs and real griefs, subjected to an entirely inauthentic mimicking of the *echt*, a piece of drama founded on the ending of the very life that gave rise to it – driven to the wall, in fact, by the metropolitan culture which is now presiding over the place where it died. Pastoral here erects a theatre over the murder it has just committed.

That isn't the sweetest of thoughts when chewing on the stub-end of a bit of summer grass, lying out in the Way Field watching the deer pause and graze above the sorrel and the buttercups. Sometimes I imagine the speech made by a hard-line landscape historicist to every-thing we have removed: the acres of concrete, the endless corrugated pole-barns, the over-large, over-nitrogenated, brutally productive rye-grass leys in the fields. How true all that was, he would say smilingly and generously, how exactly responsive to the situation those struggling dairy farmers found themselves in. They cut down the oak trees because they needed the sheds for the calves. They trashed the meadows because they needed the milk. They wanted to be as rich as you are. What you have done, Adam, is pure deceit. Landscapes reflect the money that creates them, and your pretensions are all for a kind of visual peasant-hood, a little Transylvanian flower-and-hedges idyll when the source of the cash used to create it is from some distant global capitalist system with its roots and tendrils in Shanghai and Frankfurt. For the last twenty-five years, you have been elaborating a lie.

Mmm. Chew on the grass a little longer. Watch the buzzard flick-cruising over the ash shaw, listen to the jays hawking in the oak wood, follow a jet down on its glide path into Gatwick, wait as the mist gathers in the river valley, look at your phone, take a picture of the pyramidal orchids for Instagram and remember something else, some earlier way of being.

Almightie and moste merciful father, we have erred and straied from thy waies, lyke lost shepe. We have folowed to much the devyses and desyres of our owne harts. We have offended against thy holy lawes. We have left undone those thinges whiche we ought to have done, and we have done those thinges which we ought not to have done, and there is no health in us: but thou, O Lorde, have mercy upon us, miserable offendours.

That is from the first revision of Cranmer's *Book of the Common Prayer*, added in 1552, almost exactly contemporary with the young farmer who knew these fields when they were first cut from the Wealden forest. Its measured sentences and pointed, rhetorical repetitions, its near rhyming of *devyses* and *desyres*, the yin and yang of human weakness – all would have been heard and said every week by everyone who ever lived and worked on this farm. The deep clanging of the undone-done-done-ought-not-have-done bell would have rung through their lives, either in Burwash at St Bartholomew's (the saint, flayed alive, was the patron saint of the graziers, butchers and tanners of the Weald) or at Brightling in St Thomas à Becket, the favourite of the anti-establishment, independent woodcountrymen of the Weald. Over 400 years, after walking or riding back from matins or evensong on the day of rest, those sentences would have echoed in the minds of the Perch Hill people, self-repeating around their long hard days as they ditched and hedged, mowed and stacked, milked and threshed their way through their lives. Done, undone, ought to have done; done, undone, ought to have done: the calendar of a year, or a lifetime. No health in us.

That, maybe, is what this farm sounds like in its heart: a way of thinking a thousand miles from my own pastoral vanities. There is nothing in that of my lightweight ability to drift and pick, to engage and disengage as if nothing much depended on it. Here is the kind of seriousness and embeddedness I see in the mute enquiring eye of a cow as she comes up to me in a summer field, the flies all over her muzzle, the gloss of summer on her flanks, the most wonderful animal intimacy I know as she breathes milky gales all over me, a set of giant grass-fuelled bellows in a forge. Hello, her simple eye says. So you are still here too? We are doing what you have asked us to do, eating the grass, allowing our calves to suckle, being here, getting fat. Is that what it adds up to?

Again and again, in the order of service laid down by the great Tudor archbishop and martyr, the congregation were reminded of their own insignificance. Human beings were not as good as the universe God had made for them. Time and the things of this sublunary earth were their enemy. 'There was never any thing by the wit of man so well devised, or so surely established,' Cranmer told them, 'which (in continuance of time) hath not been corrupted.' This was a world in decline, whose only possible redemption was not in anything material but in the understanding that eternity was neither here nor now. The people were instructed to pray that everything around them should 'speake good of the Lord'. Showers and dew, the winds of God, fire and heat, winter and summer, dews and frosts, frost and cold, ice and snow, nights and days, light and darkness, lightnings and clouds, the earth itself, and all the green things upon it, the wells, the seas and floods, the whales and all that move in the waters, all the fowls of the air, all the beasts and cattle, the children of men, the spirits and souls of the righteous, the holy and humble men of heart: all these huge and potent presences were to join in one grand obeisance to a God for whom, let it not be forgotten, 'all hearts be open, and all desires known and from whom no secrets are hid'.

This landscape of comfort was nothing of the kind: it was a world of terrifying uncertainty overseen by a just-as-terrifying surveillance system. This farm, in other words, was not a landscape of power or sweetness but of humility, even of humiliation; not a place in which a vision of contentment could be casually imposed, but somewhere from which, while a living had to be wrought, nothing but a sense of vulnerability and transience could be absorbed. 'Lay not up for yourselves treasure upon the earth, where the rust and moth doth corrupt and where theves breake through and steale,' Cranmer told them, 'but lay up for yourselves treasure in heaven; where neither rust nor moth doth corrupt, and where theves do not breake through and steale.'

The archbishop, speaking through his parish priest, could not have made the binaries clearer: each half of his sentence was identical except for one simple negative applied to the earth, one simple positive to the world above. Here on this farm was not the place where value was to be found. To attempt to lay it up here was a futility. Cranmer's image of goods laid up, stuffed into the fuggy dark of the farmhouse attic, is as canny as it gets. Precious things pushed up there feel hidden and secure, invisible to man, but just as God is all-seeing and all-knowing, the three forces of destruction Cranmer mentions – the moth, the rust and the thief – are those that know all too well about objects festering in the attic, vulnerable there even as you hoard them, a dark place of cupidity and guilt.

Do you store up treasure in this world? Or do you remember your insignificance? Do you loll in silks? Or restrict the vanities of self-adornment? It is the great choice, the difference over which Englishmen fought a Civil War in the seventeenth century. When Charles I came to his execution in Whitehall in 1649, among the most shocking revelations for Milton and the other Puritans hinged on this difference. The book the King took with him to the scaffold for his last moments on earth was not the Bible but a copy of Philip Sidney's *Arcadia*, a book so relentlessly dedicated to the beauty and entrancement of this life, this world, the beautification of this landscape and the people in it, that heaven or the world to come didn't get a look-in. It was the defining fact for Milton of Charles Stuart's wickedness: he had traded the next world for this.

In that cavalier way, we have dressed up this farm as if it were a slice of perfection. But should we, like good Puritans, have looked beyond worldly décor and understood this life as something of passing and fragile beauty, one over which we as human beings have little or no control? That is the way the Puritan frames the choice: which will you have, hubris or humility? Make it beautiful or serve your time? Self-delusion or self-realisation? Arcadia or significance? Picnics or cosmic reality?

A few years ago, in one part of this farm, our hands were forced. I had always loved one of our smallest fields called Hollow Flemings, tucked down away in one of the small side valleys with which the land is pleated here. Dyers' greenweed grew in the summer grasses and Meadow Brown butterflies used to flitter across it in June and July, pairs of them dancing around themselves as they fled across the hillside in dark, double, guttering flames. It was where I would often go to read and write.

Then, one very wet winter, two things happened. The stream at the foot of the field, gorged with winter rain, started to cut deeply down into its bed. At the same time the springs in the field itself were running hard, lubricating the upper layer of clay in the field. A gap was created at the bottom, a readiness to slide over the whole field, and one morning I found about three acres of Hollow Flemings slipped, a little cliff at the top of it, a tumble of fallen and half-fallen trees at the bottom where the clay was now clogging the stream. Over the next weeks, still more of the land slumped downwards. It was clear that the use of that field was now over. We couldn't mow it or even fence it, and so we let it go. It was no longer any part of the farmed world.

What Wordsworth called 'the calm oblivious tendencies of nature ... the silent overgrowings' started to take over Hollow Flemings. Brambles bubbled up into thickets which no deer could enter. Willows were the first to sprout beneath them, followed by the blackthorn and birches. Within a year or two young ash trees were raising their heads above the thorns. Now young oaks, some fifteen feet high, stand around the old landslip, the tips of their branches just beginning to touch. Deer graze in the narrow tongues of grass that persist between the clumps of new woodland. And then, this last spring, two nightingales made the brambly thickets their territories, one at each end of the landslip, sigh-shouting at the night sky for any wives that might be passing.

In one way, that field is ruined; in another it is reaching for a kind of wholeness. If the two earlier versions of this farm are presided over by Cranmer and Sidney, Wordsworth is the king of Hollow Flemings. In the late 1790s, in despair over the collapse of his hopes for the Revolution in France, and filled with guilt over his desertion of the young Frenchwoman who had borne his child, he wrote 'The Ruined Cottage'. It is his first great poem, and the first modern meditation on the relationship between our own ambitions, our failings and the ever-lasting facts of nature. He takes on the voice of a 'wanderer' who looks back to the time when, coming to the abandoned cottage, he had seen wild plants growing where the inhabitants had once cultivated a neat and human order. The wanderer remembered 'that those very plumes, / Those weeds, and the high spear-grass on that wall, / By mist and silent rain-drops silver'd o'er' had seemed not an image of 'what we feel of sorrow and despair / From ruin and from change, and all the grief / The passing shews of being leave behind', but something both far larger and slighter than that: 'an image of tranquillity, / So calm and still', which 'looked so beautiful / Amid the uneasy thoughts which filled my mind', that he turned away from them, from the ruin and from the resurgence of nature, 'And walked along my road in happiness.'

It is the most beautiful recognition that abandonment is not aban-donment, and that there is a third place between the Puritan world of submission and the Arcadian landscape of pleasure. A huge time-perspective floods into this farm in the wake of that understanding. A kind of tranquil everlastingness seems to be here now, a fusion of a worldly Arcadia with a Puritan heaven. We are irrelevant but we are not waiting for death. This place shifts and I shift. We co-evolve. Trees die, buzzards and kites arrive, the thistles, miraculously, retreat, the oak wood reclaims its own. Woods we planted now have to be thinned. New hedges are now old enough to be laid. Chestnut fence posts I remember smelling bitter with tannin when new-cut have now rotted and must be replaced. And I age as the farm cycles through its lives. Time is running through me when I look at these fields, as if I were a watergate in its stream, my bars fixed, the hum and quiver of my life nothing but the pouring of that liquid through me.

ESTUARINE

Sean O'Brien

The sea had gone away round a corner, leaving the huge door open, the hard blue sky taller and the vast khaki-coloured flats in a state of shimmering uncertainty. Pools big enough to swim in waited as noon approached. Surely it wasn't allowed? Streams ran urgently in near-silence on secret errands in the folds of the sand and mud. There seemed to be no directions.

We too were uncertain, left to amuse ourselves without orders, in a place, if that was what it was, that we had never seen before. We found we could hardly speak. The father slept among the dunes by the road, far off, in his white overall, the newspaper over his eyes. His work was done in bringing us here. The rest was up to us. The terrible liberty leaned like a god out of the stopped sun: *well then, well then?*

Somewhere at the back of us, behind the sand and stray wire and the old military road, on the far side of the landspit, the sea could still be found in a different dispensation, a bright breeze skating over the low waves as they marked time against the gravelled shore, carrying it away handful by handful. We had seen the sea for a few moments earlier on our way in. But that was not here, and it was hard to bring persuasively to mind as we knelt at the edge of a pool out on the flats of the estuary, settling without a word to make a dam, though whether to keep the water out or in I no longer know. The younger of the two brothers had a shit nearby, as though it was a point of honour to do so. The long turd was the colour of the mudbank.

All the time we were listening: there was a sound that was not happening – it would be like a warehouse full of ride cymbals being stroked to a tall silver roar, behind which everything else was gathered. It was an education in fear, in awe. The hard light was about to turn into noise. At a loss, we returned to the landspit.

The older brother smirked as we walked back on to the sandy margin. He was a thug and a bully, easily bored. At some point his father would hit him again.

We passed the sleeping father and pushed back inland until we found the airfield. In those days, when people said 'disused airfield', the phrase had something epic to it. These bomber fields had sprung up everywhere after 1939 and just as swiftly turned to phantoms of themselves. Here locked blockhouses sank among rotting sandbags whose contents had turned solid and then gradually blown away. The runway had cracked under the pressure of weeds. The control tower was a wreck, all the windows out. You could get in at the ground floor but no further. To be there was like being implicated in a crime we were too young to understand. No one would tell us the rules.

The older brother was bored. He threw a chunk of brick at the younger, hitting him on the head. We trailed separately back to where the father lay, so that the older brother could be punished. It was done, a formality of rage. Snot ran down the older boy's face on to his Aertex shirt. Time to go.

Somehow it had become a grey-purple evening as we drove back in the Jowett Javelin between the hedgerows on the white roads under mauve clouds. The car seemed to absorb the father's affection. He was a mechanic. To his sons, and to his wife, who looked like Diana Dors, he seemed to be just a formal black-haired Brylcreemed presence in a white overall.

The place we were leaving was part of the unconscious of the city, like the gravel ponds to the north, and the long, nearly immobile open drains that worked in parallel to the streets, weaving their slow brocade of cresses. The zone was bounded by the river, and by the curve of the chalk Wolds rising at the edge of the mud plain that had formed at the last Ice Age. What happened beyond that was someone else's business.

In the great silence on summer days, the air wavered in the heat. Long afterwards I discovered a reason for the peculiar empty quiet of the land (it may be what Larkin has in mind in 'wheat's restless silence'): it is a war grave for those who did not return from the Western Front. A lifetime later, on the way to Little Gidding, I found the same sense of elegiac disquiet in the empty fields on the Cambridge–Northants border, depopulated by plague. We had our own plague pits, in an ancient wood on the western edge of the city. We challenged each other to climb down to the parched forest floor among the twisted hawthorn trees. Risk it, go on.

After the trip to the landspit, that hinterland would be present to the imagination. Sometimes I would come to a blank halt in the back garden and sense what seemed like an alertness, an onlooking. It was present around the foul old drains we fished in by the bridges further down the street, and then further off in the deeper, more purposeful stretches that found their way to the sea or the estuary. When eventually the drains were filled in, the water simply rose to its original level whenever it rained. Water, said the water, this is what water is like. Watch it, smell it, think about it when you're somewhere else. Turn on the tap and hear its ceaseless conversation with itself.

We were always seeking permission to dig holes, to see the water arrive and gaze back at us. The boys' father had forbidden them to dig in the back garden behind their flat in the street of Dutch-fronted houses, but the older brother disobeyed him, and by the end of the day the pair of them had a neat circular pit in the clay, five feet wide and maybe three feet deep. The water had filled it to within inches of the top. The boys studied their handiwork, and the rest of us, who had heard the rumours, came to see what might follow.

For a time I stared into the ochre-yellow water, but what really drew my interest was a rotting tree stump nearby. It seemed to have been torn open. It was full of black insect eggs which no one could identify. The eggs were somehow terrifying, like stuff from outer space. The late-summer afternoon – it was one of those white, oppressive days that seemed peculiar to the city – wore its way onwards to teatime, and nothing happened. We lingered as long as we dared. Only as we trailed away down the street did we hear the shouting start. The father was home; the punishment could begin. That seemed part of the law: you never got to witness the whole thing, the whole story, the reasoning behind the anger and the hoarse cries the old brother made when being belted.

It was a summer that seemed unable to end. We might never get back to school. We sat on the high back wall of someone's garden, looking down into the tenfoot, one of the local concreted back lanes. It ran for half a mile between the rear gates of houses on adjacent avenues. In some sense the tenfoot belonged to us. Few people owned cars and those who did rarely used them. It was the era of the despised 'Sunday driver'. Adults were scarce on the tenfoots. If they appeared there they seemed to be off their proper ground.

Now we gazed down and along. A heavy silence had fallen. In the distance there was a disturbance in the air as if a mirage were forming. It seemed to be coming closer, bringing with it a hushing sound at first so faint as to seem beyond the limits of hearing – an idea of itself, a warning, a promise. Rain. The mirage was a wall of rain advancing steadily up the tenfoot. We watched it come, thrilled and delighted. Twenty yards away, ten feet, arm's length, and then it passed through us or over us, for a moment dividing the front of the skull from the back. I hoped that we and the rain might freeze in this position, evidence of a local, earthly miracle to which we were the only witnesses.

When the front of the rain passed by we dropped down into the garden. We knew without needing to discuss it that the deep trench we had been digging had become useful, as had the disused door we kept on hand for a purpose we had only then discovered. We climbed into the trench and pulled the door over us like the lid of a coffin. Much later I would read of how US soldiers in the Ardennes and Hürtgen Forest in winter 1944 wove nets of branches to protect their foxholes from the treebursts caused by German artillery. Down in our own foxhole under the coffin lid of the old blue door, we were on a permanent military footing. We were at war in the school playground with endlessly replenished armies of Germans and Japanese. Our mission underneath the door was to wait out the bombardment of rain. For some reason the water in that pit did not engulf us from beneath.

There was a breach. The reasons for it were not apparent but I spent much of the next summer in solitary amnsements.

I felt like a castaway on the island of the huge back garden that came with our ground-floor flat. It was a garden that someone had worked on a good deal before the house was divided up. There was a lawn edged by brittle Conference pear trees, with mossy concealed paths and a narrow jungle of elders next to a high wall. Beyond the lawn rose a parterre on which a dry fountain stood between two mature walnut trees, with a vast copper beech and an equally large mulberry tree in the offing. Beyond that lay the orchard. I had never seen anything like this place.

The fountain was obviously important. The fact that it no longer worked was taken as a given. This was the 1950s, when many things didn't work or were unavailable, and when, although rationing had finally been lifted, an austerity of possibility seemed to go unquestioned. Since I had the garden I had nothing to complain about. When I studied the fountain, with its wide drystone bowl like an ashtray full of black leaves, I saw that its pastness was what made it important. The unknown what-had-been underwrote its stillness. I found such places in books, too, in bits of de la Mare's poetry and, somehow, in the late-Victorian Lewisham where E. Nesbit's *The Treasure Seekers* was set. I think it was this place that tilted me in the direction of poetry.

When I first went with my mother to see the flat she was arranging to rent, I was sent out to explore the garden. Its sheer size, and the wooded obscurity of its remote far end, made me afraid. But gradually I acquired the ground and began to undertake some exploratory digging. Tiring of that I entered the large empty garage – this really did feel like trespass – to be dazed by the heat it stored like a battery, and beguiled by the narcotic smells there – turpentine, paraffin, boot polish, rust.

There was more fruit than we or our neighbours could find a use for: apples, pears, cherries, mulberries, gooseberries, redcurrants, black-currants, and the mysterious loganberry which I first encountered there. My father climbed into the Bramley tree and shook it for minutes on end while the fruit thundered down. A neighbour came with a ladder and a wheelbarrow and carted mounds of apples away. Still there was too much. Burrowed by wasps, fruit rotted on the ground, then froze in autumn.

We lived in the house of a suicide, though only much later did I discover this. The owner, a prominent businessman and local councillor who tried to break the General Strike, was disgraced when it turned out that he had been involved in extortion and improper dealings in the acquisition of land for housing estates. He gassed himself in 1932 while under investigation. What I knew as a child was the History Room, the large library in the ground-floor flat. It was panelled, and had stained-glass windows, and a tall wooden fireplace decorated by leering heads of Silenus gazing down as I sat reading by the fire, which was lit when autumn came.

Autumn required the acquisition of fireworks from compliant back-street shopkeepers, followed by an excursion to the Woolsheds. This vast wasteground of pitted asphalt and overgrown bramble bushes and bloodstained dock leaves had served some purpose, but none of us knew what. Though it was open land, this too felt like trespass. We might encounter groups of older boys who would want to fight, but it was worth it to empty all our bangers on the hardstanding by one of the old air-raid shelters and set the black powder alight. It was a military activity, into which the whole landscape was drawn, from the radiator factory to the railway goods line that bounded the Woolsheds on the southern side.

When the fireworks were finished we would squeeze behind a blank advertisement hoarding near the railway bridge, then scramble up the clinkered slope when a train approached. We lay there watching the great wheels grinding out sparks. If we followed this line we would eventually come to the docks, from where the landspit could be imagined, beyond the flares and glittering pipework of the refinery. When we slid out from behind the hoarding, filthy and exhilarated, we would wander the ground until we located the stream that slowly snaked its way southwards before it disappeared into a culvert and continued to some imagined confluence with a larger version of itself, and so on via glimpses at garden ends and from the steps of leaking, mould-white cellars, on to the river whose sudden tides swept over the silver mud. The pull of the water – river, sea, drainage – was irresistible. We knew that in some way we were its creatures, our task to keep wandering there until one day, suddenly, childhood was done with, and the smells of heat and rot and earth and waters, and even the names of our chance companions, were lost to us. We were leaving the flat because my parents could not raise the sum (£2,000 seems tiny nowadays) required to buy the whole huge house when the current owner decided put it on the market.

Nowhere else has ever seemed entirely real in comparison, or as amenable to being discovered and claimed. Many years later I stepped off a train at one of the little local stations. It was unmanned now, its buildings boarded, a new main road cutting it off from the river. But behind the traffic, in the huge sky, there was once more that absence of sound, with the sense of something about to happen, ever-ready. Water, mudflats, earth, grass, rain, an ancient hoarded heat and the long view down to the landspit – all this had waited with patient indifference and now once more required homage.

209

The Four Wents of Craster

Dexter Petley

1

In a house called Kia-Ora, the last tenant had left a clothes peg, a knitting needle and a blue mirror, like a mermaid's moonlight flit. Our winter let, this fish-box of gutted rooms, flipped by tides upon a rocky shore, the frost already at the gate. We ate off tea chests, made a bed of straw, then slept in the window that first night, September 1994, to watch the sea snarl at us like guard dogs on the end of a rusty chain.

Our first storm threw caution to its winds. We listened to breakers threshing oil drums from Tyneside, boat sticks, lobster pots, ship's furniture, a chandler's-worth of rope, telegraph poles, railway sleepers, whole pine trees lathed of their skins by rolling salt. Next morning, the horizon was a jagged edge as waves unfurled like ballroom carpets over the stone pier.

2

October's sun rose on dropped wind, peeled its orange rim off the world, the North Sea like a Sunday painting, dawn in salt on the window glaze, frost rind slowly visible on thistle cupulae, the low tide dubbed over skerry crusts blackened and slippery. The skyte of giant kelps, sea belts, tangles and furbelows, edges and tips which lipped and flicked like carp in summer ponds, or rudd at the evening's hatch. No cold blue winter sky quite yet, only hushed reds stained the yellow of piss on snow. Stilled white boats rode eight furlongs off Muckle Carr, two perfect swans low-flying south, nailed to the paper sky.

3

Harry next door came across for his coal shovel, overburdened by the news: *A woman's missing, aye,* he said. *Since Sunday.* They'd had to break into her house before, *once ago, aye, overdose or summ't. Her,* he said, *never went near pub.*

Harry, aged seventy-seven, born next door in this house his father had built in 1902 with stone he lugged from the quarry. A long-shore widower, Harry said you could spot the ones who wouldn't go in the pub. Looked like death, they did, when they followed the dog along the sea path. *No good that, keeping it in thyself.* The sea was no friend of Harry's. He'd learned the electrical trade instead of hauling net on his father's herring boat. The only sea in Harry's ears came from a D-Day shell on Omaha Beach, two shattered drums and a face like it saw bodies on every other tide. When I set off after driftwood, pushing Harry's barrow, he had to say it: *Aye, an' yer might find her what's miss'n, washed up wi' the wood if wind shifts t'Sooth.*

A yellow Sea King out of Boulmer hovered half a mile out, tail swinging like a weather vane as the wind shifted east and the sea gouged at rock like a cat biting between its paws. Luxury foam bulged on the tideline, heaped into creeks till a fox of wind set it into a brown flight of sheep, breaking from the fold. Above a rim of crushed horizon-yellow, a black sky screwed down like a fruit press. Gulls bent into crow bars against the brunt.

4

A blurred photograph of the missing woman appeared in the weekly *Gazette.* We'd stowed our lobster pots away for the winter that morning, in the outside bog with the jerry cans and driftwood. The lobsters had moved out into deeper water a week before the first storm. Till then, the inshore gullies had yielded them reluctantly. Half a dozen dogger crabs in a good week, a 14 oz lobster for the bonus. Even Harry had let his bait go to bad, shot with maggots, over-salted. The lorries were out gritting lanes by night. Coach trips filled the village pub some afternoons. Trees were bare, stripped of dead leaves already. The sea tight under bleached candescent suns. The overflow iced solid, drains clogged in frozen hair, puddles like toenails of ice.

She lived alone in one of the coastguard's cottages. Five feet seven inches, brown hair greying at the sides. Nobody knew what she'd been doing when she disappeared, sometime after 10 p.m. on Saturday night. Today the sea was table-flat, red tinged from a sleepless night. A lazy day. You could drop off the horizon, never be seen again on a day like this, one sharp edge of a cube. No shags on the long rock, no gulls on the pier. Glass pools and new shiny furrows caught the sunlight, made a mud sea, white glints like stacked plates, a thousand seagulls following the plough. From our distance, in the low slanting light, we saw a cotton field in the light's trick. In the same way, who dared see anything in the photograph? Perhaps her mother had taken it with a handbag camera, free with five coupons off the soap. She might be standing anywhere, dutiful and featureless. It could be yesterday, or 1950. She might've been her own remains, a face beyond a salted window.

5

The clocks went back. I missed the sunrise. The first day of winter fledged on a calm sea, a bed sheet under yellowing blue sky. The bereavement sea on a sensitivity card; sad, loss-white gulls in gentle soul-shaped flight. Rest in Peace rocks. Ezekiel 36:16 on a paper scroll in the grass, dropped there by a walker.

Night fell at six o' clock now, muffling out the sea, my watch cut short by double glaze, a riot shield, undertaker's glass. Behind drawn curtains, you couldn't guess the sea was there, just fifty yards off. It might have been a brass plaque, on a wall behind the curtain, in memory of the lost, the drowned; or coffin rollers, an incinerator pit, or simply nothing, the bottomless dream itself. Was this how Harry saw it, as the village waited for one of their own to come ashore? You couldn't help but feel a tension seething, tide-like, around the house. I ran from

room to room trying to find its beginning. The cats flew in two directions as I careered into Alice's study. One astonished face beside a
screen, but the cats decided to run with me, and Alice laughed and
joined us. We all ran outside, flattened against the darkness, and there
was Harry in his slippers, mossing out to the coal shed to feed his fire,
one shovel at a time. He saw us pale as moons. *Aye*, he said, *did yer see,
man? They took a body oot the sea this afternoon. The life-boot an' the helicopter.
Aye, tha's aboot reet. They coom up, them bodies, seven o' ten days after.*

6

Once through the swing gate, each passer-by paused below my window.
To wipe dog egg off a shoe, cup hands and light a smoke, drop a tissue,
point a camera. But always, at some point, looking up at the house for
sale behind them. Behind, because they always stood and faced the sea.
'For Sale', only it had been five years on the market. Our landlady and
her aunt had quarrelled over the asking price and the division of spoils.
A dream view in a postcard village, famous for its smoke-house kippers.
A drab and shabby house on private links protected by the National
Trust, behind a padlocked five-bar gate. Roof shot, no insulation,
unheatable, corroded metal windows, cracked pebbledash, a yellow front
door you never opened. Their Kia Ora, our Shangri-la: we had an open
fire in the parlour, straw mattress, no furniture, just boxes and a five-
quid peach-coloured sofa from *Loot* which we'd strapped to the Land
Rover roof and driven home from a thousand-acre housing estate in
Newcastle.

Glen passed my window, a dozen times a day. Duffel coat and
schoolboy hair, ex-hotelier, simplified by a stroke. Sometimes his sister
kept him company, but she preferred to walk the dog alone, a chapel
spinster, waxed jacket, tartan skirt, marching by like her life's task was
to ring the Inchcape Bell. Once, they stopped together out front. She
took Glen's comb from his duffel-coat pocket and ran it through his
hair as he made a suffering face for me to see. Glen waved up at me
each time he passed. Sometimes he'd wave at a blank window, or it was
so salty he didn't know if we were in, or which room he should wave

at. If it was cold outside, he made exaggerated semaphore just to let us know, rotating arms which hugged and strummed his flanks. He had a word for everyone he passed, usually about his stroke six years ago, how stopping work and taking the sea air had saved his life.

A widower collected driftwood in a handyman's cart with pram wheels. *Took it bad, him*, Harry said. *Dooz'n' mix, avoids pub, he.* I watched him push his bodge at dusk like it was his wife's hearse. Black cap tight and low, looked neither right nor left. As darkness took over, the sea sounded like a city at night, hum-visible through the deaf glass, when all these widowers must have wondered, more than once, if jumping in would make it stop.

7

On 5 November, a fog rolled in from Forties, Tyne and Dogger, screening sea from house. There was nothing in the paper about a body. The day was warm but from the east. They said, according to Harry, that the cold was there, in front. You could see them coming, the calm, cold days; slow bulks on the horizon, the seagulls all at sea. Harry said a Polish trawler ran aground once. The whole commie crew legged it across the fields in the dark, were never heard of again. The villagers looted the boat. It broke free and sank, but the captain's chair washed up below the house and Harry nabbed it, stuck it by his hearth. *Come through*, he said, *I'll show it yer if yer not busy. Kettle's on.*

It was in the *Gazette* the following Friday.

MISSING WOMAN'S BODY IS WASHED UP

… on a County Durham beach. Jennifer Pauline Jobling, aged 47, was last seen on Saturday 16 Oct in the village of Craster …

She'd gone a long way, staying with the tide as far as Seaham. The tide ran south and today the wind pushed against it. The body Harry saw had been a practice dummy. I watched a sheet of white board skit along a wind-lane, following the course taken by the lobster boat. At one point it lifted clear and somersaulted corner-to-corner for 200 yards.

The low tide ruffed white over slippery rocks covered in truncheons of seaweed stem, its own push no match for the wind.

8

Scant timber washed up in a north-east wind, none at all in a westerly. The signboard from the castle came ashore below the house. Someone must have sawn it clean through, then dragged it 200 yards to the cliff edge and toppled it over into the sea fifty feet below. Some boat sticks came in, split middles discarded in the harbour after a hard launch just across the way. The puddle at our gate enlarged, dug out by nobbled treads on the farmer's pick-up. He dropped bales twice a day for the sheep, counting his raddled ewes. The grazing hardened. Dead crisp packets whipped against the fence and into the sea. The sheep went far and wide, beyond the headland, rarely near the house now the grass was yellow. Shags deserted the shoreline, keeping to the Carrs at low tide. Anglers' lanterns burned all night now the codling were inshore and taking peeler crab. Oystercatchers bradawled the inland mud for lobworms, running all the way in pairs. These were dark mornings and we rose before the sun now. I'd drop Alice at the station in the dark, an early train to Newcastle. Two calm hours of flat sea before a red sun became lost in the drizzle of grey sacking clouds. Mid-morning, a wind drove them back to harbour and the horizon was a dark, indigo bar.

9

The day of her funeral was *Dreadnought*-grey. Coasters on the horizon, some bright red and blue, the sea at rock-face like washing suds, Christmas emptiness about the grass and muds, the puddle a broken side window, single shatterings too thick to prize out, its ridge-backs frozen in. The village had been invited to 'open house' at Keeper's Cottage, the incumbent widow's sixtieth birthday. Two women in black were there, up for the funeral of Jenny Jobling, her last hours served with port and sloe gin. She'd gone to Lesbury to talk to the vicar, left him at seven-thirty, walked the seven miles home, in the dark through cold wind and rain, then jumped into the sea below her cottage. The

New Year, still weeks away, was already poised to grow over this bare patch of time.

10

A shower of frozen salt-grit pecking on the window woke us Christmas Day. It turned to snow, powdered the mud. A robin stabbed at the cat food. Harry said: *The postman delivered her cards, man.* Whose cards? *Her, her what come oot the sea.* The snow passed like a Christmas wedding. New Year's Day slammed gates, rained in your eye and made side flares of your trousers. On the Hough, a wind to slit the dead woman's cards open.

11

Eastern snow, yellow January skies mid-morning, till on a white foam sea waves looked like mountain ranges, foam and snow tumbling off walls, sleet driven horizontal, gulls frenzied along the spume line. The cat watched ice run down the window, his paw always tentatively drawn. He preferred to configure it thoughtfully before touching the glass and failing to connect with what he didn't recognise. Like it was his first invention, he'd never seen snow before. Likewise, the sea was just a noise in our eyes. The cat might see in the dark, but like me he couldn't see through a blizzard.

The full moon held steady in a gale, high over the puddle first, the puddle water running like roach fry fleeing a pike, darker when the wind lulled, silver-swiped when the gale dived across it. The sea stretched silver like the puddle. I could see the horizon at midnight. Ships passed through it. I could see a coaster's rivets a league offshore. You could follow gusts for a hundred yards. The sea became the moon. I could jump into the moon. I cut the picture of dead Jenny Jobling from the *Gazette* and stuck it to the wet window.

12

In February, the rough sea was like a great slice of veined fat. The 'For Sale' sign disappeared one night, the gate blown flat off its hinges, face down in the mud. The game that afternoon was to kick the football off the cliff edge, into the gale, then watch it snatched back and fly by, spinning uphill behind us for a hundred yards. Just putting a hat on knocked your teeth out. A wind to split the cat in half, the salt skinned your face, our knees trembled. It took two to shut the door or fetch the coal, and walking with the storm behind was like being under arrest, frog-marched into a whirlwind. And in the night, again, we heard fragments of the village join the corrugated roof of the woodshed to escape over the fields like Polish mariners as waves pounded across the village.

In the clean-up days, we joined the wader count, collecting bodies for the ranger, counting guillemots and razorbills, washed up in their emaciated thousands. We stacked them into the fish boxes which had come ashore with them, and as we did so we heard the bleet of lambs below the Hough on the westerly, a spring wind, and saw a fox passing in a quandary. The curlews walked from rock to rock again, the west wind blew the sea flat, sounding like the all-clear after an air raid. A school of dolphins jammed the wind lane off the Carrs, rolling in pairs, wearing the new sea on their backs. Driftwood burned blue from the drying salt.

13

The first day of spring, and Harry had one bad night in every two. He said the daffodils wouldn't appear till it was summer everywhere else. The wind blew off the land now, making desert waves, mackerel-backs of sea. It threw vapour like smoke in shots across the surface, and the sun cast milky rainbows, colours flashing as they moved. The plughole gurgled constantly.

Dunstanburgh Castle re-opened. *National Toast*, as Harry called it. It was a human world again. The visitors returned, as if from hibernation, still unsteady on their feet. The first weekend a woman with blood on her hands ran to our front door. Her son had slipped on the rocks. An hour later, another woman ran through the gate shouting for help, past our house, away along the sea path towards three people half a mile away.

Then one mild afternoon a third woman ran, this time from the castle. As she passed my window, her face was hard and white and grim. She returned in a car, with the castle keeper's wife, behind a four-wheel-drive ambulance, and you could tell by the lack of urgency. Two lads, laying their lobster pots off the rocks for the first time that year, stood and watched it all the way. In the yard, Harry and I stood side by side. Harry said the salmon were running close, up along the gullies. He wouldn't mind betting there'd be a net or two going out the night. Then the ambulance returned and he shut up. John the keeper was already dead, a man I waved to as he passed each morning, walking the mile and a half to the castle, swinging one of the sticks he carved himself, his jacket freshly waxed, his trout bag with its flask of tea and sandwiches.

14

Next day, canoeists were driven back into harbour by a shift in the wind. Lambs huddled in the lushest grass. A cold wind, still vicious enough to slash open weak shirt collars and race up ungloved cuffs. The foam remained unspent.

On Easter Saturday, the farmer sprayed nitrogen pellets over two women pushing babies. No driftwood on the spring tide, yachts instead of coasters, fox droppings of bunny fur, radishes pushing through. Harry buried his onion sets, pushed deep or have them blacken in the wind. This was no renewal. A stillborn, shrivelled month, the long struggle into a short cold summer. Harry faced his seventy-eighth year in the same window. I was forty and the novel was dust. Alice had finished her dissertation. Then a man with a cold knocked on the back door. He said he was a writer too, had watched me typing in the window several times in winter. I said I'd kept his seat warm, when he said he'd come to buy the house.

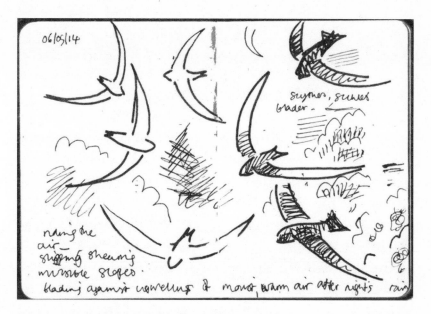

swifts arrival sketched from the allotment, early may

peacock butterfly, brambles & thistle, june

common-spotted orchid & yellow rattle, late may

REDLAND, BRISTOL

Greg Poole

Our house is on one of Bristol's many hills. Looking down our road, if it was a river it would be flowing fast north-east. Its left 'shore' rises quite steeply facing south-east, and so catches most of the sun that is on offer. Much of the slope is covered with allotments. Despite all the horticultural digging, between the plots there are still plenty of yellow meadow-ant nest mounds. Green woodpeckers furtively probe the anthills with dibber bills and long ant-licking tongues. They leave behind droppings that look like cigarette ash from a tightly packed roll-up. Walk to the top of the slope and you get a great view over the city.

I moved back to Bristol in 2004 to live with my partner, Susan. With much effort we destroyed the old Anderson bomb shelter at the end of the garden and erected my printmaking studio in its place. Around the same time we started to cultivate the allotment which is just the other side of the back gate. I was a novice gardener, and treated the project of clearing what was something of a wasteland more as groundwork than gardening. I made a series of stepped beds using boards hauled from skips, copying the approach that has been adopted all over the allotments.

One part of the allotment escaped my pickaxe-and-shovel approach. There was an area of lawn about the same footprint as my studio, about 4 x 4 metres, and we weren't really sure who it belonged to. Our allotment neighbour used to mow it; another neighbour would occasionally picnic on the lawn with his young children. Both moved away, and I carried on the mowing tradition. Then in 2012 I noticed the purple blotched basal leaves of two common spotted orchids. Although not rare plants they seemed 'wild' in this tamed terrain, and got me really excited. If there were orchids there, what else might grow? I asked the council allotment manager if it would be OK to cultivate this area as a wildflower meadow, and got the permission to go ahead.

In the autumn of that year I mowed 'the meadow' as close to the ground as I could, raked it vigorously, then sowed yellow rattle seed onto what was pretty well-scalped ground. The rattle is well known as a parasite on the roots of the coarser, more vigorous grasses, suppressing them and consequently allowing space for slower-growing, less thuggish species to move in. So in spring 2013 I watched anxiously to see if the rattle would come up. Because the spring was so cold it was very slow to appear, but by the end of March there were lots of seedlings. The rattle has a distinctive leaf even when first sprouting. It has tiny round teeth, and the segments between veins are cushioned like a more succulent plant. Lots of their seed lies on the surface right through the winter, and more recently I've been able to see their tawny, ravioli seed pods break open and the first white filament of a root come snaking out, coated with minuscule hairs. It took more strongly in some areas than in others. An area near the orchid leaves was reduced to a mat that already looked more like downland, a bed of clover hosted a jungle of rattle. It did what it was supposed to, leaving a lot more open areas and reducing the crowding effect of the coarser grasses.

The square of turf morphs through the growing season. Through the winter it could pass for poorly maintained lawn and is a lumpy 'flat' space. By the end of March the surge has begun, the green flowering tide is rising. 'High water' is reached somewhere around early June, and the level is up by over a metre. The raised 'surface' is a shifting cloud of delicate grass heads and flower forms. Up to the high-water mark there is a tendency for the flowers to be in the yellow spectrum (rattle, trefoil, daisies, dandelions), which then spills gradually into magentas and purples (orchids, thyme, knapweed, scabious, self-heal).

One of the effects (symptoms) of cultivating the mini-meadow has been hours of staring at 'lawn', gradually learning to identify the basal leaves of each species. Sketching has helped with this. In that first rattle spring I noticed more tiny orchid leaves (up to fifteen so far), minuscule and without spots, but clearly orchids. At first I wondered if they might be a different species of orchid. After hunting for ages in books and online the best description I found of the common spotted orchid's lifecycle was in the seed catalogue. It produces dust-like seeds which need to come into contact with a particular fungus soon after germination to help them get nutrition. The pair then live underground together in a symbiotic relationship for two or three years. So my little unspotted leaves were the first showing above ground of a process that is already two years minimum in the making. Despite my best efforts most of those little leaves got grazed off by slugs. Just one of these 'new' orchids has produced a flower spike (it has now flowered for three successive years). The new one is a much more delicate affair than the beefy mature specimens. So it seems you might be able to age orchid spikes? I'm hoping that despite the slug casualties the others are fortifying themselves under the soil, and that one year there will be a mass flowering.

At the same time as sowing the rattle I'd bought varieties of wild-flower seeds that corresponded to species I see locally on similar terrain. With more patience I could have just waited to see what emerged, but I greedily wanted an instant mini-meadow covered with ant mounds along with the plants that I associate with them. Thyme, ladies' bedstraw and above all bird's-foot trefoil.

Oddly, four years on, although I've learned more patience and real-ised that things take their time, I've also realised that some species are quite easy to proliferate. Cut off a 'branch' of bird's-foot trefoil with a promising bit of root, poke it into the ground a bit further along, and it will usually take pretty well. It is a hardy, deep-rooted plant. It is also easy to snip off a bit of thyme, a section that has little rootlets on the underside of its creeping stems, poke it into the top of an anthill, and four times out of five it will take. With these successes I started to feel more of a connection with the plants.

The bird's-foot trefoil was abundant by 2015. I took out all those boards that I'd used to hold up the banks and planted the sloping soil with trefoil, thyme, rock rose, etc., to stop the banks collapsing. I figured that anywhere a mower couldn't go I would try to make a wildflower bank. I was cultivating flora and insects instead of slugs and snails (which used to hide behind the boards).

One of the first gratifying effects of the burgeoning flora was seeing Common Blue butterflies egg-laying on the bird's-foot trefoil, their main food plant. Before the arrival of the trefoil, we would see the occasional blue, but they would be transient. This year (2016) I started to be able to identify them individually. I was hoping that there would be swarms of them, but in fact only around ten appeared. They vary quite a bit in colour, from a thin sky blue to something with more violet in the mix. After only a day or so they get nicks or rents in their wings and are pretty easy to get to know on first-name terms. Cookie-cut left hindwing, Rip-right forewing, etc. Knowing them in that way meant I could tell how short their lives as an adult were. None lasted over two weeks, and I only saw two females. I didn't witness any mating or egg-laying, but saw much feeding and basking on the bird's-foot trefoil. Small Coppers are still passers-by, and I haven't managed to get their food plant, common sorrel, to grow as yet.

Small Skippers have been around from the start. According to the great Jeremy Thomas and Richard Lewington guidebook they lay their eggs in the stems of Yorkshire fog grass, and the caterpillar spends the winter in a cocoon inside the stem. To reduce the fertility of the ground I mow the meadow in late summer and remove the grass. Unless those skipper caterpillars are very low down in the grass stems then I'll be removing them too. So far small skippers keep materialising in June, but I'm not quite sure how. Each butterfly species has its favourite food plant, and they vary a lot in their strategies for getting through the winter. One will exist as an egg, another as a caterpillar buried in the soil (I think Common Blue is one of those), some as a chrysalis and a few as hibernating adults. It's hard to get a handle on which needs what to make it through the bleaker months.

There is potential for conflict having a wildflower meadow on an allotment. Some of the veg growers might see the meadow as a weed breeding-ground. One plant that really gets people going is common ragwort, with its reputation of being poisonous to livestock and children. There aren't any livestock up there, and children are really unlikely to graze on ragwort (apparently it would take huge amounts to do any damage), but the plant still has a bad name. Lots of the insects that are mentioned here seem to love to feed or rest on ragwort flowers (sucking up nectar), and with a slight mind shift they are a really handsome spike of flowers. To strike some kind of political middle ground I now hoik them out as they start to seed.

One insect that does more than suck ragwort's nectar is the Cinnabar moth. A bold red-and-black fluttering in the meadow is likely to equal Cinnabar moth. Vivid red bars run along the leading edge of the satin black forewings, the almost completely red hindwings are tucked away on landing. Its caterpillars are banded yellow and black and decimate ragwort leaves, leaving behind just a bare stalk. Since leaving the ragwort to flower on the meadow I see more Cinnabar moths each year. Perhaps there is an optimal balance between Cinnabar moth and ragwort numbers, and in due course maybe there will be enough moths to keep the weed bashers happy.

Before studying this scrap of 'meadow' so intently I'd never learned to distinguish between species of bumblebee. There is a great app available for phone and tablet, and by using that it wasn't long before I could identify six common bee species on the allotment. Buff-tailed, Common Carder, Early, Garden, Red-tailed and Tree. Amazing how things that were once a generic 'bumblebee' can become distinct characters with a very particular identity. Garden and Buff-tailed for example: both black with yellow and white stripes. At first I would distinguish them with a kind of bar-code mentality, but then, with more watching, they start to seem very different creatures. The Garden bumblebee moves faster, and is smaller and blacker. Black bear to the Buff-tailed grizzly, I think its yellow is less warm too. The app tells you about head shape and tongue length, which I thought must be for identifying captured specimens. Then one day I realised that I could see the tongue of the Garden bumblebee hanging down as it flew from one rattle flower to another. The Buff-tailed visiting the same rattle flower is lumbering in comparison to the nimble Garden. It weighs down the whole flower and, because it hasn't got a long tongue, it has to go round the back of the flower and bite a hole to get access to the nectar. Common Carder (more of a ginger, striped affair) and Garden were by far the commonest feeders on the rattle.

When I'm up there digging, sketching or in turf-watch trance it is very handy to have the equivalent of guard dogs to alert me to any birds of prey that may pass overhead. The local herring gulls pursue any passing raptor, making a persistent mewing alarm call. They go particularly nuts for osprey or heron. So twice in early April I've been alerted to osprey heading north. Usually it is only the commoner species, buzzard or sparrowhawk, but several times they have chased red kites (who have almost always been drifting due east). Just once while watching newly arrived swifts moving ahead of a band of rain I saw a hobby following along.

The micro meadow isn't really big enough to give a home to larger creatures, but both foxes and badgers pass through. The foxes occasionally bask in a sunny spot, or on frosty winter nights I hear their mating calls from the studio. We rarely see the badgers, but they leave their mark. When the meadow flora is at high tide some large creature goes rolling around, flattening swathes of it. I'm pretty sure it must be baby badgers. I've just once seen the youngsters chasing each other around our vegetable beds at dusk.

A few years ago I bought a bat detector. This converts the high-pitched calls of bats to a much lower frequency, easier for us humans to hear. We had regularly seen tiny pipistrelles hawking for insects. I think having the detector forced me to pay more attention and it wasn't long before I noticed a larger species of bat. It looked a bit like a snipe doing its display flight. I traced its path through the binoculars held in one hand while pointing the detector with the other. The funky, lip-smacking sound coming from the detector was like a soundtrack to my demented pitching and rolling trying to keep up with the bat flight. When I checked on its identity, the frequency and lip-smacking quality were enough to identify it as Leisler's bat, the UK's second largest species.

The bat detector also came in handy for locating and identifying grasshoppers and crickets. Fairly annoying for anyone else in the vicinity, it sounds like cranked-up static on a CB radio. Each orthopteran species has its own distinctive calling pattern, and many are at quite different frequencies. The one that really dominated the airwaves on my first excursions was the long-winged conehead. It sounds like a helicopter coming into land, and drowns out the more gentle sounds of meadow and field grasshoppers. The coneheads prefer ranker grass and they are difficult to spot, but by moving the speaker around I could gradually home in on them. Long-winged conehead is rapidly extending its range, and has probably only been in these parts for ten years or so. Now there seem to be huge numbers of them.

Years ago I had a phase of painting up sheets of coloured paper for making collage. After painting lots of sheets in tints of red, to then go out and see a post box was like some kind of electric shock for the eyes. I was reminded of this with my recent studies of the individual Common Blues. After an afternoon squinting through close-focus binoculars (Pentax Papilios) at the Blues I then went out jogging in the local parkland that borders the Avon Gorge. I'd read on an interpretation board that there were both Small and Chalkhill blue colonies around the gorge. I couldn't quite believe it – these are scarce species, and this is only a mile or so from home. In hope I took a detour from my run, Papilios in hand, and went looking near the interpretation board, which seemed as likely a place as anywhere. There, resting on a woolly kidney vetch flower head, was a paler blue butterfly. The spotting on the underside was radically different from 'my' Common Blues. The creature is actually minuscule, but these spots looked huge, and then it opened its wings and the soft, celestial 'Chalkhill' blue nearly took my head off.

There is a sense of the Incredible Shrinking Man about all this study of the plot. Insects are the worst for bringing out the nerd in me. This year I've bought a guide to the 270 species of British bees, and another for a similar number of hoverflies. A whole range of previously unnoticed or unidentified species are now revealing themselves. Just for starters there have been Nomad and Mason bees, and a Leafcutter bee made its nest in the door lock of my studio.

Part of the value of cultivating the mini meadow has been getting to know individual species more intimately, their annual cycles and how they change their appearance with time. The sustained close observation of the inhabitants leads to a sensitisation that has made a trip into the wider countryside a heightened experience.

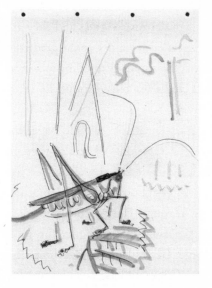

long-winged conehead, September

13/05/13

green woodpecker yaffling from
lookout post

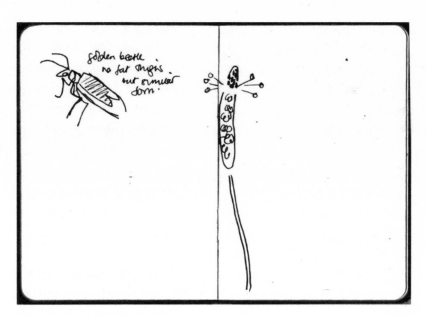

golden beetle.
no fat thighs
but similar
form.

flower beetle and plantain, june

About Time

Fiona Sampson

We live halfway up a valley. The stream that made it is small and easily dammed – by a wooden fruit crate, a dead sheep – though after heavy rain it can fill the lane and make it impassable for cars. The banks are is lined with oak and ash trees, and immediately in front of our gate there's a tall perry pear. The valley is narrow enough to feel deeper than it is; its fields are steep, but such good grazing that it's mostly cattle rather than sheep that are turned out on them.

We've lived here for three months. No one in the valley goes back more than a couple of generations, although the family who used to own it still lives and farms locally. But the place has been settled for millennia. The faint fold of a bank rings our hill, trace of the earliest settlement. The stone-lined runnels into which our neighbour Russell's cattle sometimes stumble, coming down heavy-footed to the stream to drink, are said by the county's archaeology team to be Roman. In Saxon times this ford at the valley's shoulder also supported a mill. At the top of the lane, a mile or so further upstream, is a pond that's clearly man-made. Like the one set next to an abandoned church a few miles west of here – which is obviously, and creepily, still used for ritual purposes – this pond makes no geological sense. But its situation does: set on high ground with wide views, it marks a cross-roads leading to four villages.

Today, unusually, the wind's from the south. It blows up the valley, stirring the trees with a rushing roar that's echoed by tractors harvesting the maize just over the ridge. In the autumn brightness every leaf and blade of grass, and every sound, has a dazzling clarity.

It's hard to talk about living in such a new place. Nothing here yet casts what I picture as a sort of shadow, the perspective knowledge we rely on (without realising we do) to give our experience order, or depth. Things here are overwhelmingly themselves; they aren't backlit by having been repeated over and over. I had no idea how important this kind of repetition was until we moved here. Then I found that all the connectedness of my daily life had suddenly stopped: no more wind off the Severn. No glare across the fields at dusk. No more hearing the stream behind the elder hedge.

I'd lived in our old home for seventeen years. It was time to move. Still, seventeen years turns out to be a stretch: long enough, anyway, to have been paradoxically foreshortened by the repetition that came from living it. In the old house, what was happening in any given *now* had begun to collapse into a sequence of all the other times it happened, and often I could no longer separate individual events – or even days, weeks or months – from each other. This was true above all of annual occurrences, like raising the beanpoles or picking sloes, the first pipistrelle that jinks around the eaves on a spring evening (it turns out that we have them here, too) or the first cry of a returning lapwing, faint and electric in a March wind. Such moments felt both new and old, fresh and familiar. But it became true also of daily repetitions: walking the dog on the back track past the Dutch barns. Blackbirds' alarm calls at dusk.

Here, by contrast, both past and future have disappeared. In a way, moving to the valley is a return to childhood. I don't know what tomorrow will be like, or the winter. I don't know the order in which the orchard trees will turn yellow. I've no idea where the footpaths will become slippery in autumn. I don't know where smoke lingers and where it drifts, nor which fields drain where onto our lane.

Because we're living in a place whose routines and repetitions are new to us, we take notice of them in new ways. Last week the beef herd that browses the big front field at Kilforge got separated. One afternoon we noticed Alan at work, loading the weaners into his lorry.

After weeks of being fattened together on summer grazing, the young were being taken away from their mothers. I've seen this separation innumerable times before but only with sheep, never cattle. So I was taken completely by surprise when, at dusk, the valley echoed with groans, shouts and howls, the herd sounding as if it were about to break through the hedges, each beast gone as mad and dangerous as her size warranted. The bellowing went on all night, haunting and distorting our dreams. Maybe cattle don't understand that they're being farmed: perhaps it's true that they don't recognise the abattoir. But with the loss of their calves a contagion of grief – whether or not it was truly realisation, whether or not just some kind of mood – passed violently to and fro on the hills above us.

From the top of our own hill the calves had looked oddly immaculate. I used to imagine I could pick one up between my thumb and forefinger, like a piece from a toy farm. It's already become one of our daily pleasures to watch the herd of pale, pinkish-white Charolais on the slope opposite. They've worn three red paths, ringing the field above the valley trees at nearly regular intervals like contour lines on an OS map. Whenever I look up – as now – the cows are there, pacing vaguely along and all of them heading in the same direction as each other.

Why is this dreamy kind of repetition so comforting? It almost feels as though, if you knew a place well enough, it could shelter you from time. Living here, I'm learning that old buildings – houses, barns – old chairs and tables and even tools (a second-hand spade, the shears my parents bought when they set up home together) do this too, creating a kind of shortcut into repetition. As I move around this house it comforts me to know I'm repeating gestures that have been made here over and over by generations of unknown predecessors.

Sometimes the landing window stands open at evening, letting in the changing light and particular noises. If I forget whatever it is I was meaning to do and pause to watch dusk fill the orchard, I know I'm doing so in the very spot where those earlier inhabitants stood. When what I can see contracts, first to the near trees and at last to the stumpy damson nearest the house, I know it contracted for them too. Like them, I hear the birds run through their alarm calls – blackbirds on the wing with their clockwork *chakachakachaka*, pheasants cocking up one after the other all the way down the valley – then gradually quieten. Like them, I hear that pause as a last aftershock of the evening chorus.

Living in a place means letting it carry you forward. *Habitat* seems a good word for this. It suggests living going on, rather than our *doing* living. A few nights after they lost their calves, the cows were roaring again. This time another kind of estrangement – or perhaps it was simple astonishment – set them off. After its week of practice runs, the full harvest moon had risen at the end of the valley, on and up over Ballingham Hill. It was swollen and yellow with harvest dust, and it filled our roof light like a beacon.

I got out of bed and went to the window. The herd, crisply visible on the hill opposite, were grey-white silhouettes in a grey-white field. As I watched, first one cow and then another stretched her neck to groan, and really it seemed to sing. Calling to the moon, each became a long-necked, implausible beast. The singing cows, ardent and off-balance, were surely monsters out of somebody's dream. But not yet, I thought with a kind of surprise, out of mine.

Moonlight has a strangely affectless quality – I can't think of any better way to describe this than humourlessness – something it shares with fluorescent light. I was still watching the cattle from our attic window when I noticed that we were all facing downstream together, as if in some bizarre congregation. When the first cow on the ridge raised her muzzle and thrust forward her lower jaw in a trumpet of astonishment, I could even feel as if, for want of a more accurate way of putting it, I agreed with her. Of course, even in my own dazed, nocturnal state I didn't imagine the cattle were having thoughts like *congregation* or *downstream*. But I did feel as though I was thinking like them. It seems my old mammal self isn't so very evolved after all. For what could I do but feel a burst of moon-madness, the kind of longing that resembles nothing in the world so much as a roaring cow?

I let down the blind and got back into bed. *Finished?* asked P. sleepily. As if *I* were the trumpeter on the hilltop; as if I *had* been unable to keep my feelings to myself. *All done*, I said, and he rolled over and was asleep again.

But I didn't find it easy to fall sleep. Perhaps I was *not* all done. The moonlight deposited its large white squares on the ceiling. Just beyond the triple glass of the roof light, the night was still busy. The barn owl from Justin and Caroline's place was making desultory conversation in the wood. There was the occasional *whoop!* of a tawny owl. Closer at hand, the nightjar skirred away so loudly that I almost thought he was perched on the roof ridge itself.

He's probably halfway to Africa by now. But the thought of him makes me smile, reminding me as it does how panicked I was the time I first heard that uncanny call. We were sleeping out in the old garden, which lay among Oxfordshire water meadows. (At the time, I didn't think of this as eccentric.) I was woken by a strange flutter-tonguing, a sound unlike any bird song I knew. It kept moving round and around us, low to the ground, until at last it entered my dream-fugue – as alien landing craft.

So the other night, when P. began to snore, I slipped out of bed again, restless and eager for more, even if not quite to be scared. I opened a window, shifted a cushion onto the sill and swung my feet up beside me. As I looked out once more across the little valley, I wondered again who else had done this before me, and whether they too were sometimes unable to sleep and would get up to spy on the night valley and its inhabitants.

Now I saw that the herd on the Kilforge acreage had begun to move. Slowly, as befitted their size, Alan's giantesses were drifting once again towards Ballingham. Here and there one or two paused to lift a head and give a last, thoughtful bellow. Mostly they had fallen silent. They slowed, grazed, and moved on, according to their own mysterious logic: just as they're doing this morning, up there once again.

THE PLASH

Adam Thorpe

Everything could be seen down there, right to the bottomless depths. Even your face was visible until you withdrew it, distorted like an astronaut's pulled down by the G-force of the launch. It was a place of wonder, in full colour, tinted gold by autumn. It was generally in autumn that this far more perfect world came into view, and sometimes in spring. In winter it was hidden by solid ice that my stamps of Tuf heel (with built-in compass) could barely crack.

The ensuing Arctic thaw brought danger. Setting out over the creaking wastes, I had nothing to hold on to – just balance and pluck. There'd be the sound of a latch dropping, and the trapdoor would tip in a single solid piece, icy water lapping over one edge, the other lifting a few inches free from brown tufts of couch grass. 'Oh no,' I would shout to my invisible companion, the nameless essence of loyalty, 'I think I'm a goner!'

Smashing the frozen seas with my heel was like the punching-in of a window: it was associated with theft. I felt a certain regret. That the ice had survived the passage of tractors or the odd Land Rover was already a miracle. Few vehicles came this way. After all, the only reason to turn off White Hill onto the track was to go to the farm. Steeper than any road I knew, White Hill started in the market town of Chesham, with its pet shop and toy shop and the Embassy cinema and the family optician's where my mother worked as a receptionist. The town still felt rural fifty years ago, yet it was directly connected to London's heart, being the furthest stop on the Metropolitan Line. Puffing back up the hill took you to our row of houses at the top, just a minute or so further than the sign which said, TO DUNGROVE FARM.

The track was pot-holed. My adventuring seas were a mundane puddle. 'Puddle' sounds diminutive, too like 'piddle': the language lacks a word for something bigger, unless we revive 'plash'. My plash filled the chasm of an exaggerated rut. It lay several hundred yards along the track, just where the latter curved to the right: the farm was visible on the low crest. To the left was a stile half buried in the verge, leading through arable fields along a footpath that eventually, after two unpeopled miles of the rolling Chilterns, came to my Sunday school, little St George's church and, more importantly, the Five Bells pub. My parents would have their ritual Sunday pint there after the service. My sister and I, banned from the interior, would play in a beech copse across thick pasture until a shout from the far-off stile would drag us back to the stuffy little Simca, now smelling of beer and tobacco.

I never went into the farm. The courtyard made me nervous: it was eerily silent, although it was a working place with cows and arable, exhaling urinous suggestions of manure. I didn't know at the time that it was farmed centuries earlier by Thomas Harding, one of the last Lollards condemned to the stake. His chief crime was to insist that the Bible should be rendered into the native tongue. He was executed almost within sight of Dungrove, halfway up White Hill, in 1532. Spared the agony of the flames by an onlooker who knocked his brains out with a faggot, he is remembered these days with a carved stone marking the spot. In similar vein, perhaps, our path to Sunday school is now part of a Heritage Trail.

Water attracts boats. Haphazard dinghies of leaves; tree-bark galleons with salty crews. Sometimes I press-ganged ants, or ladybirds who would flee the deck by air. My brother, eight years older than me, would come along now and again and fashion me a sail from a leaf and a mast from a twig, adept with his penknife. It would generally keel over at the first breath of a breeze. Rafts were more successful – twigs lashed together with wiry stems – but they lacked romance unless my laser imagination etched a castaway waving his shirt. His vessel was not much bigger than a king-size postage stamp.

The flinty contours were the outlines found on a seafaring map: they included the odd island and various harbours. Amazingly, I never acted God and adjusted the coast. Heroic journeys were started. Reefs were washed by tropical seas. I was often alone because, perhaps mistakenly, I felt my intense fantasies would be diluted by sharing them with a friend, who'd drag me back to a world of beehive hairdos and the Beatles thrumming from the tranny in the kitchen. At times a blue sky threw a squall of glitter over the surface: puddle as Mediterranean glamour. At others I sensed the infinity of space the wrong way up, small clouds slipping between, birds become fish. I stared into a giant lens.

Its position on a bend meant that it was maintained over and over by the wheels that took the curve leaning in, exerting more force on one side, the increased weight gouging the seabed minutely deeper. Perhaps only some ten years earlier the wheels would still have been wooden and iron-rimmed, accompanied by punching hooves. No repairs were ever carried out: no gravel, no bitumen, no sludge of builder's sand or crushed bathroom tiles. It was understood that the defect was permanent. I was fascinated by this persistence because I feared that any day now the track would be spread with the ultimate tedium of tarmac, like a blank screen. But the track remained unmetalled. The gash in it was timeless, in a way. It might well have been there since the Tudor era of Thomas Harding – or even earlier. Stubborn and refractory, it would have been familiar to the farmworkers in the wagon or the kids in the cart as a bouncing of the boards a few minutes from the yard. Tiny flies came to sup on the brackish water, as did birds. There were no tadpoles, however: the water was too ephemeral.

When it began to recede, the inlets showed their banks, as ribbed as a giant ammonite fossil. Not tyre treads but cultivated terraces. Soon, the places where my torpedo foot had stirred explosive billows of underwater smoke were turned to desert rock. A gulley buttressed by flint outcrops. Real rock showed: the gulley was serious enough to be bedded here and there with what I imagined were the tectonic plates of the planet. At school we'd studied Pompeii and the marks of wheels in cobbled streets, the hard stone worn away to grooves as smooth as sculpture, natural rails for the traffic. Who was to say that the Romans hadn't travelled up here to an earlier version of Dungrove, or to some fancy country villa with statues?

Without water, or the waters of my imagination, the rut could turn embarrassing. A shallow depression. I didn't like to look at it. Sometimes I had to wait weeks for proper rain. Or else the rejuvenation occurred during school weekdays in the winter, when it grew dark too soon for me to reach that distance up the track after tea. By the weekend, the water would often be gone, leaving only a tantalising glint of mud.

The track itself was tantalising, right from its beginning at White Hill: it was bordered on either side by a broad and grassy verge foamed in the summer by cow parsley, spreading at the foot of brambled hedgerows several feet wide, whose clustered blackberries we would strip for jam every September. To the right were huge sloping fields, cowpat-spattered; to the left, at least for the first half-mile, the hedge concealed the long back gardens of Cheyne Walk, a 1950s lollipop close that had stretched its tentacle into the former fieldscape. We lived on the corner of the close. My London mother would insist that we were not actually part of Cheyne Walk: she had a very English dislike of cul-de-sacs, associating them with twitching net curtains and suburban boredom. My parents met in Paris, my Derbyshire father was bilingual. Our family car was the small Simca, but tucked behind our garage door was a 1938 Type 57 Bugatti, gleaming black, bought during our time in France – old cars – even Bugs – were cheaper than new ones in the 1950s. We were, in many ways, in the wrong place.

One of my mother's best friends, however, hailed from the close. Mrs Crisp was the plump and jolly Avon lady. She would give me sixpence for feeding her hairless sausage dog when she was away. Woofie was an unappealing creature who would yap and tremble as if mildly electrocuted the moment I appeared. Needless to say, we had a plethora of unused Avon scents in the house. When, in my gap year, I took a job for three months as a machine operator in a Chesham factory making neon bulbs, the women packers all wore Avon. For some chemical reason the perfume would go stale by the lunch break, and that distinctive powdery muskiness is inextricably bound up with my Buckinghamshire youth.

To be honest, there was very little difference between the houses of Cheyne Walk and our own road that led into it, except for the semi-detached element. We belonged to a row of about ten identical homes built at the end of the 1950s by an architect impressed by Moorish arches in Spain: every box-like house boasted a deep and curved front porch in white stucco. Large cracks would appear in them, for reasons no builder could ever quite fathom. Some fifty years on, this mildly pleasing and repeated motif, something which gave me an obscure sense of reassurance and belonging as I walked past our neighbours, has mostly disappeared behind an anarchy of fiercely individual extensions and improvements.

I'm looking at our house on Google Street View. The porch has gone, and the garage is now a downstairs room, but the all-over rendering (if less chalky white), the drainpipes, the roof tiles, the diamond-shaped leading in the windows, these are the same. I travel the length of the garden where our fence consistently teetered over in strong winds. The fence has changed, and where I'd swing like the child in Thomas Hood's 'I Remember, I Remember', and similarly think 'the air must rush as fresh / To swallows on the wing', is now the garage. The area's electricity generator, humming under yellow skull-warnings of death beyond what was the foot of our lawn, appears identical. At the front, we were separated from White Hill itself (finally arrived on the flat summit) by a raised swelling of grass, so we weren't really a street. Beyond was the road and then some rather stockbrokerish houses, one of which held a Colditz survivor who would reminisce with my parents about the war. Behind us, the close gave way to a welter of fields and woods spreading over the hills as far as the eye could see.

It was all very English. When I first arrived at the age of five, I had spent most of my brief life in Paris, Beirut and Calcutta. England felt chilly and grey and somehow less friendly or exuberant. 'Exuberant' was a word beyond the pale of my limited vocabulary, of course, belonging to all that I was yet to explore: a hinterland of glittering riches. I was learning to write properly, tracing repeated letters on lined paper; pegging the alphabet onto its washing-line. Even now I can feel the almost physical thrill of those apparently tedious lessons. As if even the individual letters themselves, clumsily pencilled into being, were plump with entire poems and stories: seed-grains of towering trees and intricate flowers.

On the 1877 OS map of the immediate area, all you can see on either side of the road's slow-travelling worm is the unblemished white of fields. They are bordered by tiny bobbles of cartographic trees, deemed solid enough to cast an etcher's flick of shadow. Oak? Elm? Beech? The creaking shuffle of horse and plough, the summer haywains, a kiss under the wagon. My bedroom faced those phantom fields when I first read, at the age of eleven, Laurie Lee's *Cider with Rosie*. That book, more than any other, inspired me into writing. It also deepened a sense of loss: that an entire rural existence, a way of being and of knowledge, had been erased in the name of progress – both social and scientific. When our own modest lawn insisted on sprouting the stems of wheat or oats, as well as wild plants like bird's-foot trefoil and 'eggs and bacon', my father – who knew the old ways as a boy on the moors – explained that it was the old field pushing through, its dormant seeds reviving. After all, our house was only a few years old, sheltered by a young silver birch I had always imagined to be ancient.

This revenance excited me for reasons that had nothing to do with botany. I would look out from my room over the shallow roofs and out towards the tops of the oaks that marked the farm track trailing away to the south, and imagine the suburban post-war houses vanished – including our own. It surprises me now, that this palimpsestic, historical impulse started so young. Wasn't this my home, cosy and familiar? The green double-decker London Country bus, having chugged gamely up steep Eskdale Avenue, would deposit me at Codmore Cross (a name that still conjures the warm-muffin feel of school's end), and I'd race back to slump in front of *Blue Peter* or *Crackerjack* or *The Adventures of Robinson Crusoe* in fuzzy black-and-white. Why did I wish it all gone, depopulated, the clock spun back to tussocks or crops or unbroken beech wood?

That past was exciting mainly because it was lost, in the way treasure gains a magic from being buried on a coral island. It was not as if the present-day fields thrilled me that much, except as playgrounds. The steep pastures that dropped down from Dungrove Farm to the thick hedgerow of White Hill offered wonderful views over Chesham to the sloped horizon beyond, but they were chiefly enticing as the site of my international sledging championships in the freezing winters of the 1960s. They were also the aerodrome where my brother's balsa-wood plane, weeks in the making on a table in our bedroom, its tissue stiffening under the vaporous dizziness of dope, stalled at a point higher than the crowns of the bordering oaks and crashed ignominiously into a cowpat.

1877 seems impossibly far back, yet neither the track nor the field boundaries had budged a lifetime later, according to a 1952 OS map shorn of those thoughtful trees. Now, apart from the cul-de-sac's ganglion and the zip-like grey of further buildings along the roads and lanes, they haven't budged in the six decades since. We arrived in 1962, just four or five years after the building works had ceased. I vividly recall imagining the science-fiction feel of the date 1965, when it would all be white spacesuits and pills for food. A relentless optimism reigned, a complete faith in scientific progress. The Cuban crisis and myxomatosis were hiccups. Yet I rebelled against this very early on, and I'm not sure why. A handful of tradesmen still used horses. We had our own Steptoe, clomping past with his blinkered pony and flatbed cart, yelling something unintelligible that we eventually deciphered as *Any old rags, any old lumber?* I was already nostalgic for ploughhorse and haycock, which in our area might still have been visible just a few years earlier. Hayricks were certainly around, and I was to help build them when home from university a decade later following my parents' move to the edge of the Berkshire downland – more securely rural yet within earshot of the M4 motorway.

At any rate, I felt I had just missed out. The puddled track to Dungrove carried me back. Tracks and paths are as stubborn as wood and field boundaries, stitched into history, into the older landscape. They share something of the vanilla-and-dust aroma of those maps I'd call up in later years from local libraries: evidence of bottled-up time. At thirteen, in anticipation of my parents' move to Africa, I was sent to board in Wiltshire amidst downland thick with prehistoric mysteries.

The house was swapped for a maisonette down in the valley on the Berkhamsted road, near a straggling beech hanger. The wood was sufficiently large for me to roam in it every day as a brooding adolescent, dreaming of girls and poetry, pencil-sketching the hills and vales into uncertain permanence.

These days, to enter the archives of the past, I just tap on my keyboard. I don't need to move at all; not even to explore my old childhood haunts. At time of writing, our row of houses and Cheyne Walk have been trapped in an amber of miserable grey. Low cloud, little shadow. It has probably rained over the last few days. 'Cluttery' weather, as the old farmhands would say. It makes my revived memories depressing, even dismal. I click my way back to the entrance to the track. The sign proclaiming DUNGROVE FARM has gone. The sun comes out, suddenly. It gleams brilliantly on tall and full-flowering cow parsley. I advance fifty yards in three taps: all that I'm permitted. The odd new house has been squeezed in between the track and the fields and even Cheyne Walk (somebody preferring money to a garden), but the great hedgerows are intact. The gift of sunshine stays.

I peer forward into the virtual distance, impossibly far from my adventuring seas, my reefs and dreams, my other-world fantasies of deep-down nymphs and bottomless heavens. It all seems both close enough to touch and simultaneously vanished for good, never to return. Granted another few hundred yards, perhaps we would see the flash of it: the unlidded lens, bright as a living eye, catching the light and casting it back, mirroring the world while it can.

At the Edge of the Tide

Michael Viney

The screensaver on my computer shows the strand on a sunny autumn morning, the sea calm for once and unfurling on the sand in slow, gleaming doorsteps of foam. Whatever the real weather on the shore below, it offers an encouraging start to the day. It reminds me of early walks on the strand with my eyes closed, the sun a warm vermilion in their lids and the rustle of the waves on my right to keep me straight. For all but a handful of days in the year, there's no one else to bump into.

'Strand' is Ireland's word for beach, which speaks to me more of the massed and clattering, sometimes lickable, pebbles at Brighton, where I was young. The only stones on this strand are scattered platters of green sandstone, carried in with the holdfasts of kelp wrenched up in winter storms. The stones are embossed with white hieroglyphs, calcareous tubes of seabed worms. Their bright rococo doodling made me gather enough to clad the chimneybreast above the woodstove, a typically laborious endeavour when we settled here some forty years ago.

That was the time for such middle-aged departures – 'deep ecology' from Arne Naess, 'self-sufficiency' from John Seymour. An acre on the wilder coast of County Mayo, on a final tendril of road, seemed the right setting for effortful experiment: hens, goats, potatoes, peat-cutting, fishing with a spillet, all that. The view – mountains, islands, an infinite ocean – was sustaining in itself.

So was the rawness of this corner of the coast: a great delta of sand curving back round the dunes, its fringe of fields framing a pair of lagoons, one shielded by a dark, ivied cliff. Between lakes and dunes, the astonishing, wind-levelled lawn of the *machair*, the geographers' 'plain' from the Gaelic, on north-west shores of Ireland and the Hebrides.

Even the strand was suitably untamed. To reach it, down the stony lane – the boreen – to the shore, meant fording, first, a little river from the mountain, at times just a rattling splash, at others a surging, impassable flood. A little way on, past drying furls of seaweed from the last spring tide, the main flow from Mweelrea carves a long, curving channel to the sea. The crossing-place from the boreen is marked by a row of rocks, once set hopefully as stepping stones. Now one has to follow, sometimes in thigh boots, the shifting consensus of tractors taking feed across the channel to sheep on the *duach*.

The farmers' homes are strung out towards the mountain on narrow acres striped up the hillside a century ago. Above our own small house the land is corduroyed with grassed-over ridges that grew potatoes and oats before the Famine: they need a prance from one ridge to the next. Also preserved, among marshy rushes and erratic glacial boulders, are foundations of the old crowded cabins. Three hundred people lived in this townland where a dozen or so dwell today. On one boulder I can picture, a set of little stones is clasped in a matrix of moss. They were gathered, I must suppose, by a petticoated toddler, helping to clean a field some two centuries ago.

The history of this hillside includes clearance of the land and its families for a Scottish rancher's blackface sheep. The dislocation can be read into what's left of a wreck on the strand, the points of its ribs sticking up, now and then, from the sand. Just once, in our memory, a big storm stripped enough sand away to expose it right down to the keel, scattered with lumps of limestone ballast and shards of black pottery. It was probably an old coaster and probably pre-Famine, but nobody can say when it was blown ashore. That's telling in itself: folk history or even common fancy should account for every quirk of local landscape. Less and less of the wreck survives. A number of the big oak ribs, pierced for dowelling, have been dragged away by tractor to serve as gateposts in the fields behind the shore.

The sea has erased another somewhat uncertain monument. When we came to live, the big delta of the strand had as its odd focal point a pyramidal mound as high as a house. Originally a tide-severed spur of the dune system, it supported the last few square metres of a small and ancient monastic chapel and its accumulated graves, some of drifting war-dead salvaged from the sea. As the spring tides undermined it, the mound began to sink, spilling out bones and headstones. Eventually, chewed to the sandy core by a January storm surge, it collapsed, leaving stones in a jumbled circle on the strand. We salvaged a headstone, a rough-edged slab of slate inscribed by a journeyman mason in the early 1800s. The surname still thrives in the parish, but no family cared to claim it. It survives in the garden path, face down.

The strand is so exposed to gales and breakers that fishing in the tarred canvas currach has dwindled to the use, on occasional calm Sundays, of a very few boats, lashed down to rocks in niches of the headlands. Our own hauls of rays and flounders, for the freezer, were made with a long line of mackerel-baited hooks, set parallel to the shore, anchored at the very bottom of one tide and recovered at the ebb of the next. Such efforts, in weather that could utterly change overnight, diminished with the years. They were mocked by a memorable event in which a storm left the strand littered with fish, gills snapped forward in the undersea maelstrom that drowned them. We gathered weighty bags of fish for the freezer – pollack, ling, cod, haddock, hake, whiting – and left the prickly rockfish to the gulls.

For the hillside community, the sea's offerings were led by Laminaria, the offshore forest of kelp. Uprooted by storms or in annual senescence, it is tossed ashore in toffee-brown drifts. The fronds are good as fertiliser on the land, but their real value lay in the stems, the 'sea rods', worth wading in for, waist-deep, in competition at dawn. Stacked to dry and burned in stone 'ovens' on the shore, their charred clinker was the raw material of iodine, the burnings rolling pungent smoke inland. The eclipse of iodine by antibiotics is already good for reappraisal in the running battle with sepsis. The kelp is now harvested for alginates, smoothers of ice cream and toothpaste.

The shore's more enduring gift has been the sand itself, rich in calciferous marine fragments – 'the dry shells, the toe- and fingernail parings of the sea' in Michael Longley's poem. Carried up by horse and cart, the sand made a soft bed for cattle in the byre and a liming of land as their manure was spread. That was before tractors grew as powerful as tanks and the scale of sand quarrying became insupportable. In the finite budget of a bay of sand, great withdrawals by winter storms are held offshore, to be repaid in summer's soft selvedges. Steal too much from the sand budget and the ocean claws even harder at the dunes.

There is another grand recycling between the strand and the machair, the broad, green sward behind the dunes. Dunes and machair abound in snails, from the big, brown kind known to gardeners, through smaller sorts ringed with bright bands of colour, to rare and miniature whorled species no bigger than a match-head, surviving from post-glacial times. What delighted me was to realise that the land snails build their shells from the calcium of their lost ocean cousins, carried on winds from the strand. In winter, I have found long lines of 'garden' snails wedged into the leeward cracks of driftwood fence posts, their shells sand-blasted to delicate shades of blue. On some mild, moist mornings in early summer, walking the dunes risks crunching on copulating molluscs.

I have beachcombed most hopefully in winter, often in the wake of gales, wind hissing around my boots and leaving worm-stones and otter shells balanced on pedestals of sand. In the early years of smallholder mechanics, I marched the tideline with an improvising eye. Spanish fish boxes, New England milk crates, swathes of fishing net and tangles of rope, stray buoys, colourful trawler-balls. I was rarely first along, following instead the close-stitched prints of fox or stoat at dawn (for dead seabirds and crabs) and tractor tracks of the farmer who lives beside the strand.

Now that ships' cargoes are carried in containers, there is rarely much cast up that's of use to the community. There was, once, a great arrival of clean, finished timber – stout planks for roofs or scaffolding. They vanished in a day. Then, even more mysteriously, came hundreds of little cedar tiles, like the lids of school pencil boxes. These, at least, were left to me, fragrant and challenging for some better purpose than wedging rocking furniture on a bumpy flagged floor.

So much for the material, Swiss Family Robinson side of things. More importantly, as one might hope, the strand has been my primer in marine life – or rather, death. Our windowsills are heaped with predictable bric-a-brac: sea urchins, dolphin vertebrae, bird skulls, crab carapaces. Some things are fragile and beautiful, as in the ocean-drifting, translucent violet snails, *Janthina*, that Rachel Carson pursued on her side of the Atlantic. I keep mine safe in a clear plastic box. In another is the little skull of a Ridley's turtle, winter vagrant from the Caribbean. And hanging on my study wall, like a ribbed African shield, is the carapace of a big loggerhead turtle, salvaged from the strand in a wheelbarrow and left buried for months at the bottom of the garden.

What's rare can be a matter of who's around to see. In the 1980s I came upon the seventh recorded stranding (then another, a few years later) of 'True's wonderful beaked whale', *Mesoplodon mirus*. The early common name for this slim animal, a rare deep diver after squid, reflected the delight of Frederick True, a Smithsonian curator who described the new species from a corpse washed up in North Carolina in 1913. A solitary pair of conical teeth at the very end of my whale's lower jaw warranted the call to a distant zoology professor, who came to confirm their distinctive shape (as if squeezed between finger and thumb).

This first whale was salvaged for its skeleton by the Ulster Museum. Great chunks were neatly butchered by a mammal technician, then wrapped in plastic bags and ferried up the fields to his rented van. His work, conducted on a rainy Sunday in a pit dug around the whale, was watched attentively by my farming neighbours, standing together carefully upwind. When the technician dropped his big knife, it was returned to him gingerly, at the tip of a spade.

The number of Ireland's whales, alive or stranded, has since become a national wonder, thanks to the leadership of the voluntary Irish Whale and Dolphin Group. Leaping humpbacks and blowing fin whales are now regularly spotted from southern headlands; cast-up corpses are promptly noted and available for autopsy. Two recent True's, which are still very rarely stranded, carried plastic fragments in their stomachs.

A singular, lentil-sized pellet of raw plastic is called, for some reason, a 'nurdle', of which more than 100 million tonnes are produced every year. Shipped around the world in this form, the pellets have been spilled into the ocean by the billion and gulped for zooplankton by seabirds, fish and other marine life. I noticed them first in 2000, among seaweed at the strand's furthest lap of the tide.

I was stirring the weed, as usual, in the hope of adding another sea bean to my dish of them: sea hearts, horse-eyes, nickars. They are fruits spilled into rivers from tropical pods in Cuban or Central American forests, reaching our islands on the North Atlantic Drift after perhaps 400 days at sea. The glossy brown skin of the sea heart invites fondling, like a worry bead, and its toughness once served the teething of babies of this coast.

It's ages since I added another, but how long since I really looked? Perhaps drift-seeds have grown fewer, the forests of the Caribbean cleared for golf courses and celebrity homes. I still host, however, from transatlantic drift, a couple of coconuts still in their husks and a box fruit, *Barringtonia asiatica*, a four-sided fistful with a husk like Shredded Wheat. It was the first ever recorded on a European shore and reached a children's programme on telly.

My passion for the natural world has long had the company of two close friends in this landscape. One is an ornithologist, David Cabot, who lives across the lake, his lifelong study the barnacle geese that winter on north Mayo's islands. The other is the poet Michael Longley, who comes from Belfast to borrow Cabot's cottage and immerse himself in the landscape.

David and I made a film about him, where I had him paddle in a chill November surf, framed against a fiery sunset, to recite his poem 'Sea Shanty'. As the shot ended, the camera still ready on its tripod, a young otter chose to dash along the shallows, straight past us: a magical conjunction. Again, filming with my wife, the dog seated beside us at the crest of the dunes, an otter gave us a whole digital minute of its life. It climbed the dune from the strand and paused within our long winter shadows, then dashed off through the marram to the distant lagoon.

Rinsing off the sea salt with a swim in fresh water restores the insulation of the otter's soft underfur. But retreat from the sea to the cover of the dunes can have another end. Once, slowly walking the tideline with the sun behind me, I watched an otter bound from the surf with a flounder in its jaws and lollop up into the dunes to eat. Crouched among the marram, it was swooped upon by a raven that tried to bully it off its meal. At last, giving up on the whirring assault, the otter skidded back down the sand, fish flapping from its jaws, the raven skimming it back to the sea.

Such explicit drama is rare. I look for footprints leaving the tideline (a neat arc to each paw, the pads rounded and separate, impressed like petals). At the bank of a stream running into the strand, a tall, green tuft of well-fertilised grass is topped by a new wisp of spraint, black and glistening with chitin. I sniff its musky scent, content the otters are still there.

In Ireland's conservation texts, this sprawling corner of the coast is named as 'Dooaghtry', for a little, reed-fringed lake behind the dunes – one the otters sometimes wash in. They are given passing mention in the ecological synopsis of the National Parks and Wildlife Service, along with choughs, the buoyant, carolling crows whose red bills prod the machair, and the whooper swans of winter that croon to the echoes from the cliff above their lake.

In the botanical priorities of habitat conservation, Dooaghtry's special claim is its exceptional wealth of a liverwort, *Petalophyllum ralfsii*, a European rarity, its lettuce-like beauty best judged under a hand lens. Reduced to a scatter across Europe, it thrives in carpeted thousands on the moist sands of Dooaghtry. Michael Longley suggested this 'snail snack, angel's nosegay' for my farewell wreath.

One change in the landscape we mourned together moved him to these lines:

> Now that the Owennadornaun has disappeared
> For you and me where our two townlands meet,
> The peaty water takes the long way round
> Through Morrison's fields and our imaginations.

The Owennadornaun was the little river whose ford near the bottom of the boreen was so rich in the spirit of place. A sill of rock made a shallow waterfall just above the crossing, with the sun above the mountain to catch each ripple and splash. It was here I saw my first dipper, walking under water, and where, in summer, sand martins came to nest in holes in the bank. There were pied and grey wagtails dancing at the edge and, once or twice, a sandpiper.

This has all gone. The ford's loose cobbles, rolling beneath the tyres of summer cars, were thought an affront to tourism. And it's true that many 4x4s did press on, through the channel to the strand, there to spin great circles for fun or get stuck in the soft bits with the tide coming in. These transgressions were erased by the big spring tides of September. But a car park behind the strand, with a summer loo, was clearly essential to setting up the Wild Atlantic Way. It meant diversion of the little river and a road bridge built above its bed, this now remaining dry and quite birdless.

We are three ageing men, Cabot, Longley and Viney (me the oldest by a hare's leap), but we have shared a life and a landscape out of time, an ecosystem lean but lovely and enduring. We have a pact for the sequential scatter of our ashes on the little promontory fort above David's lake – a sprinkle of more calcium for the snails.

BINSEY

Marina Warner

The sanctuary where the high altar stood was out of bounds for us girls at the convent; women could arrange the flowers, but only boys could be servers. The Second Vatican Council was to redraw the rules in the mid sixties and allow females to help the priest saying Mass and, later, give out communion and even speak. But in those days before 1965, priests were the only men we saw apart from one or two gardeners: once a week in the shadowy, hushed booth, another holy enclosure, the confessor would be hazily outlined behind the colander of the dividing screen, surrounding him with a constellation of little haloes around his head as we whispered our sins. Every morning, wearing a long, rough-spun, brown robe with a rope knotted thrice for the three vows of the Franciscans, a friar would come and, as I stuck out my tongue to receive the wafer, I would peep, from lowered eyes, at Father Alfred's big strong hairy toes and thick ridged nails in sandals. He was our favourite because he got through the service quickly; some of the older monks were more devout and lingered on every word, and we schoolgirls were hungry for our breakfast; not infrequently, one of us would faint into the aisles. When I asked my friend Lindsay what it was like, losing consciousness, she answered, 'It's like going to Africa.' After that, I wanted to go to Africa, too, but when I did pass out, I found nothing except plummeting seasickness and loud thrumming in my head. On special occasions a Jesuit would be invited from Farm Street in London to give a sermon or take us on a three-day retreat; these were men who wore black suits and shiny, covered shoes.

249

Our nuns had been known as 'Jesuitesses'; Mary Ward, the founder of their order, had led a turbulent life, caught up in religious struggles, first with the Reformers in England and then with successive popes, because she wanted to teach girls, just as boys were taught by Jesuits. Jesuits had also been persecuted for being clever – we knew the history.

When I first arrived in Oxford at Lady Margaret Hall, the most celebrated poet-priest and Jesuit since Gerald Manley Hopkins was living at Campion Hall, but, unlike Hopkins, Peter Levi was infinitely glamorous, his prodigious gifts and his family history and his celibacy making him an irresistible object of desire for many, many people of every gender and age. His father had a business in oriental carpets, inherited from his father, who had come to England from Constantinople; Peter's stature was much enhanced, in the eyes of his many admirers, by his origins and expertise in Greek-Mediterranean-Levantine culture in all its polyglot variety. But it was his mother, Edith Tigar, a fervent Catholic from Yorkshire, who was the dominant influence: Peter's older brother Anthony had also become a Jesuit and his sister Gillian a nun. The triple surrender of the siblings to divine love, the family's self-fashioning according to the religious ideal and its constraints, marvellously amplified the pulsing aura around Peter. I knew a woman who was genuinely, determinedly, in love with him, and several others who were eager to try to make him surrender. I was fascinated myself, but I was struggling to abandon the faith that had ruled my whole life so far, and I was wary: it didn't feel right to me that a priest should be so alluring and have a taste for good clarets and eating out in restaurants (including the most expensive in town, the Elizabeth). He enjoyed his own seductiveness to others, like a beautiful girl who toys with her conquests. I never heard then of any consummations – and this invulnerability added to the perturbation that I felt around him.

We met in a field near Heythrop College where he was making a retreat and couldn't wait to be interrupted, or so I'd been told. It was early summer with high blue skies and a silky gleam on the crops and he came through these fields up the hill towards us, with a slight limp from a childhood attack of polio. It was the year he was ordained, I've now learned from the biography by Brigid Allen, and he was struggling with his superiors, who weren't happy about his lack of obedience.

The clandestine rendezvous – the tryst – had been arranged by Alasdair Clayre, folk-singer-songwriter, the English Joan Baez and Bob Dylan in the making (this was 1964), who happened also to be a Prize Fellow at All Souls. Alasdair was about ten years younger than Peter, and had a car – a rare thing among students in those days; how he managed to make the assignation to meet at that spot, beyond the grounds where Peter was meant to be enclosed, has vanished from memory – but there we were on a ridge in the Cotswolds, joyfully meeting the poet-priest. I was a bit shocked; I was intrigued; I was awed.

Peter Levi wasn't Father Alfred, or anything like the Farm Street confessors who had come to my school. He was then thirty-three years old, nearly twice my age; he was smooth-skinned and lissom, and had what's called an olive complexion, though no olive, either in fruit or leaf, ripe or unripe, oil or soap, is ever that colour: he was appealingly sheeny brown like a sweet chestnut when you first open its spiky shell to see it lying in its cottony nest, and he spoke confidingly and self-effacingly and rapidly, the chevrons of his brows punctuating the flow of put-downs and thumbs-ups from a fabulous range of reading and looking – all the while quoting, poetry especially, in many languages.

Later that term, he took me to see the medieval shrine at Binsey by the Isis, as the Thames is called there, where it flanks Port Meadow and runs into the capillary streams and canals that web the fields: I remember him pointing out a small building drifting in the meadow below us (we must have been approaching from Godstow and had been visiting the ruined abbey there), and talking about hermits and sacred wells and sanctuaries and places that are holy over long stretches of time. Later, in what is his longest-lasting work, he translated Pausanias's *Guide to Greece* for World Classics; he also went travelling – on horseback – in Central Asia with Bruce Chatwin. But that day at Binsey, he was telling me about the allée of trees running from the village to the little church, which had been cut down in 1879 and inspired Hopkins to write his impassioned lament and praise-song, 'Binsey

Poplars', with its unexpected but precise image of the sun, caught in branches, and made all the more fiery by rubato syncopation:

> My aspens dear, whose airy cages quelled,
> Quelled or quenched in leaves the leaping sun,
> All felled, felled, all are felled;
> ...
> Ten or twelve, only ten or twelve
> Strokes of havoc unselve
> The sweet especial scene,
> Rural scene, a rural scene,
> Sweet especial rural scene.

For my generation, Hopkins was the voice – and the eyes – of a radiant English dreamworld in which Blake was the pre-eminent seer, but which included many other intense spirits with local connections to Oxford: Pre-Raphaelites and Ancients, whom I felt were my elective affines, for they had foreseen the hopes and dreamed the future my friends and I were thinking we could bring about. Hopkins's great requiem, 'The Wreck of the *Deutschland*', sounds all through the feverish world of Muriel Spark's *The Girls of Slender Means*, which is set in 1945 but came out in 1963. At least, this is how I remember the feeling of discovery and the longing for enchantments beyond the dull and risk-less mainstream, with Peter talking to me about Samuel Palmer, and directing me to see Palmer's paintings and drawings in the Ashmolean, his ripely glowing suns in small hallucinatory rural scenes, as sweet and especial as Hopkins could have wished for. I was urged by both Alasdair and Peter to read David Jones, the poet and the painter – *In Parenthesis* and *Anathemata* were up there with Dante and Keats, far more cherished than Shakespeare (condemned by another of my mentors in those days, the historian Richard Cobb, as 'coarse, ruffianly stuff'). Hopkins, Palmer and Jones – these were luminaries, points of reference intersecting quite often with Catholicism, but not invariably.

There was more, much more – Peter was an ebullient and generous mentor; later some of these thoughts flowed into the lectures he gave as Professor of Poetry at Oxford. He imparted thoughts, not inner feelings – at least to me – and I had no inkling of his troubles, that he was so much at odds with the vows he'd made; I thought he was just a worldly priest. But at a party Alasdair Clayre gave in All Souls, Peter had already met Deirdre, the wife of Cyril Connolly, and it seems to have been a *coup de foudre* for both of them; after Cyril's death, he left the priesthood and married her. He was by all accounts much, much happier, but his unsettling aura was dimmed, not only for me.

For many years I avoided churches, and even wayside shrines and religious music made me uneasy, but now, with the years of Catholic daily life long past, I can enjoy visiting such places again, and I'm attracted to many aspects of them; setting aside the interest I have in the buildings themselves and their interiors, there's quietness, a quietness that often hums with centuries of voices. So in some ways I still envy those who can pray, but am reconciled to the spectral echoes that old sanctuaries sound for me. Walking to Binsey across the meadows and the river has become my favourite walk in Oxford; the last time I went, the hedgerows on the lane to the church had been slashed by a machine – a chainsaw? – and the dense, deep tangle of elder, dog rose, hornbeam, hazel, snowberries and hawthorn was mangled, left in broken stems to die down on the earth floor as compost. This is the country way of doing it, no doubt, but it gave the early-autumnal rural scene, still fruiting, still flowering, a battered, neglected look. Hopkins's words, when he cried out, seem to have lost no point:

> O if we but knew what we do
> When we delve or hew –
> Hack and rack the growing green!
> Since country is so tender
> To touch, her being só slender,
> That, like this sleek and seeing ball
> But a prick will make no eye at all,
> Where we, even where we mean
> To mend her we end her ...

Still, that summer bryony was mantling it all, exuberantly covering up the clumsy human husbandry, and on the last stretch of the lane, as it leads to the chapel itself, an avenue of lime trees has recently been planted; the third generation since Hopkins's aspens dear, they're still so small their crowns are globular, somewhat like standard roses.

Very old, cobwebby yews grow close in to the chapel in the churchyard. There are a few Victorian tombs and some more recent arrivals, including an infant which is under a tiny wooden marker; over the drystone wall a small herd of goats graze in an enclosure, the billy often leaping up, like the rampant, golden, Babylonian goat eating a thorn bush in the British Museum, with two nanny goats and a few kids usually at his side. On the north side of the church, some wrecks of river craft are slowly rotting in what remains of a boatyard for vessels working the web of streams and cuts that run into the Thames and its 'wind-watering weed-winding banks'. A peahen puffed up her salt-and-pepper feather cloak and shrilled furiously to ward us off her patch.

Apart from the farmhouse and the ramshackle outbuildings, the stoved-in boats and straggling animal pens that run up to the churchyard walls as if rising against a breakwater, the little gabled church with its double bell tower stands alone, a destination and an end in itself. It's a hidden place, shaded and old, built to a human, not divine scale; a speaking place even in its silence.

The shrine began in Anglo-Saxon times as an oratory, dedicated to St Margaret of Antioch, but its popularity since the twelfth century as a site of pilgrimage arose because of the well in the churchyard – the treacle-well – which is sacred to St Frideswide, the patron saint of Oxford. Margaret was one of the most beloved saints of medieval Europe, the special protectress of women who are being harassed because she resisted a pagan king who wanted to marry her and was then attacked by the devil in the shape of a monstrous dragon, and swallowed alive; but her holiness was so strong that the devil couldn't digest her and so regurgitated her safe and sound.

Gory miracle stories such as Margaret's were the staple of my childhood; mostly featuring indomitable heroines (abused children, maltreated virgins, wronged queens), they're often bizarre, sadistic and stark, very

close to fairy tales in mood and matter. The legend of St Frideswide is
no exception. Her name means 'strong hope' or, according to another
source, 'bond of peace', and she was a high-born heiress – the daughter
of a sub-king, Dida of Eynsham, and his wife Safrida; her dates are
conjectured at 680 to 727 or 735. She had lost her mother when she
was a child, and wanted to become a nun; but she was being pressed to
marry another potentate, Algar. She didn't want to, in any case, and
certainly not Algar (this is an unexpectedly common situation in fairy
tales, too). In other versions of her legend, she is pursued by several
suitors; sometimes they come accompanied by a throng of soldiers. As
in many stories of early female saints, the rejected suitor seeks revenge
and sets out to rape her (marriage by abduction), then putting her in a
brothel to punish her. 'Since she has thus rejected me,' Algar declares,

> 'I will commit a wrong against her;
> And when I have done all the lechery I desire with her,
> I will give her to whoever wants her – [to] flagrant and bold
>   lechers,
> [So] that when she leaves me, she will be [a] common whore!'
> He leaped upon his palfrey and took the way forward.

But Frideswide calls on the help of St Margaret, and escapes. She
takes a boat down the Thames and lets it drift; it carries her safely and
sets her down at Binsey; there she conceals her aristocratic birth and
becomes a swineherd (again resembling Peau-d'ane – Donkeyskin – in
the fairy tale, best known from Charles Perrault's spirited verse narrative,
but a widely known medieval legend). Algar still comes after her, remorse-
lessly, but when he reaches her refuge, he's struck by lightning and
blinded. Soon after, he's thrown from his horse and breaks his neck.

The posse he's brought with him are all struck blind too, but Frideswide
shows mercy on them, prays to St Margaret, and a spring instantly wells
up. With its sweet and fragrant water she restores their sight.

The word 'treacle' now conjures up golden syrup; its old significance,
as balm and salve, has been lost. The well at Binsey was 'for long
collapsed and fouled', according to T. J. Prout, who served as vicar for

thirty years and in 1874, five years before Hopkins wrote 'Binsey Poplars', purified it in the spirit of Anglo-Catholic enthusiasm for the old cult practices (holy water, bells, prayers to saints and belief in their miracles) previously abhorrent to Protestants.

The well itself is now again a murky sump, like a blind eye deep down in the ground, under a Gothic arch with steps leading down, green and slidey with mosses and draped with the delicate quatrefoils of rambling penny royal, but still catacomb-like, damp and eerie. A well of this kind isn't far from a privy in appearance, a meeting-point between foul and fair, wild nature and human organisation, yoked together by need, a disturbing memento of our creatureliness.

The miracle of this cure and many more that followed brought great fame to Frideswide, as a holy woman, healer and abbess. After her death, a cult grew up attended by many miracles; so many that the little church at Binsey proved too humble for the crowds and her bones were transferred to a far more beautiful and magnificent priory church in Oxford; the city of Oxford was given into her care, and her tomb became a great medieval healing shrine, specialising in eye problems and in psychological troubles.

Young women were especially attracted to seek the saint's help. Some were suffering from rejection by a man they wanted, yet others were bitterly disappointed in their hopes for a loving partnership. The symptoms reported are remarkably recognisable for us today, though we would term them 'hysterical'. Pilgrims reported illusions and mental troubles arising from sexual problems: Alveva had gone mad after sexual intercourse; Beatrix, from Wiltshire, had suffered from a headache for two years after sex with her husband; Helen, who had lived with a priest for three years and then been rejected by him, had fallen ill with sleeplessness and internal pains; Cecily had had a phantom pregnancy. A girl called Mathilda had become blind for six years and been 'spurned' by her family, but in the shrine she bled from her eyes and found her sight restored.

In 1524, as the Reformation under Henry VIII was beginning, Cardinal Wolsey dissolved St Frideswide's Priory and took the proceeds for a new foundation, Cardinal College, named after himself. After his fall from power, this would become Christ Church, the seat of the cathedral of Oxford (the famous bell in Tom Quad, a landmark of the city, was originally the bell of St Frideswide's priory, and was moved to the college in 1684). St Fridewide's tomb was smashed and her relics scattered.

Hopkins doesn't allude to any of this in his poem, but it's interesting to contrast the Anglo-Catholic effort to redress the history of past desecration with Hopkins's contemporary vision of iconoclasm as nature damaged, as transcendence forfeited by a heedless act of vandalising trees, trees which used to catch the god-like sun in their branches. The restoration of the cult and the fabric did not compel his attention; instead, like Monet in his garden, he set down with marvellous sensitivity the movement of light and water under the vanished trees

> That dandled a sandalled
> Shadow that swam or sank
> On meadow & river & wind-wandering weed-winding bank.

I walked there again recently because I thought the shrine would appeal to the friend who'd given us lunch that day, a friend who had been a nun at one time long ago at my school. But she didn't want to swap stories about miracles and holy places and treacle-wells. Instead she took one quick turn through the chapel and left, saying, 'It doesn't have the right smell.'

The fissure that opened up between Rome and Canterbury half a century ago was not narrowed by the Oxford Movement's revival of liturgy and cult; it was a case of *les extrêmes se touchent*, but the stand-off continued. It was only when my friend seemed so irritated by the trappings of the old religion at Binsey that I realised I had come back with her because there was a kind of logic across the years, after my first encounter with the chapel through a priest who would also give up his calling. I was disappointed she didn't feel the enchantment of the place, and it dulled it for me too, a little, seeing her distaste.

The streams that run through the town and its surrounding fields and meadows have carried stories with them over the centuries, and Binsey now is much more celebrated for its connections with *Alice in Wonderland* than with Frideswide. Yet the two young women are closely entwined, as Lewis Carroll, being himself a deacon in the Church of England during the period of intense medievalising religious renewal, drew on local legends for the odyssey he imagined and recounted to his audience of little friends.

In 1856, Alice Liddell's father Henry had taken up his post as Dean of Christ Church and its cathedral, so when his daughter Alice and her siblings were growing up, they would have often heard their father preach by the tomb of St Frideswide, which had been newly restored; Alice would have recognised that Lewis Carroll was only teasing, in that knowing and whimsical way of his, when he talked about the treacle-well that afternoon in 1864 as they took the same course downstream to Binsey that Frideswide had centuries before.

During the Mad Hatter's Tea Party, the Dormouse starts telling a story about three children who lived at the bottom of a well. Why? Because it was a treacle-well. 'Why?' asks Alice again. Because, says the Dormouse, they were drawing treacle.

It's baffling, another of those maddening impasses that Alice keeps encountering in Wonderland. The sensible girl replies that the children would be very ill if they lived on treacle.

Maybe some images from the trip when Alice Liddell gathered 'dream rushes' from the riverbank helped inspire a sculpture that she carved when she was grown up: a bas-relief on oak which decorated a door in the mission church in Poplar, London, that Dean Liddell established; it was bombed in World War II, and has since been demolished, but the panel was rescued and brought to Oxford, to the church on the Botley Road dedicated to St Edmund and St Frideswide. It's a huge edifice, far too huge for the community that lives around there now, and no longer in use, so I had to write a letter requesting permission to visit, and one afternoon the retired vicar came with the key to meet me and show me around. We found, leaning against a wall, the wooden bas-relief that Alice Liddell carved. It's an ogive panel, and unexpectedly skilful – did Alice Liddell miss her vocation? – and shows St Frideswide looking like a Virgin annunciate kneeling and praying, with a single oar untended in its rowlock as she drifts towards Binsey in a swan-necked skiff between the wind-wandering weed-winding banks of the Thames.

Note

I would like to acknowledge the help of Cressida Connolly; Brigid Allen, 'Levi, Peter Chad Tigar (1931–2000)', *Oxford Dictionary of National Biography*, Oxford University Press, 2007; online edition, 2011, http://www.oxforddnb.com.ezproxy2.londonlibrary.co.uk/view/article/73779, accessed 29 August 2016; Brigid Allen, *Peter Levi: Oxford Romantic*, Signal Books, 2014; Josh Spero, *Second-Hand Stories*, Unbound, 2015; Henry Mayr-Harting, 'Functions of a Twelfth-century Shrine: The Miracles of St Frideswide' in *Studies in Medieval History presented to R.H.C. Davis*, eds., Moore, R. I., Mayr-Harting, Henry (London: Bloomsbury, 1985, pp. 193–206); and Sherry L. Reames, ed., *The Legend of St Frideswide of Oxford, An Anglo-Saxon Royal Abbess* in *Middle English Legends of Women Saints*, University of Rochester, 2003. For Hopkins's 'Binsey Poplars', I accessed https://www.poetryfoundation.org/poems/44390/binsey-poplars.

THE ECHOING GREEN

Ken Worpole

Such, such were the joys
When we all, girls and boys,
In our youth-time were seen
On the echoing green.

William Blake

1

'Without common land no social system can survive,' wrote the architectural historian Christopher Alexander in 1997, a prescient warning at a time when the privatisation of public assets was gaining increased traction as the new political common sense. More recently, in July 2016, a House of Commons Select Committee on 'The Future of Public Parks' began public consultation by asking 'what the advantages and disadvantages are of other management models, such as privatisation, outsourcing or mutualisation.'

What have voters done to deserve this resurgent ideological attack on the public realm? Parks are almost the last symbols of common land rights left in towns and cities, and perhaps this is why they attract so much ideological opprobrium from free-market economists, for whom the commons is now an antiquated and outdated ethical sphere.

Having lived close to Clissold Park in Hackney for nearly fifty years, I know only too well how much the park's majestic chestnut and plane trees, wide skies and open horizons, undulating grassland, ornamental lakes and gardens – along with the regular *passeggiata* of familiar and unfamiliar faces – have provided a source of pleasure and refuge to the many who use it, often daily. As with the woodland glade in *A Midsummer Night's Dream*, parks are places of enchantment from which visitors emerge refreshed, changed or renewed.

For the three million visitors it attracts each year, Clissold Park is one of the larger public open spaces in this part of London, and has been so for more than a hundred years, but its future is once again threatened. This is because the provision of public parks remains a 'non-statutory' service, which means municipal authorities are not required to provide them if they feel they can't afford to, and in an 'age of austerity' non-statutory provision is the first to suffer, as is now happening.

Cuts to parks budgets are biting deeply across the UK, according to the Heritage Lottery Fund's report, *State of UK Public Parks 2016*. While more popular than ever – with over 90 per cent of families with children under five and 57 per cent of all adults using them regularly – parks services across the country are being outsourced to community groups or their management, and maintenance handed over to private contractors in order to save money. In 2014 Liverpool City Council, for example, announced that over the following three years its annual £10 million parks budget would be cut by 50 per cent. Many other councils have announced similar levels of reduced funding. 'Parks take a long time to fall apart,' says Dave Morris, chair of the National Federation of Parks and Green Spaces, adding that 'it's not immediately noticeable, like a library closing'. But over time the effects are just as socially (and environmentally) disastrous. Sooner or later there is a danger that many city parks will take on the character of the bleak, deserted grasslands of those edgeland prairies, where only dog walkers, footballers and joy-riders venture.

The amount of public parkland in any town or city is an accident of history: some places have prodigious amounts of open green space, while others have just pockets. To complicate matters, there are distinct typologies of urban parkland, ranging from the ornamental garden to the prestigious civic park, and from the garden square to the public commons or recreation ground. Allotments, canal towpaths, closed burial grounds, memorial gardens, bowling greens and many other serendipitous green spaces add to the urban mix. Each has its own history and customary 'rules of engagement', which are often implicitly understood by their users, occasionally reinforced by local by-laws. These typological distinctions are fascinating, each bringing with it rich historic associations, not just with aesthetic issues, but also differences in their respective 'moral economies'. A park is never simply just a green space, but an ever-changing *mise-en-scène* of social theatre.

Clissold Park itself is a classic *hortus conclusus*, a former enclosed private house and grounds, that over time has mutated into a modern city park, a successful hybrid of the Renaissance 'public garden' and the historic recreational space of the English commons, where markets are held, sports played, and funfairs and travelling circuses encamp for a short while. It is intriguing how these historic typologies of cultivated and open land have been commandeered and re-purposed in recent times by the internet with its 'walled gardens' and 'creative commons'.

The park and its mansion, Clissold House (Grade II-listed), originated as a family estate in the 1790s, under the ownership of a Quaker banker, Jonathan Hoare. After several changes of ownership during the nineteenth century, in the 1880s the 53-acre estate ended up in the hands of the Church Commissioners, who proposed selling the site for development. A vociferous and successful public campaign led to its purchase by the Metropolitan Board of Works in 1886, and it was opened as a public park by the newly formed London County Council (LCC) on 24 July 1889. It remained with the elected London authority until 1986 when, with the abolition of the Greater London Council (GLC), house and park were transferred to Hackney Borough Council, in whose large and richly variegated portfolio of land holdings it now rests.

For some years after Hackney Council – like many other London boroughs to which the former GLC parks were transferred by government diktat – struggled to maintain Clissold Park adequately. This was for reasons of cost as well as a lack of management expertise necessary to maintain such large historic parks and their built heritage. In the 1980s anxieties about the decline of the park and mansion spurred the formation of a voluntary user group, Clissold Park User Group (CPUG). This grew in size and expertise over time, and, though starting from a fairly adversarial relationship with the local authority, now works closely with council officers. Initially this was for one reason only: the arrival of the Heritage Lottery Fund's urban parks spending programme in 1996. Whatever one's reservations about the morality of using lotteries to underwrite public amenities – and I certainly have them – there is no doubt that the HLF parks programme, which has now provided more than £800 million to UK parks over the past twenty years, has transformed many out of recognition, and provided the greatest renewal of parks seen in Britain for more than half a century.

A grant of £4.5 million to Clissold Park in 2008, matched by £4.1 million from council funds, restored the mansion to a pristine condition, and refurbished every aspect of the park and its hydrological features, together with new tennis courts and extensive play provision for young children and sports enthusiasts. The grant came with significant conditions, notably that the park and mansion required their own dedicated management team, together with on-site gardening staff, a business plan for the house, and an educational programme for working with local schools. The enhanced status that Hackney's parks service now enjoys as a result of the HLF programme has put its management team back on the top table in the council hierarchy – but for how much longer?

2

Many other city parks also have their origins in large private family estates acquired by municipal authorities in the late-Victorian era. In the history of modern cities it is the moment when the new civic gospel and the natural world came together, and in doing so created a new landscape form that has over the past hundred years been replicated across the world. The architect Terry Farrell has said that while Britain imported most of its ideas on city form and townscape from Europe and beyond, its true claim to fame is that it gave the world the public park.

The Victorian concern with formality in public life meant that the early parks were designed and managed as spaces of moral uplift and social regulation, though over time such regimes fell out of step with changing social mores. It was Sunday every day in the Victorian park: best clothes and best behaviour. Plants and trees were labelled for public edification in English and Latin; children's free play was strictly restricted to one small area, if allowed at all, and informal sports were prohibited.

Times changed, and parks had to change accordingly. Thus, when the veteran municipal socialist George Lansbury was given the minor Cabinet post of Commissioner of Works in the 1929 Labour government – he had been deliberately sidelined by Prime Minister Ramsey MacDonald, who loathed him – Lansbury took to the job with gusto. He ended up as the only minister of that short-lived government to acquit himself with an enhanced political reputation, notably through his commitment to widening access to public parks. 'Railings were pulled down, shelters for parents put up, paddling and swimming pools for children constructed, play and recreational equipment installed in the parks over which he had jurisdiction,' wrote his biographer, Bob Holman. 'Mixed bathing was allowed in the Serpentine and Hyde Park was revamped as "Lansbury's Lido". His aim was to make the parks attractive to and open to families of all kinds – and he succeeded.'

Other cities followed Lansbury. During the 1930s across Britain the Victorian park underwent a process of greater democratisation in design and amenity. This was sufficiently impressive to attract the praise of admiring observers from abroad, such as the eminent Danish architect, Steen Eiler Rasmussen, who devoted five chapters of his seminal 1937 work on London architecture, London: The Unique City, to praising the lively conviviality of London's parks, as did the great Dutch historian and philosopher of play, Johan Huizinga, in his 1938 study Homo Ludens.

Those new public parks designed from scratch, rather than adapted from existing estates, were usually part of the development of the wealthier housing districts and suburbs, and were sometimes regarded de facto as a private amenity for those living in properties overlooking or adjoining them, as had been the case with the more prestigious London parks. Conflicts between residents immediately fringing the grander parks, and users from other parts of the city, soon emerged (and still rumble beneath the surface in many places even today).

Other changes resulted during both world wars, when large areas of urban parkland were transformed into allotments for food-growing, a trend re-emerging today as community groups request permission to convert under-used parkland into productive use. For some years now the organisation Growing Communities has had its own smallholding in Clissold Park, supplying local farmers' markets and cafés with salads and herbs, while training volunteers in horticultural skills. During the Second World War people were encouraged to take advantage of 'Holidays at Home' schemes, eschewing travel abroad or elsewhere in Britain in favour of using local parks, where programmes of events and activities were provided to help sustain civilian morale.

3

Parks have their fair-weather users, as well as hardened regulars. In the summer months Clissold Park provides a popular place for picnics, informal sports, funfairs, Turkish, Kurdish and Afro-Caribbean festivals, along with a deer park and animal enclosures to visit, and swans, ducks and geese to admire on the lakes. Meanwhile people queue to be photographed against the brilliant floral displays for wedding and family photographs. There are free summer music concerts in the formal gardens, play schemes for children and young people, the butterfly tunnel is opened and one of the last surviving municipal paddling pools comes into its own.

T'ai chi, yoga, martial arts, meditation, circus skills and tightrope walking can all be seen being practised daily, alongside impromptu football games and organised matches on marked-out pitches. It is estimated that more than 500 people use Clissold Park regularly for jogging. Local surgeries promote organised 'health walks' in the park, now popular among older people from all of Stoke Newington's diverse communities, and the 'One O'Clock Club', a legacy from the post-war London County Council that installed them in all of its major parks, has provided indoor and outdoor play facilities for the under-fives for many years, as well as a much-needed meeting place for isolated parents and carers. Thanks to Lottery funding there is now a popular 'wheels park' for skate-boarders and riders of BMX bikes. No other public amenity in this densely populated area offers such a rich variety of attractions and activities every day of the year, and for free. Hence the 3 million visits each year.

Among the hardened regulars out in all weathers are dog owners and professional dog-walkers. The growing number of dogs in the park is a divisive issue locally, though owners are always keen to remind other park users that they are out in all hours of daylight and often the first to spot or report anything untoward. Nevertheless, the fact that so many dogs run freely is a problem for the Orthodox Jewish and Muslim visitors who use the park and share a common aversion to dogs as human familiars. This is where parks draw on the legacy of the commons, as places where conflicting needs and interests – and there are many – have to be negotiated. Apart from conflicts about dogs in the park, there are cyclists competing with pedestrians on the footpaths, players of team sports in conflict with those looking for peace and quiet, and festival organisers whose (strictly rationed) events cause concern for residents living nearby. Regular public meetings of the park-user group provide a mediating forum for trying to resolve such conflicts, and may indeed be one of the voluntary forum's principal functions.

This was the theme of an article by the American journalist Michael Goldfarb in the *New York Times* some time ago, when he wrote admiringly about the park he found himself living close by. 'In a world splitting at the seams, Clissold Park is like a dream,' he wrote. 'Some of the most intractable conflicts in the world seem to have been resolved – or at least temporarily ignored. Kurds and Turks, Jews and Muslims, working-class and middle-class people (this is Britain) all co-exist, enjoying the lawns, the deer park, the ponds, the rose garden and the wading pool.'

Not all use is negotiable, especially after dark. Despite the fact that the park is locked at night, its after-hours use increases in the summer months: homeless people sleep there, and it provides a setting for sexual encounters and drinking schools. To my knowledge at least two people have hanged themselves from the trees, to be discovered by distressed park staff the next morning. Some years ago it was also the scene of a frenzied stabbing attack on a woman jogger after dark, which proved serious but not fatal. The morning after the police closed the park for a fortnight, and every gate was sealed and permanently guarded. An air of gloom settled upon the immediate neighbourhood. On the Sunday after re-opening the minister of the nearby Anglican church organised a carol-singing procession through the park, led by a professional jazz trumpet-player. It was a large, ecumenical gathering in which several hundred people processed along every park footpath and avenue, holding candles and lamps, singing. With this largely spontaneous ritual the park was reclaimed from its enforced sleep.

Despite such rare and shocking events the park remains overwhelmingly a sanctuary and safe haven. At its busiest it is used by thousands of people in the course of a day without any formal policing, in sharp contrast to many other public spaces in the city which now seem to swarm with private security guards. For me, this attests to the moral economy of traditional park culture, which acts to temper behaviour in the interests of the wider public comity, providing the strongest argument as to why they are safer in public rather than private hands. While conflicting uses are mostly resolved informally, the elected local authority retains the power to arbitrate on any major conflicts of use within the park, possessing as it does, in my opinion, a democratic legitimacy that a privatised or outsourced park would lack.

4

Parks also serve as proxy memorial gardens, and in some towns in recent years this has reached critical proportions, especially where sites of burial or cremation are located some distance away. A handful of local authorities have embargoed the installation of further park memorial benches, after complaints that their parks were acquiring the ambience of remembrance gardens. Some years ago the anthropologist Leonie Kellaher and I interviewed a number of park managers on the ways in which parks were increasingly being used for these purposes. Apart from dedicated benches and memorial trees, we were told of people surreptitiously interring ashes in areas previously favoured by the deceased. Furthermore, many of the trees planted without permission were of an inappropriate species, planted at the wrong time of year, dying soon after.

As a result, many local authorities now ask that those wishing to dedicate a tree to the memory of a loved one sponsor a species already designated as part of the park's long-term planting programme. They are also asked to forgo individual memorial plaques, which, it is felt, compromise the communal aesthetic of the public park or garden, and the unanchored, amorphous spirit of this *rus in urbs*. A park can be a place of memory without words.

What gives parks this privileged status as one of the few remaining 'sacred spaces' in the modern urban landscape? Primarily there is a perceived connection to a pre-existent and enduring natural world – tenuous though the municipal park version of 'nature' may be – and thus with more seasonal rhythms of life, increasingly distinct from the digital timetable of the 24-hour city. This may be especially important for people who have come from rural cultures and who retain a strong pull to being outdoors whenever possible. And while the seemingly immutable world of Clissold Park has nevertheless witnessed enormous changes at its borders – the Georgians, Victorians and Edwardians have come and gone, tower blocks have risen at its perimeter, been demolished, and today rise again – it remains for many a still centre in an otherwise fast-turning world.

Finally, of course, there is the crucial factor of the weather. 'Weather is the chief content of gardens,' wrote the idiosyncratic artist and land-scape designer Ian Hamilton Finlay, 'yet it is the one thing in them over which the gardener has no control.' The same is patently true of the sensual *au plein air* world of the public park, which can possess a crowded festive air in the heat of a summer's afternoon, but at dusk on a winter's day can exude an other-worldly melancholy.

The year 2016 commemorated the 500th-anniversary year of the publication of Sir Thomas More's *Utopia*, and there has been much discussion as to where any residual utopian impulses or visions in the world might still be found today. Inequality is on the rise, and London's socially mixed communities are under continuing pressure from 'the invisible hand' of the housing market to segment even further into discrete enclaves of wealth and lifestyle. Yet parks remain among the last places in the city where all users are equal, and preferential terms of access or treatment cannot be purchased or parlayed. These outbreaks of arcadia hark back to ancient commons rights, and continue to embody the spirit of Blake's idyll of the echoing green: a rare place of enchantment open to all.

Further Reading

G. F. Chadwick, *The Park and the Town: Public Landscapes in the 19th and 20th Centuries*, Architectural Press, 1966.

Hazel Conway, *People's Parks: the Design and Development of Victorian Parks in Britain*, Cambridge University Press, 1991.

Travis Elborough, *A Walk in the Park: The Life and Times of a People's Institution*, Jonathan Cape, 2016.

Gareth Evans & Di Robson (editors), *Towards Re-Enchantment: Place and Its Meanings*, ArtEvents, 2010.

Liz Greenhalgh & Ken Worpole, *Park Life: Urban Parks & Social Renewal*, Comedia & Demos, 1995.

Heritage Lottery Fund, *State of UK Public Parks 2016*, HLF, 2016.

Leonie Kellaher & Ken Worpole, 'Bringing the Dead Back Home: Urban Public Spaces as Sites for New Patterns of Mourning & Memorialisation', in *Deathscapes*, edited by Avril Maddrell & James D. Sidaway, Ashgate, 2010.

Margaret Willes, *The Gardens of the British Working Class*, Yale University Press, 2014.

CONTRIBUTORS

Barbara Bender is Emeritus Professor of Anthropology at UCL. She spent twenty-five years researching and teaching landscape across disciplinary boundaries. Her books include *Stonehenge: Making Space* (Berg); *Stone Worlds*, co-author (Left Coast Press); *Contested Landscapes: Movement, Exile and Place*, editor (Berg). She has also spent twenty-five years working with the oral/archival Branscombe Project, a communal endeavour.

Julia Blackburn has written two novels and ten works of non-fiction. Her books are a mixture of memoir, biography and travel writing, alongside the process of thinking on the page. She has approached all sorts of subjects, but perhaps the unifying factor is her interest in people who are caught in a predicament of one sort or another. A Box of Shells' is an extract from *Time Song: Journeys in Search of Doggerland* which will be published by Jonathan Cape in 2019.

Sean Borodale works as an artist and writer. His first collection of poems, *Bee Journal*, was shortlisted for the T. S. Eliot Prize and the Costa Poetry Book Awards. He keeps bees in Somerset.

Hugh Brody's books include *The People's Land, Maps and Dreams* and *The Other Side of Eden*. His films include documentaries made with indigenous peoples of northern and western Canada: *Nineteen-Nineteen*, starring Paul Scofield and Maria Schell, and *Tracks Across Sand*, a set of sixteen films made with the Khomani San of the southern Kalahari. He holds the Canada Research Chair in Aboriginal Studies at the University of the Fraser Valley in British Columbia.

John Burnside's novels include *The Devil's Footprints* (2007), *Glister* (2008) and *A Summer of Drowning* (2011). He is also the author of two collections of short stories, three memoirs and several prizewinning poetry collections, including *Black Cat Bone*, winner of both the Forward and the T. S. Eliot prizes in 2012. His most recent novel, *Ashland & Vine*, was published alongside a new collection of poetry, *Still Life with Feeding Snake*, in February 2017.

Mark Cocker is an author, naturalist and environmental teacher who writes and broadcasts on nature and wildlife in a variety of national media. His eleven books include works of biography, history, literary criticism and memoir. The latest is *Our Place*, a personal journey into British environmental history.

Peter Davidson is Senior Research Fellow at Campion Hall, University of Oxford. His most recent book is a cultural history of twilight, *The Last of the Light*, published by Reaktion Books. He is working on a book about lighted windows in the dark, and on a further collection of poems for Carcanet. He lives in Oxford.

Nick Davies is Professor of Behavioural Ecology at the University of Cambridge and a Fellow of Pembroke College. He has studied cuckoos in the fens for the past thirty years and his book *Cuckoo – cheating by nature* is published by Bloomsbury.

Paul Farley is a poet and broadcaster. He has received many awards for his work, including the 2009 E. M. Forster Award from the American Academy of Arts & Letters, and is a Fellow of the Royal Society of Literature. His *Selected Poems* was published in 2014 by Picador.

Tessa Hadley has written six novels and three collections of short stories. Her novel *The Past*, published in the UK in 2015, won the Hawthornden Prize; a collection of stories, *Bad Dreams*, was published in 2017. She publishes short stories regularly in the *New Yorker*, reviews for the *Guardian* and the *London Review of Books*, and is a Professor of

Creative Writing at Bath Spa University. In 2016 she was awarded a Windham Campbell Prize for Fiction.

Alexandra Harris is the author of *Romantic Moderns, Virginia Woolf* and *Weatherland: Writers and Artists under English Skies*. She is Professorial Fellow at the University of Birmingham, and a Fellow of the Royal Society of Literature. Her radio programmes include a series on Woolf's walks in different landscapes and *A British History in Weather*.

Philip Hoare is the author of eight works of non-fiction, including biographies of Stephen Tennant and Nöel Coward; *Leviathan or, the Whale* (winner of the 2008 Samuel Johnson Prize for Non-Fiction) and *The Sea Inside*. His latest book is RISINGTIDEFALLINGSTAR. He is co-curator, with Angela Cockayne, of mobydickbigread.com, and is Professor of English at the University of Southampton. @philipwhale

Richard Holmes is a Fellow of the British Academy. He is the author of *Footsteps: Adventures of a Romantic Biographer*, and biographies of Shelley, Coleridge and young Dr Johnson. His study of scientists and poets, *The Age of Wonder*, won the Royal Society Prize for Science Books (UK) and the National Book Critics Circle Award for Nonfiction (USA). He has also written about ballooning in *Falling Upwards*. His most recent book is *This Long Pursuit*.

Tim Ingold is Professor of Social Anthropology at the University of Aberdeen. He has written on evolutionary theory, human–animal relations, environmental perception and skilled practice. He is currently exploring the interface between anthropology, archaeology, art and architecture, and is the author of *Lines* (2007), *Being Alive* (2011), *Making* (2013) and *The Life of Lines* (2015).

Richard Long is an artist of landscape and nature. His work takes many forms, but is essentially about making walks in both rural and wilderness landscapes which articulate ideas of time and distance. He often also makes sculptures of place along the way, marks of passage.

He has worked on all five continents. Since 1968 he has had over 250 one-person exhibitions worldwide. He was born in Bristol in 1945.

Richard Mabey is the author of some forty prizewinning books, the most recent being *The Cabaret of Plants: Botany and the Imagination*. In 2002 he moved from the Chilterns to Norfolk, swapping wood for water and a slim-line electric boat. He is a Fellow of the Royal Society for Literature, and Patron of the John Clare Society.

Helen Macdonald wrote the bestselling memoir *H is for Hawk*, which won the 2014 Samuel Johnson Prize and Costa Book of the Year, and was a 2015 Kirkus Award and NBCC Award finalist in the USA. She has also published collections of poetry and works of cultural history. She is a contributing writer for the *NYT Magazine*.

Patrick McGuinness is the author of two books of poems, *The Canals of Mars* and *Jilted City*, and the novel *The Last Hundred Days*, about the fall of the Ceaușescu regime. His memoir, *Other People's Countries: A Journey into Memory*, appeared in 2014. He teaches French and comparative literature at Oxford University.

Andrew McNeillie's seventh collections of poems, *Making Ends Meet*, was published in 2017. His memoir *An Aran Keening* was published by Lilliput Press in 2001. He is the founding editor of the literary magazine *Archipelago* and runs the Clutag Press.

Philip Marsden is the award-winning author of books that include *The Bronski House*, *The Spirit-Wrestlers*, *The Chains of Heaven*, *The Barefoot Emperor*, *The Levelling Sea* and, most recently, *Rising Ground*. He is a fellow of the Royal Society of Literature and his work has been translated into more than a dozen languages. He lives in Cornwall with his family and a number of boats.

David Matless is Professor of Cultural Geography at the University of Nottingham. He is the author of *Landscape and Englishness* (Reaktion 2016, first published 1998), *The Regional Book* (Uniformbooks 2015) and *In the Nature of Landscape: Cultural Geography on the Norfolk Broads* (Wiley-Blackwell 2014). His work explores the relationship of landscape and culture, with a particular interest in the landscapes of East Anglia, the landscapes of English identity, and the cultural geographies of the Anthropocene.

Andrew Motion was UK Poet Laureate from 1999 to 2009. He is now a Homewood Professor of the Arts at Johns Hopkins University and lives in Baltimore.

Adam Nicolson was born in 1957 and has written about the English landscape and its owners, the Hebrides, Homer, 17th-century England and the sea and its birds. Since 4 May 1994, he has lived at Perch Hill Farm in the Sussex Weald, where he keeps a small herd of Sussex cattle and a flock of sheep of mixed parentage. He is presently writing a book on the year Coleridge and Wordsworth spent together in the Quantocks and another on life between the tides.

Sean O'Brien is a poet, critic, novelist and short-fiction writer, Professor of Creative Writing at Newcastle University and a Fellow of the Royal Society of Literature. His poetry collection, *The Drowned Book* (2007), won the Forward and T. S. Eliot Prizes. Among his most recent publications are *The Beautiful Librarians* (2015), which won the Roehampton Poetry Prize, and his second novel, *Once Again Assembled Here* (2016).

Dexter Petley is the author of four critically acclaimed novels: *Little Nineveh, Joyride, White Lies* and *One True Void*. His latest book, *Love Madness Fishing*, is a memoir of boyhood among the rural poor in a 1960s Weald of Kent. Angling writer and mushroom-gatherer, he lives in a yurt in a Normandy forest, where he is working on a nature detective novel.

Greg Poole – artist – printmaker – illustrator – naturalist – was born in Bristol in 1960. A long-time council member of the Society of Wildlife Artists (SWLA), he is widely travelled, including several Artists for Nature Foundation (ANF) projects. His work features in numerous nature/art publications, and a one-man book was published in French: *La Riviera* (Gallimard). He writes a blog on his website: www.gregpoole.co.uk

Fiona Sampson has received numerous national and international awards and been widely translated as a poet. She also writes non-fiction including biography, writing about place, and criticism. Among her recent books are *Limestone Country*, *In Search of Mary Shelley* and *The Catch*.

Adam Thorpe is a poet, novelist, translator and critic. He was born in Paris and brought up in Beirut, Calcutta, Cameroon and England. His first novel, *Ulverton* (1992), is now a Vintage Classic. *Voluntary*, his sixth poetry collection, was a Poetry Book Society Recommendation in 2012. A work of non-fiction, *On Silbury Hill* (Little Toller), was a BBC Radio 4 Book of the Week in 2012. His latest novel, *Missing Fay*, was published by Cape in 2017.

Michael Viney, author of *Ireland* in the Smithsonian natural history series, moved from English to Irish journalism in 1962 and has written 'Another Life', a weekly column on ecology and rural life, in the *Irish Times* since 1977. His books include *Ireland's Ocean: a natural history* (Collins Press), written with his wife Ethna. He was elected to the Royal Irish Academy in 2017.

Marina Warner writes fiction and cultural history. Her most recent books are *Once Upon a Time: A Short History of Fairy Tale* (Oxford University Press) and *Fly Away Home: Short Stories* (Salt). She is Professor of English and Creative Writing at Birkbeck College, London, and is working on a book about Cairo in the fifties. In 2015 she was awarded the Holberg Prize, and in 2017 became President of the Royal Society of Literature.

Ken Worpole is the author of many books on architecture, landscape and social history, and works as a writer and researcher in the field of public policy. He lives with his wife, the photographer Larraine Worpole, in Hackney, where they have both been active in local social and environmental campaigns since the late 1960s. www.worpole.net